Book on

EXPERIMENTAL SPIRITISM.

Book on Mediums;

OR,

GUIDE FOR MEDIUMS AND INVOCATORS:

CONTAINING

THE SPECIAL INSTRUCTION OF THE SPIRITS ON THE THEORY
OF ALL KINDS OF MANIFESTATIONS; THE MEANS OF
COMMUNICATING WITH THE INVISIBLE WORLD; THE
DEVELOPMENT OF MEDIUMSHIP; THE DIFFI-
CULTIES AND THE DANGERS THAT ARE
TO BE ENCOUNTERED IN THE
PRACTICE OF SPIRITISM.

BY

ALLAN KARDEC.

TRANSLATED BY EMMA A. WOOD.

SAMUEL WEISER, INC.

York Beach, Maine

First published in 1874

First published in 1970 by
Samuel Weiser, Inc.
Box 612
York Beach, Maine 03910-0612

First paper edition, 1978
This printing, 2000

Library of Congress Catalog Card Number: 77-16630

ISBN 0-87728-382-6
MG

Printed in the United States of America

The paper used in this publication meets the minimum require-
ments of the American National Standard for Permanence of Paper
for Printed Library Materials Z39.48-1984.

TRANSLATOR'S PREFACE.

In offering to the public a translation of a work of so celebrated an author as Allan Kardec, and one so much beloved among spiritists in foreign countries, not only for his scientific attainments in spirit studies, but for his purity of life and character, I feel my own incompetency for the task — my own incompetency but for the assistance received from the Spirits who are interested in my undertaking. I have endeavored to render faithfully the exact meaning of the original, and I can truly say the work of translating has been a labor of love, to be fully repaid to me by the good I am sure it will perform among our own people.

E. A. W.

I

CONTENTS.

4 *CONTENTS.*

INTRODUCTION

Today, as in the past, misinformation coupled with misinterpretation regarding the phenomena of Spiritism remain the foremost and greatest difficulties to surmount. Often both the medium and the sitter have failed to agree on the subject and on its practice. Mediums, themselves, have been at variance. It remained for Allan Kardec to make an exhaustive study of all phases of Spiritism, reducing it to a simple, forthright, understandable language.

Perhaps an almost overpowering desire on the part of those who endeavor to pursue the practice of Spiritism is to contact the spirits of the so-called dead. Thus one who is sensitive, even to a minor degree, assumes the role of mediumship, and the seeker, often with reservations despite his desires, becomes a sitter hopefully asking for a crumb of encouragement from a departed dear one.

As the work of Allan Kardec points out, there is no royal road to mediumship. There is no how-to-do-it directory describing how to become a successful practising medium. A ouija board or a planchette, a pencil in a willing hand or pairs of hands resting lightly on a table may bring results for the occasional sensitive, but generally, even though following the usual meager directions, the participants are usually disappointed.

Never-the-less, every individual, within himself, possesses the innate qualities that lead to mediumship. Naturally these qualities manifest in different degrees. A so-called hunch may be all the individual will ever have, but even that, in itself, is sufficient proof that the essence of psychic ability is present, and not entirely dormant. Not every musician will become a Mozart. Not every poet will become a Tennyson. Not every artist will become a Michelangelo. So it follows that not every sensitive will become a Mrs. Piper.

During the past fifty years, there has been a growing interest in Spiritism. What was once confined to small, selected groups meeting secretly to witness spirit manifestations, direct voice mediumship, spirit photography and table-turning, to name only a few of the phenomena which claimed the attention of psychic research workers, is now brought out into the open. Colleges and universities examine the evidence and dignify it by the name of parapsychology. It is no longer an interest to approach surreptitiously—it is rather a phase of man's becoming that engages the minds of some of our most respected philosophers and psychologists.

Yet in spite of this undisguised and commendable interest, there is grave danger in the desire to know what happens in the Spirit World. That danger is the inexperience of those who wish to contact this invisible plane. The novice is too prone to accept everything told him without investigating the veracity of the informant. The fledgling sensitive is often puzzled by the evidence of early experiences. Either he casts it completely aside, or practices without seeking assistance. In either case he has reached a mistaken conclusion.

Therefore, this work by Allan Kardec is without peer. It is a book of exceptionally practical instructions, not to be read superficially. After a thorough study of it the student will better understand the effects of his experiences. Perhaps the most significant thing about this work is—it is not expressly for mediums. IT IS FOR ALL WHO ENTERTAIN A GENUINE DETERMINATION TO UNDERSTAND SPIRITISM.

A study of Kardec's work will bring the dedicated medium to a recognition of his talent. Clairvoyance and clairaudience may be readily recognized. However, there are many categories in which the sensitive, if properly guided, operate. To mention only a few—the pneumatographists, who produce writing directly by the spirit without handling pencil and paper; mediums who produce material phenomena; somnambulists who act without a guide; mediums who give their lives to spiritual healing; and the inspired medium who receives messages by thought communications foreign to his preconceived ideas. The sensitive will eventually realize the fulfillment of Plato's admonition: "Know thyself!"

To the one who seeks consolation and advice from the spirits, this work will assist him in recognizing the selfless medium whose prime objective is service. It will give him confidence and assurance when he is privileged to have a sitting. If the sitter lacks rapport with the medium, the spirits must surmount this.

As has been pointed out, the practice of Spiritism is beset with many difficulties, and even possible dangers. Therefore, dilettantism is discouraged. Serious study is the only road reaching to the ultimate goal of communication with the invisible world. To make a sport of such practice, as is often the case among sophisticated, uninformed people, is looked upon with disfavor. Also, to make an effort to communicate with the spirit world out of mere curiosity to see if it can be done is another practice that is frowned upon. The study should be accompanied by gravity and deep respect for the communicator and the communicant.

In this work the many advantages acquired through conscientious study and experience are presented to the devoted student of Spiritism.

Even though it is submitted here with some hesitation, there is one important point to make, even though it is applicable to only a few. Never make an experiment with levity or without special cause. To the novice the effect may be disastrous. He may become critical or even repelled without a valid reason. He is robbed of his desire to approach the subject seriously, and he is deprived of the solace which Spiritism could have given him in times of grief and stress.

Today there is very little time spent in table-turning and kindred approaches. Spiritism has brought the investigators to a higher level; in fact, it is thought of as philosophical in many instances. Often the medium is empowered to bring an entire teaching of a high spiritual quality to those privileged to be members of the Circle. Through the medium's voice invaluable instructions are received. The tape recorder has captured these fine lectures, and now many outside the Circle are benefitted by them. The spirit world readily accepted and appropriated the tape recorder. To them the earthlings were slow in using this mechanical device to more accurately record their messages. They were ready all the while—they were patiently waiting for their loved ones to find a facile way to capture in sound the messages from the invisible world.

In this BOOK ON MEDIUMS by Allan Kardec, who was greatly acclaimed for his scientific spirit investigations and his integrity, the practical side of Spiritism is emphasized. Whether the reader wishes to take part in manifestations, or merely to pass unbiased, critical judgment on any phenomena that may have been witnessed, this work is invaluable. Fortified by this detailed knowledge, any question that might possibly be encountered can be averted successfully.

After the publication of the first edition, Kardec felt there might possibly be some discrepancies. Quite naturally he turned to the spirit world. It is known that they heeded his call, and the spirits, themselves, meticulously corrected anything which did not meet with their approval. They, also, added some instructions which proved of inestimable importance. It can be said beyond question, that this book, to a marked measure, is their work, for on nearly every page they are indirectly quoted. Occasionally direct quotations are discovered. Therefore, the Invisible World chose Allan Kardec to author their instructions for the spiritist, and encouraged him to identify himself with its publication. Because he was such a devoted Spiritist of unequaled humility the work has continued to live on. Since 1874 it has been in constant demand. So eagerly was it sought that it became a collector's item. Now once again, it has become available to the present day student. It deserves serious, intensive study.

NY 1969   SIBYL FERGUSON

EXPERIMENTAL SPIRITISM.

PART FIRST.

PRELIMINARY IDEAS.

Chapter I.

ARE THERE SPIRITS?

1. THE doubt respecting the existence of spirits has for its first cause ignorance of their true nature. They are usually thought of as beings apart in the creation, and whose necessity is not demonstrated. Many know them only by the fantastic tales heard in their childhood, almost as one knows history by romances : without seeking to find whether these tales, stripped of ridiculous accessories, rest on a foundation of truth, the absurd side alone strikes them : not taking the trouble to strip off the bitter bark to find the almond, they reject the whole ; as, in religion, some persons, shocked by certain abuses, confound all in the same reprobation.

Whatever may be one's idea of spirits, this belief is necessarily founded on the existence of an intelligent principle outside of matter : it is incompatible with the absolute negation of this principle. We take, then, our point of departure from the existence, the survival, and the individuality of the soul, of which Spiritualism is the theoric and dogmatic demonstration, and Spiritism the manifestation. Let us for a moment make an abstraction of the manifestations, properly so called, and, reasoning by induction, let us see to what consequences we shall arrive.

2. From the moment that the existence of the soul is admitted, and its individuality after death, it must also be admitted, first, that it is of a different nature from the body, since, once separated, it no longer has the properties of the latter : secondly, that it enjoys a consciousness of itself, since to it is attributed happiness or suffering ; otherwise it would be an inert being, and of no use for us to have one. This admitted, this soul goes somewhere. What becomes of it, and where does it go? According to the common belief it goes to heaven or hell. But where are heaven and hell? It was said, in other times, that heaven was above and hell below : but what is above and what is below in the universe since the roundness of the earth is known ; the movement of the stars, which makes what is above at one given moment become below in twelve hours ; the infinity of space, into which the eye plunges to immeasurable distances? It is true that by low places we also understand the depths of the earth ; but what has become of those depths since they have been searched into by geology? What, too, of those concentric spheres, called " heaven of fire," " heaven of stars " ? since it is known that the earth is not the center of the worlds, that our sun itself is only one of the millions of suns which shine in space, and of which each is the center of a planetary system. What becomes of the importance of the earth, lost in this immensity ? By what unjus-

tifiable privilege should this imperceptible grain of sand, distinguished neither by its size, its position, nor any particular character, be alone peopled with reasonable beings ?

Reason refuses to admit this inutility of the infinite, and everything tells us that these worlds are inhabited. If they are peopled, then they furnish their proportion to the world of souls : but again, what becomes of these souls, since astronomy and geology have destroyed the dwellings that were assigned them ? and, above all, since the so rational theory of the plurality of worlds has multiplied them to infinity.

The doctrine of the localization of souls not agreeing with the facts of science, another more logical doctrine assigns to them as domain, not a determined and circumscribed spot, but universal space : it is an entire invisible world, in the midst of which we live. which surrounds us, and is always in close contact with us. Is there in that an impossibility — anything repugnant to reason? Not at all ; on the contrary, everything tells us it can not be otherwise.

But, then, future pains and rewards, — what becomes of them, if you take away their special places ? Remark that incredulity as to the place of these pains and rewards is generally excited because they are presented in inadmissible conditions : but say, instead, that the souls find their happiness or misery within themselves, that their lot is subordinated to their moral state ; that the reunion of good and sympathetic souls is a source of felicity ; that, according to the degree of their purification, they penetrate and see into things that vanish before gross souls, — and every one will understand it without trouble. Say, again, that souls reach the supreme degree only through the efforts they make for self-improvement, and after a series of trials which serve for their purification ; that the angels are souls that have reached the highest degree, which all may attain by effort ; that the angels are God's messengers, charged to watch over the execution of his designs throughout the universe; that they are happy in these glorious missions, — and you give to their felicity a more useful and attractive object than that of a perpetual contemplation, which would be nothing more than a perpetual uselessness. Say, again, that demons are but the souls of the wicked, not yet purified, but which can be, like the others ; and that will appear more conformable to the justice and to the goodness of God than the doctrine of being created for evil, and perpetually devoted to evil. Still again, this is what the severest reason, the most exact logic, in a word, good sense, can admit.

But these souls that people space are precisely what are called *spirits: spirits*, then, are but the souls of men stripped of their corporeal envelope. If spirits were beings apart, their existence would be more hypothetical ; but if we admit that there are souls, we must also admit spirits, who are naught else but souls : if we admit that souls are everywhere, we must equally admit that spirits are everywhere. The existence of spirits, then, cannot be denied without denying the existence of souls.

3. This, it is true, is only a theory, more rational than the other: but it is much to have a theory contradicted neither by reason nor science: still more, if it is corroborated by facts, it has for itself the sanction of reasoning and experience. We find these facts in the phenomena of spiritual manifestations, which thus are the proofs patent of the existence of the soul, and

its survival of the earthly body. But with many persons belief stops short at that point ; they fully admit the existence of souls, and, consequently, of spirits ; but they deny the possibility of communicating with them, for the reason, they say, that immaterial beings cannot act on matter. This doubt is founded on ignorance of the true nature of spirits, of which a very false idea is generally conceived ; for they are wrongly imagined to be abstract, vague, and indefinite beings, which they are not.

Let us first speak of the spirit in its union with the body. The spirit is the principal being, since it is the being that *thinks* and *survives ;* the body is, then, only an *accessory* of the spirit — an envelope, a clothing, which it abandons when worn out. Besides this material envelope, the spirit has a second, semi-material, which unites it to the first : at death, the spirit strips off the first, but not the second, to which we give the name of *périsprit*. This semi-material envelope in the human form constitutes for the spirit a fluidic vaporous body, but which, invisible to us in its normal state, does not the less possess some of the properties of matter. The spirit, then, is not a point, an abstraction, but a being, limited and circumscribed, to whom is wanting only the properties of being visible and palpable to resemble human beings. Why, then, can it not act upon matter ? Is it because its body is fluidic ? But is it not among the most rarefied of fluids, those even regarded as imponderable, — electricity, for instance, — that man finds his most powerful motors ? Does not imponderable light exercise a chemical action on ponderable matter ? We do not know the specific nature of the périsprit ; but let us suppose it formed of electrical matter, or some other equally subtile, why should it not possess the same property when directed by a will ?

4. The existence of a soul, and that of God, — the consequence one of the other, — being the base of the whole superstructure, before entering into a spiritual discussion it is necessary to assure ourselves if the interlocutor admits this base.

If to these questions, —

Do you believe in God ?

Do you believe you have a soul ?

Do you believe in the survival of the soul after death ? — he answers negatively, or even if he simply says, "*I don't know; I hope it may be so, but I am not sure,*" — the most frequent equivalent to a polite negation, disguised under less offensive form to avoid shocking too abruptly what are called respectable prejudices, — it would be equally as useless to go further, as to undertake to demonstrate the properties of light to a blind man, who would not admit the existence of light ; for, finally, spiritual manifestations are naught else but the effects of the properties of the soul : with such a person quite another order of ideas should be entered upon, if one would not lose one's time.

If the base is admitted, not as a *probability*, but as a positively declared, incontestable thing, the existence of spirits naturally flows from it.

5. There now remains the question to know if the spirit can communicate with man ; that is to say, if he can exchange ideas with man. And why not ? What is man, if not a spirit imprisoned in a body ? Why should not the free spirit communicate with the captive spirit, as the free man with one who is enchained ? While you admit the survival of the soul, is it rational

not to admit the survival of the affections? Since souls are everywhere, is it not natural to think that the soul of a being who has loved us during his life should come near to us, and should use for that purpose the means at his disposal? During his life did he not act on the matter of his body? Was it not he who directed its movements? Why, then, after his death, being in accord with another spirit bound to a body, should he not borrow this body to manifest his thought, as a dumb person uses a speaker to make himself understood?

6. Let us for a moment make an abstract of the facts which, for us, render the thing incontestable; let us admit it in the shape of a simple hypothesis; we ask that the skeptical prove to us, not by a simple negation, — for their personal opinion does not make a law, — but by peremptory reasons, that it cannot be.

We plant ourselves on their ground, and since they wish to appraise spiritual facts by the aid of material laws, let them draw from that arsenal some mathematical, physical, chemical, mechanical, physiological demonstration, and prove by a plus b, always beginning from the principle of the existence and survival of the soul, —

First. That the being who thinks in us during life should think no longer after death.

Second. That if he thinks, he should not think of those he has loved.

Third. That if he thinks of those he has loved, he should not wish to communicate with them.

Fourth. That if he can be everywhere, he cannot be by our side.

Fifth. That if he is by our side, he cannot communicate with us.

Sixth. That by his fluidic envelope he cannot act on inert matter.

Seventh. That if he can act on inert matter, he cannot act on an animated being.

Eighth. That if he can act on an animated being, he cannot direct his hand to make him write.

Ninth. That, being able to make him write, he cannot answer his questions, and transmit to him his thoughts.

When the adversaries of Spiritism shall have demonstrated to us that this cannot be, by reasons as patent as those by which Galileo demonstrated that it is not the sun that turns around the earth, then we shall be able to say their doubts are well founded. Unhappily, up to this day all their arguments are comprised in these words: " *I do not believe it ; therefore it is impossible.*" They will, doubtless, say that it is for us to prove the reality of the manifestations. We prove it to them by reasoning and by facts : if they admit neither one nor the other, if they deny even what they see, it is for them to prove that our reasoning is false, and our facts impossible.

Chapter II.

THE MARVELOUS AND SUPERNATURAL.

7. If the belief in spirits and in their manifestations were an isolated conception, the product of a system, it could, with some appearance of reason, be suspected of illusion ; but we should like to be told why it is constantly found so strongly impressed among all people, ancient and modern, in holy books and in all known religions ?   It is, say some critics, because man, in all times, has loved the marvelous.   What, then, do you consider the marvelous ?   Whatever is supernatural.   What do you understand by supernatural ?   Whatever is contrary to the laws of nature. You are, then, so thoroughly acquainted with these laws, that it is possible for you to assign a limit to the power of God ?   Well, prove, then, that the existence of spirits and their manifestations are contrary to the laws of nature ; that it is not, and can not be, one of these laws. Follow the spirit doctrine, and see if it has not all the characteristics of an admirable law, which solves all that the laws of philosophy have, until now, been unable to solve.

Thought is one of the attributes of the spirit ; the possibility of acting on matter, of making an impression on our senses, and, consequently, of transmitting his thought, results, if we may so express ourselves, from his physiological constitution ; then there is nothing in this fact either supernatural or marvelous.

When a man dead, thoroughly dead, revives corporeally,— when his dispersed members re-unite to re-form
his body, — that is something marvelous, supernatural, fantastical ; that would be a veritable derogation,
which God could accomplish only by a miracle ; but
there is nothing of the kind in the spirit doctrine.

8. Nevertheless you admit, it will be said, that a
spirit can raise a table, and maintain it in space without support ; is not this a derogation of the law of
gravity? Yes, to the known law ; but has Nature said
her last word ?   Before the ascensional force of certain
gases had been discovered, who would have said that a
heavy machine, carrying several men, could triumph
over the force of attraction ?   Would not this seem
to the eyes of the crowd marvelous, diabolical ?   A
hundred years ago, a person who should have proposed to transmit a despatch five hundred leagues and
receive an answer in a few minutes, would have been
called a fool : had he done it, it would have been
thought he had the devil under his orders ; for at that
time the devil alone was capable of traveling so rapidly.   Why, then, should not an unknown fluid have
the property, under given circumstances, to counterbalance the effect of weight, as hydrogen counterbalances the weight of the balloon ?

This, let us remark, *en passant*, is a comparison, but
not an assimilation, and simply to show, by analogy,
that the fact is not physically impossible.   Now, it is
precisely when the learned, in the observation of these
phenomena, have wished to proceed by assimilation
that they have been led astray.   As to the rest, the
fact is there : all the denials can not make it not be ;
for to deny is not to prove.   For ourselves, there is in it
nothing supernatural ; that is all we can say at present.

9. If the fact is verified, it may be said we accept it ; we accept even the cause you have assigned, — that of an unknown fluid, — but what proves the intervention of spirits ? There lies the marvelous, the supernatural.

An entire demonstration would be necessary here, which would not be in place, and besides, would make double work ; for it will be found throughout the other parts of the book. Only we will say, to sum it up in a few words, that it is founded, in theory, on this principle — all intelligent effect should have an intelligent cause; in practice, on this observation — that the phenomena called spiritual, having given proofs of intelligence, should have their cause outside of matter ; that this intelligence, not being that of the assistants, — this is a result of experience, — must be outside of them : since the acting being can not be seen, it must be an invisible being. It is thus that, from observation to observation, we have learned that this invisible being, to which we have given the name of spirit, is no other than the soul of those who have lived corporeally, and whom death has stripped of their gross, visible envelope, leaving them only an ethereal envelope, invisible in its normal state. Here, then, are the marvelous and the supernatural reduced to their simplest expression.

The existence of invisible beings once proved, their action on matter results from the nature of their fluidic envelope : this action is intelligent, because, in dying, they have lost only their body, but have retained intelligence, which is their essence ; that is the key to all the phenomena erroneously reported supernatural. The existence of spirits is not, then, a preconceived system, an imagined hypothesis to explain facts ; it is a result of observations, and the natural consequence of the existence of the soul : to deny this cause is to deny the soul and its attributes. Those who may think they can give a more rational solution of these intelligent effects, — above all, giving a reason for all the facts, — let them do so, and then the merits of each may be discussed.

10. To the eyes of those who regard matter as the sole power in nature, *all that can not be explained by the laws of matter is marvelous or supernatural*, and for them, *marvelous* is synonymous with *superstitious*. To such persons, religion founded on the existence of an immaterial principle would be a tissue of super-stitions ; they dare not say it aloud, but say it softly, and think to save appearances by conceding that there needs a religion for the people and to make chil-dren good ; but one of two things, either the religious principle is true or it is false ; if true, it is so for all the world ; if false, it is no better for the ignorant than for the enlightened.

11. Those who attack Spiritism, under the name of the marvelous, generally rest on the materialistic principle ; since, in the very denying of all extra ma-terial effect, they deny the existence of the soul : go to the very bottom of their thought, scrutinize well the sense of their words, and you will almost always see this principle, if not categorically formulated, peep from under the pretended rational philosophy with which they cover it.

Thus, in rejecting, on the score of *marvelous*, all that flows from the existence of the soul, they are con-sistent with themselves ; not admitting the cause, they can not admit the effects : thence a preconceived opin-ion, that incapacitates them from judging soundly of

Spiritism, because they start on a principle of negation for all that is not material. As for us, while we admit all the effects which are the consequence of the existence of the soul, does it follow that we should accept all the facts called marvelous? that we should be the champions of all dreamers, skilled in all Utopian projects, all systematic eccentricities? One must know very little of Spiritism to think so; but our adversaries do not look at it so closely; the necessity of knowing what they talk of is the least of their care. According to them, the marvelous is absurd; Spiritism rests on marvelous facts; hence Spiritism is absurd: this is, for them, a judgment without appeal. They think to offer an unanswerable argument when, after having made erudite researches among the convulsionaries of St. Medard, the *camisards* of the caverns, the nuns of Loudun, they have discovered patent evidences of fraud, which no one denies; but are these histories the evangel of Spiritism? Have its partisans denied that charlatanism has used certain facts for its profit? that the imagination has created, and fanaticism exaggerated much of it? It is no more responsible for the extravagances committed in its name, than true science for the abuses of ignorance, and true religion for the excesses of fanaticism.

Many critics judge Spiritism only by fairy tales and popular legends, which are its fictions: as well judge history by historical romances or tragedies.

12. In elementary logic, to discuss a thing, one must know it; for the opinion of a critic has a value only as he speaks in perfect knowledge of cause; then, only, his opinion, were it erroneous, can be taken into consideration: but of what weight is it on a matter of which he knows nothing? The true critic should

give proof, not only of erudition, but of profound knowledge of the parts of the subject-matter, of a sound judgment, and of impartiality in every trial ; otherwise any fiddler could arrogate to himself the right to judge of Rossini, and a dauber that of censuring Raphael.

13. Spiritism, then, does not accept all the facts reputed marvelous or supernatural ; far from that, it demonstrates the impossibility of a great number, and the absurdity of certain beliefs which constitute, properly speaking, superstition. It is true that in what it admits there are things that, for the skeptic, are of the purely marvelous, otherwise called superstition. So be it ; but at least discuss only those points, for on the others it has nothing to say, and you preach to the converted. In attacking what refutes itself, you prove your ignorance of the matter, and your arguments fall to the ground. But, it may be said, where does the belief of Spiritism stop ? Read, observe, and you will know. No science is acquired without time and study ; and Spiritism, which touches on the gravest questions of philosophy, on all the branches of social order, which embraces at the same time man physical and man moral, is itself an entire science, an entire philosophy, which can no more be learned in a few hours than any other science. There would be as much puerility in seeing the whole of Spiritism in table-turning as to see the whole of physics in certain toys. For whoever would penetrate beyond the surface, there are not hours, but months and years, required to probe all its mysteries. Judge by that of the degree of knowledge, and of the value of the opinion of those who arrogate to themselves the right of judging, because they have witnessed one or two experiments, most

often only by way of distraction or pastime. They will, doubtless, say they have not the leisure to give all the time necessary to this study. So be it; nothing constrains them; but, then, when they have not the time to learn a thing, let them not speak on it, still less judge it, if they would not be accused of frivolity; the more exalted a position one occupies in science, the less excusable is it to treat lightly a subject one does not know.

14. We sum up in the following propositions:—

First. All the spiritual phenomena have for their principle the existence of the soul, its survival of the body, and its manifestations.

Second. These phenomena, being founded on a law of nature, have in them nothing *marvelous* or *supernatural*, in the ordinary acceptation of these words.

Third. Many facts are reputed supernatural only by reason of their cause not being known. Spiritism, in assigning their cause, brings them into the domain of natural phenomena.

Fourth. Among the facts called supernatural, there are many of which Spiritism demonstrates the impossibility, and which it places among superstitious beliefs.

Fifth. While Spiritism recognizes in many popular beliefs a foundation of truth, it refuses positively the responsibility of all the fantastic tales created by the imagination.

Sixth. To judge Spiritism by what it does not admit, is a proof of ignorance, and destroys all the value of a person's opinion.

Seventh. The explication of the facts admitted by Spiritism, their causes and moral consequences, constitute a whole science, a whole philosophy, which requires a serious, persevering, and searching study.

Eighth. Spiritism can regard as a serious critic only him who may have seen all, studied all, explored all, with the patience and perseverance of a conscientious observer; who may know as much on this subject as the most enlightened believer; who, consequently, will have drawn his knowledge from elsewhere than the romances of the science; to whose attention *no fact* can be brought with which he is not acquainted, no argument that he has not studied; let him refute, not by negations, but by other arguments more peremptory; in a word, who can assign a more logical cause for the averred facts. Such a critic is yet to be found.

15. We mentioned the word *miracle:* a short observation on this subject will not be out of place in this chapter on the marvelous.

In its primitive acceptation, and by its etymology, the word *miracle* signifies *extraordinary thing; thing admirable to see;* but this word, like many others, has wandered from its original sense, and now it is, according to the Academy, *an act of the divine power contrary to the common laws of nature.* Such is, in fact, its usual acceptation, and it is now only by comparison, and by metaphor, that it is applied to common things which surprise us, and whose cause is unknown. It enters not into our views to examine if God has judged it useful, under certain circumstances, to set aside the laws established by himself; our aim is only to demonstrate that the spiritual phenomena, however extraordinary they may be, do not set aside these laws — have nothing of a miraculous character; neither are they marvelous or supernatural. A miracle cannot be explained; the spiritual phenomena, on the contrary, are explained in the most rational manner; they are not then miracles, but simple effects, which have their cause in general laws. A miracle has still another character; it is that of being insulated and isolated. But from the moment a fact is reproduced, so to say, at will, and by different persons, it cannot be a miracle.

Science every day performs miracles in the eyes of the ignorant; this is why, formerly, those who knew more than the common herd passed for sorcerers, and, as it was thought all super-human science came from the devil, they burned them. Now, when people are much more civilized, they content themselves with sending them to the mad-house.

That a man really dead, as we said in the beginning, should be recalled to life by divine intervention, — that is a real miracle, because it is contrary to the laws of nature. But if the man had only the appearance of death, if there remained in him some *latent vitality*, and science, or magnetic action, should succeed in re-animating him, this, in the eyes of enlightened persons, is a natural phenomenon; but in the eyes of the ignorant, the fact will pass for miraculous, and the author will be pursued with stones or venerated, according to the character of the individuals. In some countries, should a natural philosopher let fly an electrical paper kite, and cause the thunderbolt to strike a tree, this new Prometheus would be looked upon as armed with diabolic power; and it may be said, in passing, Prometheus seems to us singularly to have forestalled Franklin; but Joshua arresting the movement of the sun, or, rather, of the earth, — this is a real miracle; for we know of no magnetizer endowed with sufficient power to perform such a prodigy. Of all the spiritual phenomena, one of the most extraordinary is, without contradiction, that of direct writing, and the one that shows, in the most evident manner, the action of occult intelligences ; but, as the phenomenon is produced by invisible beings, it is no more miraculous than all the other phenomena due to invisible agents, because these occult beings, who people space, are one of the powers of nature — a power whose action is incessant on the material, as well as on the moral world.

Spiritism, in shedding light on this power, gives us the key to a crowd of things unexplained and inexplicable by all other means, and which have, in times past, passed for prodigies : like magnetism, it reveals a law, if not unknown, at least scarcely comprehended ; or, to better express it, the effects are known, for they have been produced through all time ; but the law was not known, and it is the ignorance of this law that has engendered superstition. The law known, the marvelous disappears, and the phenomena reënter the natural order of things. This is why spirits no more perform a miracle in turning a table, or in writing, than the doctor in reviving a dying man, or the natural philosopher in causing the fall of the thunderbolt. He who should pretend, by the aid of this science, to *perform miracles*, would be either ignorant of the thing or an impostor.

16. Before the causes were known, spiritual phenomena, as well as magnetic phenomena, might readily have passed for prodigies ; but as the skeptics, the free-thinkers, — that is, those who have the exclusive privilege of reason and good sense, — believe nothing possible which they cannot understand, all facts reputed wonderful are the object of their ridicule, and as religion contains a great number of facts of this kind, they do not believe in religion ; and from thence

to absolute skepticism is but a step. Spiritism, in explaining the greater part of these facts, assigns them a cause. It comes, then, to the aid of religion in demonstrating certain facts, which, though no longer possessing a miraculous character, are not the less extraordinary ; and God is no less grand, no less powerful, for not having set aside his laws. Of what jests have not the suspensions of St. Cupertin been the object! But the ethereal suspension of heavy bodies is a fact explained by spirit law: we have been *personally* eye-witnesses, and Mr. Home, as well as other persons of our acquaintance, have, at various times, reproduced St. Cupertin's phenomenon. Thus this phenomenon enters into the order of natural things.

17. Among the number of facts of this kind, apparitions must be placed in the front rank, because they are most frequent. That of La Salette, about which even the clergy are divided, is not for us an isolated fact. Assuredly we cannot affirm that it took place, because we have no material proof of it ; but for us it is possible, insomuch as millions of recent analogous facts are known to us ; we believe in them, not only because their reality is proved to us, but because we know perfectly the manner in which they are produced. Let any one look well into the theory we give, further on, of apparitions, and it will be seen that this phenomenon becomes as simple and as plausible as a host of physical phenomena which are wonderful only because the key to them is unknown. As to the person who presented himself at La Salette, that is another question ; his identity is not at all demonstrated : we simply state that an apparition *could* take place ; with the rest we have nothing to do. Every one, in this respect, may have his own convictions. Spiritism

is not obliged to meddle with them ; we say only that the facts produced by Spiritism reveal to us new laws, and give us the key to a host of things that appear supernatural : if some of those which pass for miraculous find here a logical explanation, it is one reason why we should not be in haste to deny what we do not understand.

Spiritual phenomena are contested by some persons precisely because they appear to be outside of the common law, and they cannot explain them to themselves. Give them a rational basis, and the doubt ceases. Explanation in this age, when words do not satisfy, is, then, a powerful motive for conviction. Thus we see, every day, persons who have never witnessed a single act, have never seen a table turn, nor a medium write, and who are as convinced as ourselves, only because they have read and comprehended. If one should only believe what one has seen with the eyes, one's convictions would be reduced to very little.

CHAPTER III.

METHOD.

18. THE very natural and praiseworthy desire of every believer—a desire that cannot be too much encouraged—is to make proselytes. It is with the view of facilitating their task that we propose to examine here the surest way, according to our ideas, to attain this end, in order to spare them useless efforts.

We have said that Spiritism is an entire science, an entire philosophy : he who would seriously know it should, then, as a first condition, compel himself to a serious study, and persuade himself that no more than any other science can it be learned by sport. Spiritism, we have said, touches on all the questions that interest humanity ; its field is immense, and it is most especially in its consequences that we should view it. Belief in spirits, doubtless, forms its basis ; but that belief no more suffices to make an enlightened spiritist, than the belief in God suffices to make a theologian. Let us see, then, what is the fittest mode of procedure, in these instructions, to lead most surely to conviction.

Let not believers be frightened by this word instruction ; there is other teaching than that given from the pulpit or the tribunal ; there is also that of simple conversation. Every person who seeks to persuade another, whether by way of explanations or by experiments, instructs : what we desire is, that his trouble shall bear fruit, and it is for that purpose we give some advice, by which those who wish to instruct themselves may also profit ; they will here find the means of more certainly and quickly reaching their end.

19. It is generally believed that, in order to convince, it suffices to show facts. This seems, indeed, the most logical way, and yet experience shows that it is not always the better ; for we often see persons whom the most palpable facts can never convince. Why is this ? We shall try to demonstrate.

In Spiritism the question of spirits is secondary and consecutive ; it is not the point of departure ; and there, precisely, is the error into which we fall, and which causes us to fail with certain persons. Spirits being naught else but the souls of men, the true point of departure, then, is the existence of the soul. But how can a materialist admit that beings exist outside of the material world, when he believes himself to be but matter ? How can he believe in spirits outside of himself, when he does not believe he has one within ? In vain would you accumulate before his eyes the most palpable proofs ; he would question them all, because he does not admit the principle. All methodical teaching should proceed from the known to the unknown : with the materialist the known is matter ; begin, then, with matter, and try, above all, in making him observe it, to convince him that there is within him something that escapes the laws of matter ; in a word, *before making him a spiritist, try to make him a spiritualist.* But for that an entirely different order of facts is requisite, a teaching wholly special, in which we must proceed by other means. To talk to him of spirits, before he is convinced of having a soul, is to begin at the end, for he cannot admit the conclusion if he admit not the premises. Thus, before undertaking to convince the skeptic, even by facts, it is necessary to be assured of his opinion in regard to the soul; that is, if he believe in its existence, its survival of the body, its individuality after death; if his answer is in the negative, it will be trouble wasted to talk to him of spirits. This is the rule: we do not say there is no exception, but then there are probably other causes which make him less refractory.

20. Among materialists are two classes. In the first we place those who are such *from system;* with them it is not doubt, but absolute negation, reasoned after their own manner; in their eyes man is a machine, which goes as long as it is wound up, which gets out of order, and of which, after death, there remains but the carcass. Their number is, happily, very restricted, and nowhere constitutes a boldly-avowed school; it is not necessary to insist on the deplorable results to social order from popularizing such a doctrine; we have said enough on that subject in the *Book on Spirits* (No. 147 and conclusion, § iii.).

When we say that doubt ceases with the skeptic in presence of a rational explanation, we must except pure materialists — those who deny all power and all intelligent principle outside of matter: the greater part confirm themselves in their opinion through pride, and consider their self-love engaged to persist in it. This they do in the face of and against all contrary proofs, because they do not want to yield. With such people nothing can be done; we must not even be taken by the false seeming of sincerity of those who say, Make me see, and I will believe. Some are more frank, and say plainly, I should like to see what I will not believe.

21. The second class of materialists, and by far the most numerous, — for a real materialism is an unnatural sentiment, — comprises those who are such through indifference, and one might say, for *want of better*, they are not such from deliberate purpose, and ask nothing better than to believe, for uncertainty is a torment to them. There is within them a vague aspiration toward the future ; but this future has been presented to them under colors their reason cannot accept ; from thence doubt, and, as a consequence of doubt, skepticism. With them disbelief is not a system ; show them something rational, and they accept it eagerly ; such persons can understand us, for they are nearer to us than they themselves suppose. With the former talk neither of revelation, nor angels, nor paradise ; they would not comprehend you ; but place yourself on their ground, prove to them, first, that the laws of physiology are powerless to give a reason for everything ; the rest will follow. It is otherwise when skepticism is not confirmed, for then belief is not absolutely null ; it is a latent germ, filled with ill weeds, but which a spark can reanimate ; it is the blind to whom one can give sight, and who is joyful in once more seeing the light of day ; it is the shipwrecked to whom one may extend a plank of safety.

22. Besides materialists, properly so called, there is a third class of unbelievers, who, though spiritualists without the name, are not the less very refractory ; these are *intentional disbelievers*. They would be sorry to believe, because that would disturb their quiet in material enjoyments ; they fear to see the condemnation of their ambition, of their egotism, and of the human vanities that constitute their delights ; they

close their eyes that they may not see, their ears that they may not hear. One can only pity them.

23. We will speak only from memory of a fourth category, whom we shall call *interested unbelievers*, or those *from insincerity*. These very well understand Spiritism, but ostensibly they condemn from motives of personal interest. Of them there is nothing to be said, as there is nothing to be done with them. If the real materialist deceive himself, there is at least the excuse of sincerity; he can be redeemed by being shown his error: here it is a thing settled, against which all arguments come to naught; time will open their eyes, and show them, perhaps to their cost, wherein their true interest consisted; for not being able to hinder the spread of the truth, they will be carried away by the torrent, and with them the interests they thought to save.

24. In addition to these various categories of opponents there is an infinity of shades, among which may be reckoned the skeptical *from pusillanimity;* courage will come to them when they see others are not burned; *the skeptical from religious scruples;* an enlightened study will teach them that Spiritism rests on the fundamental basis of religion, and that it respects all beliefs; that one of its effects is to give religious sentiments to those who have them not, to fortify them with those who are wavering: then come the skeptical from pride, from the spirit of contradiction, from indifference, from frivolity, &c., &c.

25. We cannot omit a class which we shall call that of *the skeptical from deception.* It comprises persons who have passed from an exaggerated confidence to skepticism, because they have experienced disappointments; then, discouraged, they have abandoned all,

rejected all. They are in the position of him who denies all sincerity because he has been deceived. Again, it is the result of an incomplete study of Spiritism, and of a defect of experience. He who is mystified by the spirits is, generally, he who asks of them what they ought not or cannot tell, or because he is not sufficiently clear on the subject to distinguish truth from imposture. Besides, many see in Spiritism only a new means of divination, and imagine that spirits are made for fortune-tellers ; so light and mocking spirits are not to blame if they amuse themselves at their expense. In this way they predict husbands to young girls, honors, inheritances, hidden treasures, &c., to the ambitious ; from thence often arise disagreeable deceptions, from which a serious and prudent man always knows how to preserve himself.

26. A very numerous class, the most numerous of all, indeed, but which cannot be placed among opponents, is that of the *uncertain ;* they are usually *spiritualists* in principle ; with the most of them there is a vague intuition of the spirit idea, an aspiration toward something they cannot define ; it is only necessary that their thoughts should be regulated and formulated ; for them Spiritism is like a flash of light ; it is the daylight that disperses the fog ; thus they seize it eagerly, because it delivers them from the agonies of uncertainty.

27. If, now, we cast a glance on the various classes of *believers*, we shall find, first, *the spiritists without knowing it :* it is, properly speaking, a variety or a shade of the preceding class. Without ever having heard of the spirit doctrine, they have the innate sentiment of the grand principles that flow from it, and this sentiment is reflected in certain passages of their

writings and discourses to such an extent, that, in listening to them, one would suppose them thoroughly
initiated. We find numerous examples of them in
sacred and profane writers, in poets, orators, moralists,
in ancient and modern philosophers.

28. Among those whom a direct study has convinced, we may distinguish, —

First. Those who believe purely and simply in the
manifestations. Spiritism is for them a simple science
of observation, a series of facts more or less curious :
we shall call them *experimental spiritists.*

Second. Those who see in Spiritism something
besides facts ; who comprehend its philosophy, admire
the morality that flows from it, but do not practice it.
Its influence on their character is insignificant or null ;
they change nothing of their habits, neither deprive
themselves of a single enjoyment ; the miser remains
sordid, the proud full of himself, the envious and jealous always hostile ; to them Christian charity is but a
beautiful maxim : these are *imperfect spiritists.*

Third. Those who are not contented with admiring
spirit morality, but who practice it and accept all its
consequences. Convinced that the terrestrial existence is a passing trial, they try to put to profit these
short moments, to walk in the road of progress which
alone can elevate them in the hierarchy of the world
of spirits, forcing themselves to do good, and to repress
their evil inclinations. What they relate is always
true, for their convictions take from them all thought
of evil. Charity is in all things the rule of their conduct. These are the *true spiritists*, or, better still,
Christian spiritists.

Fourth. Finally, there are *exalted spiritists.* The
human species would be perfect, if it would take only

the good side of things.   Exaggeration in anything
is injurious ; in Spiritism it gives too blind and
childish a confidence in the things of the invisible
world, and causes the too easy acceptation of what reflection and examination show to be absurd or impossible ; but enthusiasm does not reflect — it dazzles.
This kind is more injurious than useful to the cause
of Spiritism ; they are the less easy to convince because they doubt, and with reason, their own judgment ; they are very sincere dupes, whether it be of
mystifying spirits, or of men who wish to play upon
their credulity.   If they alone were to suffer the consequences, the evil would be but half ; the worst is,
that, without wishing it, they arm the skeptical, who
are always seeking occasions to impute to all the folly
of some.   This is, doubtless, neither just nor rational ;
but, it is well known, the adversaries of Spiritism recognize only their own reason as being good gold, and
to know thoroughly the subject on which they speak
is the least of their cares.

29. The means of conviction vary exceedingly, according to individuals ; what persuades one is nothing
to another ; some are convinced by certain material
manifestations, others by intelligent communications ;
the greater part by reasoning.   We might even say
that, for the greater part of those not prepared by
reasoning, the material phenomena are of little weight.
The more extraordinary these phenomena, and the further removed from known laws, the more opposition
they meet, and for a very simple reason, — that one is
naturally inclined to doubt a thing not having a rational sanction ; each sees it from his own stand-point,
and explains it after his own fashion : the materialist
sees in it a purely physical cause, or a superstition ;

the ignorant and the superstitious see a diabolical or supernatural cause ; while a true explanation destroys these preconceived ideas, and shows, if not the reality, at least the possibility ; they understand before seeing it ; and from the moment its possibility is recognized, conviction is three quarters accomplished.

30. Is it worth while to try to convince an obstinate unbeliever ? We have said that it depends on the causes and nature of his disbelief ; often the persistent efforts made to persuade one strengthen within him the idea of his personal importance, and become a reason for his increased obstinacy. If one is convinced neither by reasonings nor by facts, it shows that he must still suffer the trial of skepticism ; we must leave to Providence the care of bringing together circumstances more favorable for him : there are plenty of people asking to receive the light ; it is not worth while to waste time on those who reject it. Address yourselves, then, to the willing, whose number is greater than is supposed ; and their example, being multiplied, will overcome more resistance than words. The true spiritist will never lack good to do — afflicted hearts to soothe, consolations to give, despair to calm, moral reforms to effect : this is his mission ; here, also, he will find his true satisfaction. Spiritism is in the air ; it spreads by the law of events, and because it makes those happy who profess it. When its systematic adversaries shall hear it resound about them, even among their friends, they will realize their own isolation, and will be forced to be silent, or yield assent.

31. To proceed : in the teaching of Spiritism, as in that of the ordinary sciences, the whole series of phenomena that can be produced should be passed in re-

view, beginning with the most simple, and reaching, by successive stages, the most complicated; but this cannot be done, for it would be impossible to give a course of experimental Spiritism, as one would a course of physics or chemistry. In the natural sciences we operate on brute matter, manipulating it at will, and are nearly always sure of being able to regulate the effects; in Spiritism we have to do with intelligences that are free, and prove to us at every instant that they are not bound to obey our caprices; we must then observe, await the results, seize them in passing: so we here announce that *whoever would flatter himself to obtain them at will must be either an ignoramus or an impostor.* This is why TRUE Spiritism never makes a spectacle of itself, and never mounts the rostrum. Besides, there is something illogical in supposing that spirits come to make a parade, and submit to investigation, as objects of curiosity. The phenomena, therefore, may either fail altogether when we want them, or be presented in an entirely different order from what we desire. Add, again, that to obtain them we require persons endowed with special faculties, and that these faculties vary infinitely, according to the aptitude of individuals; and as it is extremely rare that one person should possess all the aptitudes, it is one difficulty the more, for we should need to have always at hand a veritable collection of mediums, which is scarcely possible.

The means of obviating this inconvenience is very simple, — it is to begin with the theory; there all the phenomena are passed in review; they are explained, can be accounted for, their possibility understood, the conditions under which they can be produced and the obstacles they may meet can be known; then, whatever may be the order into which they may be led by circumstances, there will be nothing in them to create surprise. This method offers still another advantage — that of sparing the operator numberless disappointments ; forewarned against the difficulties, he can be on his guard, and avoid acquiring experience at too great expense.

Since we have been engaged with Spiritism, it would be hard to tell the number of persons who have come to us, and among them how many we have seen remain indifferent or skeptical, in presence of the most glaring facts, and who have afterward been convinced only by a reasonable explanation ; how many others who have been predisposed to conviction by reasoning ; how many, also, who have been persuaded without seeing, but simply because they understood. Thus we speak from experience, when we say that the better method of teaching Spiritism is to address the reason before addressing the eyes. It is the one we follow in our lessons, and we can only praise it.

32. The previous study of the theory has another advantage; it shows at one view the grandeur of the end, and the sweep of the science. He who begins by seeing tables turned or rapped, is more disposed to ridicule, because he can scarcely imagine that out of a table can come a regenerating doctrine for humanity. We have always remarked that those who believe without having seen, but because they have read and understood, far from being superficial, are, on the contrary, the ones who reflect the most ; resting more on the fundamental principles than on the form, to them the philosophical part is the principal, the phenomena but the accessories ; and they say to themselves that even did these phenomena not exist, there would not

the less remain·a philosophy that alone can solve problems hitherto insoluble ; which alone gives the most
rational theory of man's past and future ; they prefer
a doctrine that explains, to one that explains not at
all, or explains badly.   A thoughtful person will readily
comprehend that the manifestations might be wholly
done away with, and thé doctrine none the less remain ;
the manifestations corroborate, confirm it, but are not
its essential basis ; the serious observer does not reject them, on the contrary, but he awaits circumstances favorable to his being a witness of them.   The
proof of what we advance is, that, before having heard
of the manifestations, very many persons have had an
intuition of this doctrine, which has but given a body,
a unity, to their ideas.

33. At the same time it would not be strictly true
to say that those who begin with the theory lack subjects for practical observation ; on the contrary, they
have plenty which should possess greater weight in
their estimation, than those that might be produced
before their eyes : these are the numerous facts of
spontaneous manifestations, of which we shall speak in
the following chapters.

There are few persons who have not some knowledge of them, if only by hearsay ; many have themselves had experiences to which they have given but
slight attention. The theory has this effect — it explains
them ; and we say that these facts have great weight
when they rest on invincible testimony, because then
neither preparation nor connivance can be supposed.
If the induced phenomena did not exist, the spontaneous phenomena would none the less be present, and
Spiritism, should it have no result but to give a rational solution of them, would be doing much. Thus, most

of those who read recall these facts, thereby confirming the theory.

34. Our ideas would be strangely misunderstood, were it supposed that we advise a neglect of facts ; it is by the facts that we have arrived at the theory ; it is true that assiduous labor for several years, and thousands of observations, have been necessary ; but since the facts have served us, and do serve us daily, we should be inconsistent to deny their importance, especially as we are writing a book for the purpose of making them known. We only say that, without reasoning, they would not suffice to produce conviction ; that a previous explanation, by destroying prejudices, and showing that there is nothing in them contrary to reason, *disposes* one for their acceptance. This is so true that, of ten persons, complete novices, who may assist at an experimental *séance*, were it the most satisfying one to believers, nine would leave it unconvinced, some more incredulous than before, because the experiments will not have answered their expectations. It would be quite otherwise with those who could understand them from a previous theoretic knowledge ; it is a means of criticising, but nothing surprises them, not even want of success, because they know in what conditions the facts are produced, and that they must not ask what cannot be given. The previous knowledge of the facts thus enables them to judge of all anomalies, but, above all, permits them to catch a multitude of details, often of very delicate shades, which are, for them, means of conviction, and which escape the ignorant observer. Such are the motives for admitting to our experimental *séances* only persons possessing preparatory notions enough to understand what is being done, persuaded that any

others would lose their time, and cause us to lose ours.

35. To those who would desire to acquire the preliminary knowledge by reading our works, we would advise the following order: —

First. *What is Spiritism?* This tract, of a hundred pages only, is a summary exposition of the principles of the spirit doctrine, a general glance, which permits us to embrace the whole in a brief outline. In a few words we see the end, and can judge of its range. Above all, here may be found answers to the principal questions, or objections, which novices are disposed to make.

This first, which calls for little time, is an introduction which facilitates a more profound study.

Second. *The Book on Spirits.* It contains the doctrine complete, dictated by the spirits themselves, with all its philosophy, and all its moral consequences; it is the destiny of man unvailed, the initiation into the nature of spirits, and into the mysteries of the life beyond the grave. In reading this it will be seen that Spiritism has a serious aim, and is not a frivolous pastime.

Third. *The Book on Mediums*, intended to direct in the practice of manifestations, by the knowledge of the proper means of communicating with spirits ; it is a guide either for mediums or invocators, and is the complement of the *Book on Spirits*.

Fourth. *The Spirit Reviewed.* This is a varied collection of facts, of theoretic explanations and detached fragments, which complete what is said in the two preceding works, and of which it is in some sort the application. It may be read at the same time, but will be more profitable and more intelligible, particularly after the *Book on Spirits*. This is all we can say. Those who desire to understand a science thoroughly must, necessarily, read all that is written on the subject, or, at least, the principal things, and not limit themselves to a single author ; they should even read the for and against, the critics as well as the apologists, to know the different systems, to be able to judge by comparison. In this connection we neither extol nor criticise any work, desiring in nothing to influence the opinion that may be formed ; bringing our stone to the edifice, we place ourselves in the ranks : it does not pertain to us to be judge and client, and we make not the absurd pretension of being sole dispenser of the light ; it is for the reader to distinguish between the good and the bad, the true and the false.

Chapter IV.

SYSTEMS.

36. When the strange phenomena of Spiritism began to be produced, or rather reproduced in these latter times, the first sentiment they excited was doubt even of their reality, and still greater of their cause. When they were proved by indubitable evidence, and by the experiments every one could make for himself, each one interpreted them after his own fashion, according to his personal ideas, beliefs, or preconceptions; from thence have arisen several systems, which a more attentive observation must reduce to their just value.

The adversaries of Spiritism have thought to find an argument in this difference of opinion, saying that the spiritists do not agree among themselves. This is a very poor argument, when one reflects that the steps of all newly-born science are necessarily uncertain, until time is given to bring together and make co-ordinate the facts that may fix opinion: in proportion as the facts become complete, and are better observed, the premature ideas are effaced, and unity established, at least on the fundamental points, if not in all the details. This is what has taken place for Spiritism; it could not escape the common law, and must, by its very nature, lend itself more than any other to diversity of interpretations. One might even say that in this respect it has advanced more rapidly than other sciences, its elders ; medicine, for instance, which still divides the most learned.

37. In methodical order, to follow the progressive march of ideas, we may place at the head of the list those that may be called *systems of negation*, those of the adversaries of Spiritism. We have refuted their objections in the introduction and in the conclusion of the *Book on Spirits*, also in the little work entitled *What is Spiritism?* It would be superfluous to enter into it again ; we will simply recall, in a few words, the bases on which they stand. Spirit phenomena are of two kinds, physical and intelligent effects. Not admitting the existence of spirits, for the reason that they admit nothing outside of matter, it may be readily conceived that they deny the intelligent effects, they comment upon them from their own stand-point, and their arguments may be summed up in the following systems : —

38. *System of Charlatanism.* Among our antago-nists many attribute these effects to fraud, because some of them have been imitated. This supposition would transform all spiritists into dupes, all mediums into cheats, without regard to the position, the charac-ter, knowledge, and reputation of the persons. If this deserved an answer, we might say that certain phe-nomena of physics have also been imitated by jugglers, and that it proves nothing against the real science. Besides, there are persons whose characters are beyond all suspicion of fraud, and one must be wanting in every vestige of good breeding and urbanity to dare to say to them that they are the accomplices of char-latanism. In a very respectable parlor, a gentleman, otherwise well bred, having permitted himself to make a reflection of this nature, the lady of the house said

to him, " Since you are not content, sir, your money will be returned to you at the door," and, with a gesture, made him understand what he would better do. Is that to say that there are no abuses in it? To think that we must admit men to be perfect.

Everything is abused, even the most sacred things ; why, then, should not Spiritism be abused ? But the bad use that may be made of a thing should cause no prejudice against the thing itself; the only way by which we can judge of men's sincerity is by the motives from which they act. Where there is no speculation, charlatanism can find no place.

39. *System of Insanity.* Some persons condescendingly wish to do away with the suspicion of fraud, and pretend that those who do not make dupes are themselves dupes ; which is as much as to say they are insane. When skeptics speak without ceremony, they say, " O, they are crazy !" thus arrogating to themselves alone the privilege of good sense. This is the great argument of those who have no good reason to bring forward. This mode of attack has so long served that it has become ridiculous, and does not deserve that time should be wasted in refuting it. Besides, spiritists scarcely trouble themselves about it ; they bravely take their stand and console themselves in the knowledge that they have, as companions in the misfortune, plenty of people whose merits cannot be disputed. It must be agreed that this insanity, if insanity it be, has a very singular character, which is that, by preference, it attacks the enlightened class, among whom Spiritism has hitherto reckoned the immense majority of its believers. If among the number we find some eccentric, it proves no more against the doctrine than the crazy religious prove against religion, the crazy

music-lovers against music, the crazy mathematicians against mathematics. All ideas have found exaggerated fanatics, and one must be endowed with a very obtuse judgment to confound the exaggeration of a thing with the thing itself. We refer, for more enlarged explanation of this subject, to our tract, *What is Spiritism?* to the *Book on Spirits* (Introduction, par. XV.).

40. *System of Hallucination.* Another opinion, less offensive, inasmuch as it has a little scientific color, consists in placing all the phenomena to the account of illusion of the senses ; thus the observer is perfectly sincere, only he thinks he sees what he does not see. When he sees a table rise, and sustain itself in the air without support, the table has not really left its place ; he sees it in the air by a kind of mirage, or an effect of refraction, as one would see a star or an object in the water, out of its real place. That might possibly be, but those who have witnessed this phenomenon have verified the isolation by passing under the suspended table, which would seem to be difficult to do if it had not left the ground. On the other hand, it has many times happened that, in coming down, the table has broken : would this also be called an optical delusion ?

A well-known physiological cause can, without doubt, make one believe he sees a thing turn that does not stir, or make one think one's self turning when one is not moving ; but when several persons around a table are carried along by so rapid a movement, that they can scarcely follow it, that some are often thrown to the ground, will they say that all of them are taken with a kind of vertigo, like that of the drunkard, who thought he saw his house moving away from before him ?

41. *System of Muscle-cracking.* If it might be thus for the sight, it cannot be the same for the hearing, and when blows struck are heard by a whole assembly, they cannot reasonably be attributed to illusion. Understand, we set aside all idea of fraud, and suppose that attentive observation has proved that they are owing to no accidental or material change. It is true that a learned physician has given a positive explanation: he says (Note 1), "The cause of it is in the voluntary or involuntary contractions of the tendon of the muscle of the ankle joint." In connection with this subject he enters into the most complete anatomical details, to demonstrate by what mechanism this tendon can produce these sounds, imitate the beating of the drum, and even execute rhythmic airs ; from whence he concludes that those who think they hear blows struck in a table are dupes either of mystification or illusion. The fact, in itself, is not new ; unhappily for the author of this pretended discovery, his theory does not hold in all cases. Let us first say that those who enjoy the singular faculty of making the ankle joint, or any other muscle, crack at will, or play tunes by this means, are exceptional subjects, while those who cause table rapping are very common, and that those who possess the last faculty scarcely ever enjoy the first. In the second place, this learned doctor has forgotten to explain how the muscular cracking of a person, immovable and isolated from the table, can produce therein vibrations sensible to the touch ; how this sound can be thrown, at the will of the assistants, into different parts of the table, into other furniture, against the walls, the ceiling, &c.; how, finally, the action of this muscle can extend to a table that is not touched, and make it move. This explana-

tion, if indeed it were one, could only invalidate the phenomenon of the rapping, but does not concern all the
other modes of communication. Let us conclude that
he has judged without having seen, or, without having
thoroughly or well seen. It is always to be regretted
that scientific men should give a hasty opinion on
what they do not understand, when the facts can give
the lie to their explanations. Their knowledge, at
least, should make them as much more circumspect in
their judgments as it removes for them the limits of
the unknown.

42. *System of Physical Causes.* Here we leave the
system of absolute negation. The reality of the phenomena being proved, the first thought that naturally
entered the minds of those who saw them was to
attribute the movements to magnetism, to electricity,
or to the action of some kind of fluid ; in a word, to a
cause entirely physical and material. In this opinion
there was nothing irrational, and it would have prevailed had the phenomena been limited to purely
physical effects. One circumstance seemed to corroborate it ; in certain cases, the increase of the power
according to the number of persons ; each one of
them might thus be considered as one of the elements
of a human electric pile. What characterizes a true
theory, we have said, is the power of giving a reason
for everything ; but if a single fact comes to contradict it, it must be false, incomplete, or too absolute.
This has happened in this instance. These movements and these rappings have given signs of intelligence, in obeying the will and answering to the
thought ; they must, then, have an intelligent cause.
As soon as the effect ceases to be purely physical,
the cause, for that very reason, must have another

source : thus the system of the *exclusive* action of a
material agent was abandoned, and is only found
among those who judge *a priori*, and without having
seen.   The main point, then, is to verify the intelligent action ; and of this any one, who will take the
trouble to observe, may be convinced.

43. *System of Reflex Action.* Intelligent action once
recognized, the source of this intelligence remained to
be accounted for. It was thought it might be the
medium or the assistants who were reflected like the
light, or the rays of sound. That was possible ; experience alone could decide. But, first, let us remark,
that this system completely sets aside the purely materialistic idea, for, in order that the intelligence of the
assistants should be able to be reproduced in an indirect way, we must admit a principle within man beyond
the organism. If the thought expressed had always
been that of the assistants, the reflex theory might
have been confirmed ; but was not the phenomenon,
even reduced to that proportion, of the highest interest ?   Thought being reflected into an inert body, and
being translated by movement and sound, — was not
this a very remarkable thing? Was there not in it
something to pique the curiosity of the learned ?
Why, then, did they disdain it, — they who exhaust
themselves on the search of a nerve fiber ?

Experience alone, we say, could show the falsity or
truth of this theory ; and experience has shown its falsity ; for it demonstrates, at every moment, and by the
most positive facts, that the thought expressed can be
not only foreign to that of the assistants, but often
exactly contrary ; that it comes to contradict all preconceived ideas, baffle all foresight ; in fact, when I
think white, and am answered black, it is difficult to

make me believe that the answer comes from myself. The argument is founded on some cases of identity between the thought expressed and that of the assistants ; but what does that prove, except that the assistants may think the same as the intelligence that communicates ? It has not been said that they must always be of the opposite opinion. When, in course of conversation, the interlocutor expresses a thought analogous to your own, will you, for that reason, say it comes from yourself ? It is sufficient to have some contrary examples well verified, to prove that this theory cannot be absolute. Besides, how explain, by reflection of thought, the writing produced by persons who know not how to write ; the answers of the highest philosophical bearing obtained through illiterate persons — answers that are given to mental questions, or in a language unknown to the medium, and thousands of other facts which can leave no doubt of the independence of the intelligence which is manifested ? The contrary opinion can be only the result of a defect of observation. If the presence of a foreign intelligence is morally proved by the nature of the answer, it is materially proved by the fact of direct writing ; that is, by writing spontaneously obtained, without pen or pencil, without contact, and in spite of all the precautions taken as a guarantee against subterfuge. The intelligent character of the phenomenon cannot be doubted ; then there is something besides a fluidic action. Finally, the spontaneity of the thought expressed without expectation, without proposed question, does not permit us to see in it a reflection of that of the assistants. The system of reflex action is sufficiently disobliging in some instances, when, in a reunion of well-bred persons, there comes inopportunely

one of those communications revolting for their grossness ; it would be a very poor compliment to the assistants to pretend it comes from one of them, and it is
probable that each one would hasten to repudiate it.
(See *Book on Spirits*, Introduction, par. XVI.)

44. *System of the Collective Soul.* This is a varia-
tion of the preceding. According to this system, the
soul alone of the medium is manifested ; but it is
identified with that of several others living, either
present or absent, and forms a *collective whole*, uniting the aptitude, intelligence, and knowledge of each.
Though the tract in which this theory is put forth be
entitled *the light* (?), it seems to us to be of a very
obscure style. We confess to have hardly comprehended it, and speak of it only from memory. It is,
besides, like many others, an individual opinion, which
has made few proselytes. The name *Emah Tirpse* is
that taken by the author to designate the collective
being he represents. He takes for motto, *There is
nothing hidden that shall not be known*. This proposition is evidently false, for there are many things that
man cannot and ought not to know : it would be very
presumptuous in him to pretend to penetrate into the
secrets of God.

45. *Somnambulic System.* This system has had
more partisans, and even yet counts some. Like the
preceding it admits that all the intelligent communications have their source in the soul or spirit of the medium ; but in order to explain his aptitude to treat of
subjects beyond his knowledge, instead of supposing a
multiple soul, it attributes his power to a temporary
excitement of the mental faculties, to a kind of somnambulistic or ecstatic state, which exalts and develops his intelligence. It cannot be denied that some

cases are influenced by this cause ; but after having seen a great number of mediums, any one will be convinced that it will not solve all the facts, and that it forms the exception, and not the rule. It might be thought so if the medium had always the air of an inspired or ecstatic person — an appearance that he certainly could always simulate, if he wished to act a part ; but how believe in inspiration, when the medium writes like a machine, without having the least consciousness of what he is writing, without the least emotion, without thinking of what he is doing, laughing or talking of one thing and another. Excitement may be imagined in the case of ideas, but it is not easy to understand how it can make a person write who does not know how to write, and still less when the communications are transmitted by rappings, or by the aid of a planchette or a basket. We shall see, at the end of this work, the part we must assign to the influence of the medium's ideas ; but the cases in which a foreign intelligence is revealed by incontestable signs, are so numerous and so evident, that they can leave no doubt in this respect. The fault in most of the hashed-up systems of the origin of Spiritism, is having drawn general conclusions from a few isolated facts.

46. *Pessimist, Diabolic,* or *Demoniac System.* Here we enter another order of ideas. The intervention of a foreign intelligence being admitted, it was necessary to know the nature of this intelligence. Doubtless the most simple means was to ask it of itself ; but some persons did not find that a sufficient guarantee, and saw in the manifestations only a diabolic work ; according to their opinion, only the devil or demons can communicate. Although this system finds few

echoes nowadays, it at least enjoyed a momentary credit from the character of those who sought to make it prevail. We must always understand that the partisans of the demoniac system should not be considered among the adversaries of Spiritism ; quite the contrary. Let the beings who communicate be demons or angels, they are incorporeal : to admit the manifestation of demons is always to admit the possibility of communicating with the invisible world, the same as with a person in this world.

The belief in the exclusive communication of demons, however irrational it may be, could not seem impossible when spirits were looked upon as having been created outside of humanity ; but since we know that spirits are naught but the souls of those who have lived, it has lost all its *prestige*, and, one might say, all probability ; for it would follow that all these souls are demons, were they those of a father, a son, or a friend, and that we ourselves, in dying, would become demons, —a doctrine neither very flattering, nor consoling to most people. It will be difficult to persuade a mother that the cherished child she has lost, and which comes after its death to give her proofs of its affection and its identity, may be an agent of Satan. It is true that among the spirits are some very bad ones, worth not much more than those we call *demons*, for the very simple reason that there are very bad men, and death does not make them immediately better ; the question is, to know if these are the only ones that can communicate. To those who think so we will address the following questions : —

First. Are there good and bad spirits ?

Second. Is God more powerful than the bad spirits, or than the demons, if you desire so to call them ?

Third. To affirm that the bad alone communicate, is to say that the good cannot : if this be so, then one of two things : it takes place either by the will, or against the will, of God. If against His will, the bad spirits must be more powerful than He ; if by His will, why, in His loving kindness, would He not permit the good to counterbalance the influence of the others ?

Fourth. What proof can you give of the powerlessness of good spirits to communicate ?

Fifth. When the knowledge displayed in some communications is cited against your theory, you answer that the demon assumes all masks, the better to betray. We know there are hypocritical spirits, who give to their language a false varnish of goodness ; but do you admit that ignorance can counterfeit true knowledge, and a bad nature counterfeit true virtue, so that nothing will be seen to disclose the fraud ?

Sixth. If the demon alone can communicate, as he is the enemy of God and of men, why does he recommend us to pray to God, to submit to His will, to endure the tribulations of life without a murmur, to desire neither honors nor riches, to practice charity, and all the maxims of the Christ ; in a word, to do all that is necessary to destroy his own empire ? If it be the demon who gives such advice, we must agree that, cunning as he is, he is very unskillful to furnish arms against himself. (8)

Seventh. As spirits communicate, it is because God permits them ; seeing the good and the bad communications, is it not more logical to think that God permits the bad to try us, and the good to advise us ?

Eighth. What would you think of a father who would leave his child at the mercy of pernicious examples and advice, and who should take from him and forbid him to see those who could turn him from evil? What a good father would not do, must we think that God, who is the perfection of goodness, would do?

Ninth. The church recognizes as authentic certain manifestations of the Virgin and other saints, in apparitions, visions, oral communications, &c. ; is not this belief at variance with the exclusive communication of demons? We believe that some persons have sincerely professed this belief; but we also believe that many have pretended it, solely with a view to prevent people from occupying themselves with these things, because of the bad communications that they are liable to receive; saying that the devil alone manifests, they would terrify them, as we tell a child, "Don't touch that; it will burn." The intention may be praiseworthy, but the end is lost; for the prohibition excites curiosity, and the fear of the devil restrains very few; they would like to see him, if only to see how he is made, and are very much astonished to find him not half so black as they thought.

Could we not also see another motive for this theory?

There are persons who think every one in the wrong who is not of their opinion; so are not those who pretend that all communications are the work of the demon, moved by the fear of not finding the spirits agree with them on all points — on those that concern the interests of this world still more than those of the other? Not being able to deny the facts, they desire to present them in a terrifying manner; but this means has arrested it no more than the others. Where the fear of ridicule is powerless, we must be resigned to let matters take their course.

The Mussulman who should hear a spirit speak against the Koran, would assuredly think it a bad spirit ; it would be the same with a Jew as to what respects certain laws of Moses. As to the Catholics, we heard one affirm that the communicating spirit could only be the devil, because it disagreed with him as to the temporal power, though, at the same time, preached only charity, tolerance, love of the neighbor, and the abnegation of the things of this world — all maxims taught by the Christ.

Spirits being only the souls of men, and men not being perfect, it thence results that there are imperfect spirits, whose character is reflected in their communications. It is an incontestable fact, that there are among them bad, crafty, and profoundly hypocritical spirits, and against these we must be on our guard ; but because we meet in the world with bad men, is it a reason for withdrawing ourselves from society ? God has given us reason and judgment to appreciate spirits as well as men. The better means to provide against the dangers which the practice of Spiritism may present, is not to forbid it but to make it understood. An imaginary fear impresses but for a moment, and affects but few ; the reality, clearly demonstrated, is understood by all.

47. *Optimist System.* By the side of those who see in the phenomena only the action of demons, are others, who see in them only that of good spirits. They supposed, the soul being disengaged from matter, no vail existed for it ; that it must have sovereign science and sovereign wisdom. Their blind confidence in this absolute superiority of the beings of the invisible

world, has been a great source of many of the deceptions ; they have learned, to their cost, to beware of
certain spirits as well as of certain men.

48. *Unisprit* or *Monosprit System.* A variety of
the optimist system consists in the belief that one
single spirit communicates to men, and that this spirit
is the Christ, who is the protector of the world.   When
we see communications of the most trifling kind, of a
revolting grossness, full of malevolence and wickedness, it would be profanation and impiety to suppose
they could emanate from the spirit of perfect goodness.   If those who believe it had never had any save
irreproachable communications, one might conceive
their illusion ; but most of them admit having had
very bad ones, which they explain by saying that dictating to them absurd things is a trial the good spirit
causes them to undergo : thus, while some attribute all
communications to the devil, who may say good things
to tempt them, others think Jesus alone is manifested,
who may say bad things to try them.   Between these
two so opposite opinions, who will decide ?   Good
sense and experience.   We say experience, because it
is impossible that those who express ideas so exclusive
can have thoroughly viewed all sides.

When we bring forward the facts of identity, which
show the presence of relations, friends, or acquaintances, by the manifestations, written, visual, or otherwise, they answer that it is always the same spirit, —
the devil, according to some, the Christ, according to
others, — who takes all forms ; but they do not tell
us why the other spirits cannot communicate — with
what motive the Spirit of Truth should present himself under false appearances, to deceive a poor mother,
making her falsely believe it is the child she laments.

Reason refuses to admit that the Holy Spirit should be degraded to play such a comedy. Besides, is it not taking from Spiritism its greatest charm, the consolation of the afflicted, to deny the possibility of all other communication? Let us simply say that such a system is irrational, and cannot sustain a serious examination.

49. *Multisprit* or *Polysprit System.* All the systems we have passed in review, without excepting those in the negative, rest on some observation, though incomplete and badly interpreted. If a house is red on one side and white on the other, they who have seen only one side will affirm that it is white or that it is red; and they will be wrong and right: but he who has seen it on both sides will say it is red and white, and he alone will be right. The same in regard to the opinion formed of Spiritism; it may be true in certain lights, and false if we generalize from partial knowledge — if we take for the rule what is only the exception, for the whole what is only a part. This is why we say that whoever would seriously study this science should see much and for a long time: time alone will permit him to seize the details, to catch the delicate shades, to observe a multitude of characteristic facts, which will be as rays of light to him; but if he stops at the surface, he may carry away a premature, and, consequently, an erroneous judgment. Here are the general consequences deduced from a complete observation, and which now form the belief, we may say, of the majority of spiritists, for the restrictive systems are now but isolated opinions.

First. The spirit phenomena are produced by extra corporeal intelligences; in other words, by spirits.

Second. Spirits constitute the invisible world; they

are everywhere : space is peopled with them to infinity ; there are some always around us, with whom we are in contact.

Third. Spirits constantly react on the physical and on the moral world, and are one of the powers of nature.

Fourth. Spirits are not beings apart in nature ; they are the souls of those who have lived on this earth, or in other worlds, and who have laid aside their corporeal envelop ; from whence it follows that the souls of men are incarnated spirits, and that, in dying, we become spirits.

Fifth. There are spirits of all degrees of goodness and of malice, of knowledge and of ignorance.

Sixth. They are all subject to the law of progress, and can ail attain to perfection ; but, as they have their free will, the time is more or less long, according to their efforts or otherwise.

Seventh. They are happy or unhappy according to the good or evil they have done during this life, and the degree of advancement they have reached. Happiness, perfect and without alloy, is the lot of those spirits only who have reached the supreme degree of perfection.

Eighth. All spirits, under given circumstances, can manifest themselves to men : the number of those who can communicate is indefinite.

Ninth. Spirits communicate through the intervention of mediums, who serve them as instruments and interpreters.

Tenth. The superiority or inferiority of spirits is recognized by their language : the good counsel only good, and say only good things ; everything about

them proves elevation ; the bad deceive, and all their
words bear the marks of imperfection and ignorance.

The different degrees through which spirits pass are
indicated in the *Spirit Scale* (*Book on Spirits*, Book 2,
Chap. 1, No. 100). The study of this classification is
indispensable to appreciate the nature of the spirits
who manifest themselves, their good and bad qualities.

50. *System of the Material Soul* consists only in
a peculiar opinion on the inmost nature of the soul.
According to this opinion, the soul and the *périsprit*
are not distinct things ; or, to speak more plainly, the
périsprit is only the soul itself gradually purified by
various transmigrations, — as alcohol is purified by various distillations, — while the spirit doctrine considers
the *périsprit* only as the fluidic envelope of the soul or
spirit. The *périsprit* being a matter, though very ethereal, the soul would thus be of a material nature, more
or less essential, according to the degree of its purification. This system invalidates none of the fundamental principles of the spirit doctrine, for it changes
in nothing the destiny of the soul : the conditions of
its future happiness remain the same ; the soul and
the *périsprit* forming a whole under the name of spirit,
as the germ and périsperm form one under the name
of fruit, the whole question being reduced to considering the whole as homogeneous, instead of being found
of two distinct parts. As may be seen, this is of little
consequence, and we should not have mentioned it,
had we not met persons disposed to see a new school
in what is, definitively, but a simple interpretation of
words. This opinion, a very restricted one, were it
even more general, would no more constitute a schism
between spiritists, than the two theories of the emission
or the undulations of light make one among physicists.

Those who would form a separate party for so trifling a question, would prove by that alone that they attach more importance to the accessory than to the principal, and that they are pressed to disunion by spirits who cannot be good ; for good spirits never breathe spite and dissension : this is why we entreat all true spiritists to guard against similar suggestions, and not to attach to certain *minutiæ* more importance than they deserve ; the foundation is the essential point. Nevertheless, we will, in a few words, explain on what rests the opinion of those who consider the soul and the *périsprit* two distinct things. It is founded on the teachings of the spirits, who have never varied in that respect. We speak of enlightened spirits, for among them there are those who know no more about it than men, and some even less, while the contrary theory is a human conception. We have neither invented nor supposed the *périsprit* to explain the phenomena ; its existence was revealed to us by spirits, and observation has confirmed us in it. (*Book on Spirits*, No. 93.) It rests also on the study of sensation among spirits (*Book on Spirits*, No. 257), and particularly on the phenomenon of tangible apparitions, which would involve, according to the other opinion, the solidification and the disintegration of the constituent parts of the soul, and, consequently, its disorganization. It would, besides, be necessary to admit that this matter, which can come within reach of the senses, is itself the intelligent principle, which is no more rational than to confound the body with the soul, or the clothing with the body. As to the innate nature of the soul, it is unknown to us. When we say it is *immaterial*, this must be understood in a relative and not an absolute sense, for absolute immateriality would be nothing ;

but the soul, or spirit, is something ; we would say that its essence is so superior, that it has no analogy with what we call matter, and that so, for us, it is immaterial. (*Book on Spirits*, Nos. 23 and 82.)

51. Here is the answer given on this subject by a spirit.

"What some call *périsprit* is only what others call material fluidic envelope. I will say, to make myself understood in a more logical manner, that this fluid is the perfection of the senses — the extension of sight and ideas. I speak here of elevated spirits. As to the inferior spirits, the terrestrial fluids are still completely inherent in them : so it is matter, as you see. From thence the sufferings from hunger, from cold, &c., sufferings which superior spirits do not endure, because the terrestrial fluids are purified around the thought ; that is to say, the soul. The soul, for its progress, always needs an agent ; the soul without an agent is nothing for you, or, rather, cannot be conceived by you. The *périsprit* is, for us wandering spirits, the agent by which we communicate with you, whether indirectly by your body or your *périsprit*, or directly to your soul ; from thence the infinite shades of mediums and communications. Now remains the scientific stand-point, that is, the very essence of the *périsprit* itself : this is another affair. Understand, first, morally, there remains only a discussion on the nature of fluids, which is inexplicable at present : science does not know it, but it will come to it if science will walk hand in hand with Spiritism. The *périsprit* may vary and change to infinity ; the soul is the thought ; it changes not its nature : in this go no further ; it is a point which cannot be explained. Think you I do not search like you?　You seek the *perisprit*, we the soul.　Wait then.　　　　　　　　LAMENAIS."

Thus spirits, who may be considered advanced, have not yet fathomed the nature of the soul : how can we do it ?　It is, then, loss of time to attempt to investigate first principles, which, as it is said in the *Book on Spirits* (Nos. 17, 49), are God's secrets.　To pretend, by the aid of Spiritism, to pry into what is not yet within the province of humanity, is to turn it from its true aim ; it is like the child who would know as much as an old man.　Let man use Spiritism for his moral development : that is the essential point : anything more is only a sterile, and often vain curiosity, whose satisfaction would not gain him one step in advance ; the only way to advance is to become better.　The spirits who dictated the book which bears their name, proved their wisdom, in keeping themselves, in all that concerns the rudiments of things, within the limits which God permits not to be crossed, leaving to systematist and presumptuous spirits the responsibility of erroneous theories more seductive than solid, and which will some day fall before reason like so many others issued from human brains.　They have said only exactly what was necessary to make man understand the future that awaits him, and by that to encourage him to good.　(See Part 2, Chap. 1, *Action of Spirits on Matter.*)

PART SECOND.

OF SPIRIT MANIFESTATIONS.

CHAPTER I.

ACTION OF SPIRITS ON MATTER.

52. THE materialistic opinion being withdrawn as condemned at once by reason and by facts, the whole question is to know if the soul, after death, can manifest itself to the living. The question, thus reduced to its simplest expression, is found to be singularly free. It might be asked, first, why intelligent beings, who live in some way in our very midst, though, by their very nature, invisible, should not attest their presence. Simple reason says there is nothing in it absolutely impossible, and this is something gained. Besides, this belief has the assent of all people, for we find it everywhere, and at all epochs : an intuition could not be so general nor survive time without resting on something. More, it is sanctioned by the testimony of sacred books and by the Fathers of the Church, and it has taken the skepticism and materialism of our age to consign it to superstition ; if we are in error, so are these authorities.

But these are only moral considerations. One cause, above all others, has helped to fortify doubt, in an epoch so positive as ours, where people believe in giving a reason for all, where they want to know the why and the how of everything; it is ignorance of the nature of spirits, and of the means by which they can manifest themselves. This knowledge acquired, the fact of the manifestations is no longer surprising, and enters into the order of natural facts.

53. The idea formed of spirits renders, at first sight, the phenomena of the manifestations incomprehensible. These manifestations can take place only by the action of the spirit on matter; this is why those who believe that spirit is the absence of all matter ask, with some appearance of reason, how it can act materially. But there is the error, for spirit is not an abstraction; it is a being defined, limited, and circumscribed. The spirit incarnated in the body constitutes the soul; when it leaves the body at death, it does not leave it entirely stripped of an envelope. All tell us they preserve the human form, and in fact, when they appear to us it is in the form in which we have known them.

Observe them attentively at the moment they leave this life; they are in a troubled state, everything around them is confused; they see their body, whole or mutilated, according to the kind of death: on the other hand, they see themselves and feel that they are living. Something tells them that body belongs to them, and they do not understand that they may be separated from it. They continue to see themselves under their primitive form, and this sight, with some, produces a singular illusion — that of believing themselves still living; experience of their new state is necessary to convince them of the reality. This first troubled moment dissipated, the body becomes for them like an old garment, which they have stripped off and no longer regret; they feel lighter, and as if disencumbered of a burden; they no longer experience physical pains, and are perfectly happy in the power of elevating themselves, traversing space, as they have a thousand times in their dreams while living. Fourth. In the mean time, spite of the absence of the body, they realize their personality; they have a form, but a form that neither troubles nor embarrasses them; they have the consciousness of their *me* and of their individuality. What must we conclude? That the soul does not leave all in the coffin, and that it carries something with it.

54. Numerous observations and incontestable facts, of which we will speak further on, have led to this conclusion — that there are in men three things: first, the soul or spirit, intelligent principle in which resides the moral sense; second, the body, gross, material envelope with which it is temporarily clothed, for the accomplishment of certain providential views; third, the *périsprit*, semi-material, fluidic envelope serving as a link between the soul and the body.

Death is the destruction, or rather the disintegration, of the grosser envelope — that which the soul abandons; the other is disengaged, and follows the soul, which thus finds itself always in possession of an envelope; this last, though fluidic, ethereal, vaporous, invisible to us in its normal state, is not the less matter, though we have not as yet been able to catch and subject it to analysis.

This second envelope of the soul — the *périsprit* — exists during the corporeal life; it is the intermediary of all the sensations perceived by the spirit, that by which the spirit transmits its will to the exterior, and acts upon the organs. To make use of a material comparison, it is the conductor, the electric thread, which serves for the reception and transmission of thought ; it is, lastly, that mysterious, unseizable agent, denominated nervous fluid, which plays so great a part in the economy, and of which too little is thought in physiological and pathological phenomena. Medicine, considering only the material, ponderable element, is deprived, in the appreciation of facts, of an incessant cause of action. But this is not the place to examine that question ; we would only remark that the knowledge of the *périsprit* is the key to a crowd of problems hitherto inexplicable.

The *périsprit* is not one of those hypotheses to which recourse is sometimes had in science for the explanation of a fact ; its existence is not revealed solely by the spirits ; it is a result of observations, as we shall have occasion to show. For the present, and not to anticipate facts we shall have to relate, we limit ourselves to say that, whether during its union with the body or after its separation, the soul is never separated from its *périsprit*.

55. It has been said that the spirit is a flame, a spark ; this should be understood of the spirit, so called, as intellectual and moral principle, and to which we know not how to attribute a determined form ; but in whatever degree it may be found, it is always clothed with an envelope or *périsprit*, whose nature is etherealized to the same degree in which it is purified and elevated in the hierarchy ; in such a manner that the idea of form is inseparable from that of spirit, and that we cannot conceive the one without the other.

Thus the *périsprit* makes an integral part of the spirit, as the body makes an integral part of the man : but the *périsprit* alone is not the spirit any more than the body alone is the man, for the *périsprit* does not think ; it is to the spirit what the body is to the man ; it is the agent or instrument of his action.

56. The form of the *périsprit* is the human form, and when it appears to us it is usually that under which we have known the spirit during his life. It might be believed from this, that the *périsprit*, disengaged from all the parts of the body, is moulded on it in some sort, and so preserves its imprint ; but it does not appear to be so. The human form, with some shades of difference, and with the organic modifications made necessary by the medium in which the being is called to live, is found among all the inhabitants of all the globe ; this, at least, is what the spirits say : it is equally the form of all non-incarnated spirits, who have only the *périsprit ;* it is that under which, from all time, angels and pure spirits have been represented : from whence we conclude that the human form is the type form of all human beings to whatever degree they may belong. But the subtile matter of the *périsprit* has neither the tenacity nor the rigidity of the compact matter of the body ; it is, if we may so express ourselves, flexible and expansible ; this is why the form it takes, though counterdrawn on that of the body, is not absolute ; it changes at the will of the spirit, who can give himself such or such an appearance at his will, while the solid envelope would offer an insurmountable resistance. Disencumbered of these shackles that compressed it, the *périsprit* is elongated or contracted, transformed, in a word lends itself to all metamorphoses, according to the will

that acts on it. It is in consequence of this property of his fluidic envelope, that the spirit who wishes to be recognized can, when it is necessary, take the exact appearance he had when living, nay, even those of the corporeal accidents which may be signs of recognition.

Spirits, then, as may be seen, are beings similar to ourselves, forming around us a whole population invisible in the normal state, because, as we shall see, this invisibility is not absolute.

57. Let us return to the nature of the *périsprit*, for that is essential to the explanation we have to give. We have said that, though fluidic, it is not the less a kind of matter; and this follows from the fact of the tangible apparitions to which we shall return. Under the influence of certain mediums, hands have appeared having all the properties of living hands, which have the heat, could be handled, offer the resistance of a solid body, which could grasp you, and which suddenly vanished like a shade. The intelligent action of these hands, which evidently obey a will in executing certain movements, in even playing airs on an instrument, proves that they are the visible part of an invisible being. Their tangibility, their temperature, in a word the impression they make on the senses, — for they have been known to leave impressions on the skin, give painful blows or caress gently, — prove that they are of some kind of matter : especially does their instantaneous disappearance prove that this matter is eminently subtile, and is like some substances that can pass alternately from the solid to the fluid state, and *vice versa*.

58. The intimate nature of the spirit, properly so called, — that is to say, of the thinking being, — is entirely unknown to us : it is revealed to us only by its action,

and its actions can strike our material senses only by an intermediate material. It has for direct instrument its *périsprit*, as a man has his body, and its *périsprit* is matter, as we shall see. It has, besides, for intermediary agent, the universal fluid — a sort of vehicle on which it acts, as we act on the air to produce certain effects by the aid of dilatation, comprehension, propulsion, or vibrations.

Seen by this light, the action of the spirit on matter may be easily conceived: we comprehend from this that all the effects that result from it enter into the order of natural facts, and have nothing of the marvelous in them. They appeared supernatural only when the cause was unknown; the cause known, the marvelous disappeared; and this cause lies entirely in the semi-material properties of the *périsprit*. It is a new order of facts which a new law comes to explain, and which, in a short time, will no more astonish any one than we are now astonished with correspondence at a distance in a few minutes by electricity.

59. It may perhaps be asked how the spirit, by the aid of a matter so subtile, can act on heavy and compact bodies, raise tables, &c. Assuredly it could not be a man of science who could make such objections; for, without speaking of the unknown properties this new agent may possess, have we not under our eyes analogous examples? Is it not in the most rarefied gas, in the most imponderable fluids, that industry finds its most powerful motors? When we see the air overthrow edifices, steam carry enormous masses, gasified powder raise rocks, electricity break trees and pierce walls, what is there more strange in admitting that the spirit, by the aid of his *périsprit*, can raise a table? above all, when we know that this *périsprit* can become visible, tangible, and behave altogether like a solid body.

Chapter II.

PHYSICAL MANIFESTATIONS. — TURNING TABLES.

60. The name Physical Manifestations has been given to those shown by sensible effects, such as noises, the movement and displacement of solid bodies. Some are spontaneous, that is, independent of all will; others are evoked.

We shall speak at present only of these last.

The simplest effect, and the one among the first observed, consists in the circular movement given to a table. This effect may be produced quite as well on other objects, but the table being that on which it was most frequently exercised, because it was most convenient, the name of *turning tables* prevailed as the designation of this kind of phenomenon.

When we say that this effect is one of the first that were observed, we mean in these latter times, for it is very certain that all kinds of manifestations were known from the most remote times, and it could not be otherwise; since they are natural effects, they must have been produced in all ages. Tertullian speaks, in explicit terms, of tables turning and speaking.

This phenomenon for some time supplied food for the curiosity of the drawing-room; then it was left for other amusements, for it was made but a subject of pastime. Two causes contributed to its abandonment — fashion for frivolous persons, who rarely consecrate

two winters to the same amusement, and who — prodigious for them ! — have given three or four to this.
For grave and observant persons, something serious
resulted and prevailed ; if they neglected the turning
tables it is because they were occupied with consequences otherwise very important in their results ;
they have left the alphabet for the science : there is
the whole secret of the apparent abandonment on
which our deriders place so much stress. However
this may be, the turning tables are none the less the
starting-point of the spirit doctrine ; and in this respect we owe them some developments, the better,
also, that, presenting the phenomena in their greatest
simplicity, the study of the causes will be easier, and
the theory, once established, will give us the key to
the most complicated effects.

61. For the production of the phenomena, the intervention of one or several persons, endowed with a
special aptitude, and named mediums, is necessary.
The number of coöperants is indifferent ; only it may
be, in a number, some unknown mediums may be
found. As to those whose mediumship is naught,
their presence is without result, and even more injurious than useful, from the disposition of mind they often
bring with them.

Mediums often enjoy, in this relation, a power greater or less, and, consequently, produce effects more or
less decided : often one person, a powerful medium,
will alone produce more than twenty others united ; it
is enough for him to place his hands on the table to
make it instantly move, stand up, be thrown over, turn
somersaults, or turn round with violence.

62. There is no index to the medianimic faculty ;
experience alone can show it to us. When, in a re-

union, a trial is desired, it is necessary simply to be seated around a table, and hold the hands flatly above it, without pressure or muscular intensity. In the beginning, being ignorant of the causes of the phenomenon, several precautions were indicated, since known to be absolutely useless ; such as, for instance, the alternation of the sexes, or the contact of the little fingers of the different persons, so as to form an uninterrupted chain. This last precaution appeared necessary while it was attributed to the action of a sort of electric current; but experience has since demonstrated its inutility. The only prescription which should be rigorously obligatory, is concentration of thought, absolute silence, and, above all, patience, if the effect has to be awaited. It may be produced in a few minutes, or it may be a half hour, or an hour ; that depends on the medianimic power of the co-participants.

63. Let us say, still further, that the form of the table, the substance of which it is made, the presence of metals, of silk in the garments of the assistants, the days, the hours, obscurity or light, &c., are as indifferent as rain or fair weather. The size alone of the table is of some consequence, but only when the medianimic power may be insufficient to overcome the resistance; in the contrary case, a single person, a child even, can make a table of a hundred kilometres rise ; though, under less favorable conditions, a dozen persons could not make the smallest stand move.

Things being in this state, when the effect begins to be manifested, there is usually heard some slight cracking of the table, which continues to be moved in various ways without contact.

Under some circumstances the table rises and

stands, sometimes on one foot, sometimes on another, then gently resumes its natural position.   At other times it is balanced, imitating the movement of pitching and rolling.   At other times, again, — though this requires considerable medianimic power, — it is entirely detached from the floor, and maintained in equilibrium in space, without support ; sometimes rising to the ceiling, so that persons may pass under it, then descending slowly, balancing itself like a sheet of paper ; or it sometimes falls violently to the ground, and is broken, which proves very decisively that it is from no optical delusion.

64. Another phenomenon, very often produced, according to the nature of the medium, is that of raps in the very tissue of the wood, without movement of the table ; these raps, sometimes very weak, at other times very strong, are heard as well in the other furniture of the room, against the walls and the ceiling.   We shall return to this presently.   When they take place in the table, they produce in it a vibration very perceptible to the fingers, and very distinct when the ear is applied to it.

Chapter III.

INTELLIGENT MANIFESTATIONS.

65. In what we have seen, nothing assuredly reveals the intervention of an unknown power, and these effects could be perfectly explained by the action of a magnetic or electric current, or of some kind of fluid. Such was, in fact, the first solution given to these phenomena, and which might reasonably pass for logical. It would have prevailed without contradiction, if other facts had not come to demonstrate its insufficiency. These facts are the proofs of intelligence given ; for as all intelligent effects must have an intelligent cause, it remained evident, that even admitting that electricity or some other fluid played a part in it, there was still some other cause. What was it ? what was this intelligence ? This is what the continuation of the observations brought to light.

66. For a manifestation to be intelligent it is not necessary that it should be eloquent, witty, or learned ; it is sufficient that it prove a free and voluntary act, expressing an intention, or answering to a thought. Assuredly, when we see a weathercock agitated by the wind, it is very certain it obeys only a mechanical impulse ; but if we should recognize in its movements intentional signals, — should it turn to the right or to the left, rapidly or slowly, at command, — we should be forced to admit, not that the weathercock is intelligent,

but that it obeys an intelligence. This is what happened with the table.

67. We have seen the table moved, raised, strike blows, under the influence of one or of several mediums. The first intelligent effect that was remarked was to see these movements obey the word of command; thus, without changing its place, the table would rise alternately on the designated foot, then, in coming down, strike a required number of blows, answering a question. At other times the table, without personal contact, would walk across the room, going to the right or to the left, forward or backward, executing divers movements, at the order of the assistants. It is very evident that we set aside all supposition of fraud, that we admit the perfect loyalty of the assistants, proved by their honor and perfect disinterestedness. We shall speak, by and by, of the frauds against which it is necessary to be guarded.

68. By means of raps, and, above all, by the inner raps of which we have spoken, still more intelligent effects are produced, as the imitation of the beatings of a drum, a small war, with rank and platoon firing, cannonading; then the grinding of the saw, blows of a hammer, the rhythm of different airs, &c. It was, as may well be supposed, an immense field opened for exploration. It was said, since there is here an unknown intelligence, it should be able to answer questions; and, in fact, it did answer Yes, or No, by means of a given number of raps. These answers were very insignificant, which led to the idea of designating the letters of the alphabet, and thus composing words and phrases.

69. These facts, renewed at will, by thousands of persons in all countries, could leave no doubt of the

intelligent nature of these manifestations. Then arose
a new system, according to which this intelligence was
no other than that of the medium, the interrogator, or
even of the assistants. The difficulty was, to explain
how this intelligence could be reflected into the table,
and translated by blows. As soon as it was proved
that these blows were not struck by the medium, they
were then by the thought ; but thought striking blows
was a still more prodigious phenomenon than the one
they had already witnessed. Experience soon demonstrated the inadmissibility of this opinion. In fact, the
answers were often found to be in complete opposition
to the thought of the assistants, beyond the intellectual strength of the medium, and even in language of
which he was ignorant, or relating to facts unknown
to all. The examples are so numerous that it is almost
impossible that any one, even slightly occupied with
Spiritism, should not have been many times witness
of it. We shall cite only one, brought to us by an eye-
witness.

70. On a vessel of the imperial French navy, sta-
tioned in the Chinese Seas, the whole crew, from the
sailors up to the staff-major, were occupied in making
tables talk. They hit upon the idea of invoking the
spirit of a lieutenant of this same vessel, some two
years dead. He came, and after various communications, which astonished every one, he said, by rapping,
what follows : " I pray you instantly to pay the captain
the sum of " (he mentioned the sum) " which I owe
him, and which I regret not having been able to repay
before my death." No one knew the fact ; the captain
himself had forgotten the debt, — a very small one, by
the by,— but on looking over his accounts, he found
there the lieutenant's debt, the sum indicated being

perfectly correct. We ask, of whose thought could this be the reflection?

71. The act of communicating by alphabetic raps was perfected, but the process was always very long; though by its means they obtained very interesting revelations from the world of spirits. These indicated other means, and to them we are indebted for written communications.

The first communications of this kind were by adjusting a pencil to the foot of a table, held lightly on a sheet of paper. The table, moved by the influence of a medium, began to trace characters, then words and phrases. This process was successively simplified, by using little tables, the size of the hand, made expressly, then baskets, card-baskets, and afterward simple planchettes. The writing was as flowing, rapid, and easy, as with the hand, but it was afterward found that these objects were really only appendices, pencilholders, with which they could dispense by themselves holding the pencil: the hand, carried along by an involuntary movement, wrote under the impulse given by the spirit, and without the concurrence of the will or thought of the medium. From henceforward, the communications from beyond the tomb had no more limits than correspondence between the living.

We shall return to these different processes, and will explain them in detail; having rapidly sketched them to show the succession of the facts, proving in these phenomena the intervention of unknown intelligences, otherwise spirits.

CHAPTER IV.

THEORY OF PHYSICAL MANIFESTATIONS.

*Movements and Levitations. — Noises. — Increase and
Diminution of the Weight of Bodies.*

72. THE existence of spirits being demonstrated by
reasoning and by facts, as well as the possibility for
them to act upon matter, it remains now to know how
this action is performed, and how they manage to
make tables and other inert bodies move. One thought
naturally presents itself, and that was our own : as it
was contradicted by the spirits, who gave us quite a
different explanation, one we were far from expecting,
it is an evident proof that their theory was not our
opinion. As to the first thought, every one, as well as
ourselves, might be likely to have it ; but as to the
theory of the spirits, we believe it never has entered
into any person's mind. It will easily be recognized
as superior to ours, though less simple, because it
gives the solution of a crowd of other facts which
found no satisfactory explanation in our idea.

73. From the moment in which the nature of the
spirits is known, their human form, the semi-material
properties of the *périsprit*, the mechanical action they
can have on matter, that among the facts of apparition,
fluidic and even tangible hands have been seen to
grasp objects and transport them, it was natural to
believe that the spirit simply used his hands to make

the table turn, and that he sustained it in the air by the strength of his arm. But, in that case, what necessity for a medium ? Cannot the spirit act alone ? for the medium, who most often rests his hands in a sense contrary to the movement, or even does not rest them at all, evidently cannot second the spirit by any muscular action whatever. Let us first allow the spirits whom we questioned on the subject to speak.

74. The following answers were given to us by the spirit of St. Louis : they have since been confirmed by many others.

1. Is the universal fluid an emanation from the Divinity ?

" No."

2. Is it a creation of the Divinity ?

"All is created, except God."

3. Is the universal fluid at the same time the universal element ?

" Yes ; it is the elementary principle of all things ? "

4. Has it any relation to the electric fluid whose effects we know ?

" It is its element."

5. What is the state in which the universal fluid is presented to us in its greatest purity ?

" To find it in its absolute purity, you must mount to the pure spirits ; in your world it is always more or less modified to form the compact matter that surrounds you ; at the same time you may say that the state in which it approaches most nearly to purity, is that of the fluid you call *animal magnetic fluid.*"

6. It has been said that the universal fluid is the source of life ; is it at the same time the source of intelligence ?

" No ; this fluid animates only matter."

7. Since it is this fluid which composes the *périsprit*, it appears to be there in a kind of condensed state, which approximates it, up to a certain point, to matter so called.

"Up to a certain point, as you say, for it has not all its properties : it is more or less condensed, according to the worlds."

8. What is the operation by which a spirit moves a solid body?

"He combines a portion of the universal fluid with the fluid exhaled from the medium suitable to this effect."

9. Do the spirits raise the table with the aid of their members in some degree solidified?

"This answer will not yet lead to what you desire. When a table is moved under your hands, the spirit evoked draws from the universal fluid what animates the table with a factitious life. The table thus prepared, the spirit attracts it and moves it under the influence of his own fluid thrown off by his will. When the mass he wishes to move is too heavy for him, he calls to his aid spirits who are in the same condition as himself. By reason of his ethereal nature, the spirit proper cannot act on gross matter without intermediary, that is to say, without the link that unites it to matter : this link, which you call *périsprit*, gives you the key to all material spirit phenomena. I believe I have expressed myself clearly enough for you to understand."

Remark. We call attention to this first phrase : *this answer will not yet lead to what you desire.* The spirit had perfectly understood that all the preceding questions were asked only to arrive at this, and he alluded to our thought, which, in fact, expected quite a different answer, that is to say, the confirmation of our idea on the method by which the spirit makes the table move.

10. Are the spirits he calls to his aid inferior ? are they under his orders ?

" Equal, almost always ; sometimes they come of themselves."

11. Are all spirits able to produce phenomena of this kind ?

" The spirits who produce these effects are always inferior spirits, who are not entirely disengaged from all material influence."

12. We understand that the superior spirits are not occupied by things that are beneath them ; but we ask if, by reason of their being more dematerialized, they would have the power if they had the will ?

" They have the moral strength, as the others have the physical strength ; when they require this strength, they make use of those who possess it. Have they not told you that they make use of inferior spirits as you do of porters ? "

Remark. It has been said that the density of the *périsprit,* if one may so express it, varies according to the state of the worlds ; it appears that it varies also in the same world according to individuals. Among the morally advanced spirits, it is more subtile, and approximates to that of the elevated spirits : among the inferior spirits, on the contrary, it approximates to matter, which is the reason these spirits of low state preserve so long the illusions of the terrestrial life ; they think and act as if they were still living ; they have the same desires, and we might almost say the same sensuality. This coarseness of the *périsprit* giving to it more affinity with matter, makes the inferior spirits more fitted for physical manifestations. It is for the same reason that a man of the world accustomed to the labor of intellect, whose body is frail and delicate, cannot carry a heavy burden like a porter. Matter, with him, is in a manner, as it were, less compact, the organs less resistant; he has less nervous fluid. The *périsprit* being to the spirit what the body is to man, and its density being according to the degree of inferiority of the spirit, it takes the place of muscular force; that is to say, gives him, over the fluids necessary for manifestations, a greater power than those have whose nature is more ethereal. If an elevated spirit desires to produce such effects, he does what delicate people amongst us do; he has it done by a *spirit of the trade.*

13. If we have thoroughly understood what you have said, the vital principle resides in the universal fluid; the spirit draws in this fluid the semi-material envelope which constitutes his *périsprit*, and it is by means of this fluid that he acts on inert matter. Is it so?

"Yes; that is to say, he animates matter with a kind of factitious life; the matter is animated with animal life. The table that moves under your hands lives like the animal; it obeys the intelligent being. It is not he who pushes it as a man does a burden; when the table is raised, it is not the spirit who raises it by strength of arm, it is the animated table that obeys the impulse given by the spirit."

14. What is the part of a medium in this matter?

"I have said it; the fluid of the medium is combined with the universal fluid accumulated by the spirit: the union of these two fluids is necessary; that is to say, the animalized fluid with the universal fluid, to give life to the table. But remark that this life is only momentary; it is extinguished with the action, and often before the end of the action, as soon as the quantity of fluid is insufficient to animate it."

15. Can the spirit act without the concurrence of a medium?

"It can act in spite of the medium; that is to say, that no doubt many persons serve as auxiliaries to the spirits for certain phenomena. The spirit draws from them, as from a source, the animalized fluid he needs; it is thus that the concurrence of the medium, as you understand it, is not always necessary; which is the case particularly in spontaneous phenomena."

16. Does the animated table act with intelligence? Does it think?

"It thinks no more than the stick with which you make an intelligent sign; but the vitality with which it is animated permits it to obey the impulse of an intelligence. Understand that the table that moves does not become spirit, and that it has of itself neither thought nor will."

Remark. We often use an analogous expression in our usual language; we say of a wheel that turns quickly, that it is animated with a rapid movement.

17. Which is the preponderating cause in the production of this phenomena, the spirit or the fluid?

"The spirit is the cause, the fluid is the instrument; both are necessary."

18. What part does the will of the medium play in this case?

"To call the spirits, and to second them in the impulse given to the fluid."

Is the action of the will always indispensable?

"It adds to the power, but is not always necessary,

since the movement can take place against and in spite of that will ; this is a proof that there is a cause independent of the medium."

Remark. The contact of the hands is not always necessary to make an object move. It is so more often to give the first impulse ; but once the object is animated, it can obey the will without material contact ; that depends either on the power of the medium or the nature of the spirit. A first contact even is not always indispensable ; there is proof of it in the spontaneous movements and displacements which no one has dreamed of calling forth.

19. Why cannot every one produce the same effect ? and why have not all mediums the same power ?

"That depends on the organization, and the greater or less facility with which the combination of fluids can operate ; then the spirit of the medium sympathizes more or less with the foreign spirits who find in him the necessary fluidic power. This power, like that of magnetizers, is greater or less. Under this relation there are persons who are altogether refractory ; others with whom the combination operates only by an exertion of their will ; others, finally, with whom it takes place so naturally and so easily, that they are not aware of it, and serve as instruments against their will, as we have already said." (See the next chapter, on *Spontaneous Manifestations.*)

Remark. Magnetism is, doubtless, the principle of these phenomena, but not such as we usually understand it. The proof is, that there are very powerful magnetizers who could not move a stand, and persons who cannot magnetize, children even, to whom it suffices only to touch the fingers on a heavy table to make it move ; so, if the medianimic power is not by reason of the magnetic, it is that there is another cause.

20. Can persons called electric be considered as mediums ?

"These persons draw from themselves the fluid necessary to the production of the phenomena, and can act without the help of foreign spirits. Thus they are not mediums in the sense attached to this word ; but a spirit can assist them, and profit by their natural disposition."

Remark. There are persons, like somnambulists, who can act with or without the concurrence of a foreign spirit. (See, in chapter on *Mediums*, the article relative to *Somnambulistic Mediums*.)

21. Is the spirit that acts on solid bodies in the substance of the bodies, or outside of it ?

"Both ; we have said that matter is no obstacle to spirits ; they penetrate everything ; a portion of the *périsprit* is identified, so to say, with the object it penetrates."

22. How does the spirit manage to strike ? Does he make use of a material object ?

"No more than of his arms to raise the table. You well know that he has no hammer at his disposal. His hammer is the combined fluid put in action to move or to strike. When he moves, the light brings you the sight of the movements ; when he strikes, the air brings you the sound."

23. We can understand that when he strikes on a hard body ; but how can he make us hear noises or articulate sounds in the air ?

"Since he can act on matter, he can act on air as well as on the table. As to articulate sounds, he can imitate them, as he can all other noises."

24. You say that spirits do not use their hands to remove the table ; yet, in certain visual manifestations, hands have been seen to appear whose fingers have wandered over the key-board of a piano, moved the keys, and caused sounds. Would it not seem that in this case the movement of the keys is produced by the pressure of the fingers ? Is not this pressure as direct and real when it is felt on ourselves, when these hands leave imprints on the skin ?

" You can understand the nature of spirits and their manner of acting only by comparisons, which give you an incomplete idea, and it is wrong to always wish to assimilate their processes to your own. Their processes must bear relation to their organization. Have I not told you that the fluid of the *périsprit* penetrates matter, and is identified with it, that it animates it with a factitious life ? Well, when the spirit rests his fingers on the keys, he puts them there really, and even moves them ; but it is not by muscular force that he presses the key : he animates it as he animated the table, and the key, which obeys his will, moves and strikes the chord. There is one thing you will have trouble in comprehending ; it is this : that some spirits are so little advanced, and so material in comparison to the elevated spirits, that they still have the illusions of the terrestrial life, and believe they act as when they had their body ; they can no more give a reason of the true cause of the effects they produce, than a peasant can give a reason for the theory of the sounds he articulates ; ask them how they play on the piano, they will tell you they strike on it with their fingers, because they believe they do strike it ; the effect is produced instinctively with them, without their knowing how, and yet by their will. When they make you hear words, it is the same thing.''

Remark. It results, from these explanations, that spirits can produce all the effects that we produce ourselves, but by means appropriate to their organization : certain forces which are suited to them take the place of the muscles which are necessary to us to act ; as gesture with the mute takes the place of speech, which he lacks.

25. Among the phenomena cited in proof of the action of an occult power, there are some evidently contrary to all the known laws of nature ; does not doubt, then, seem to be permitted ?

" It is because man is far from knowing all the laws of nature ; if he knew them all he would be a superior spirit. Every day, however, gives the lie to those who, thinking they know everything, presume to set bounds to nature ; and they are none the less haughty. In constantly unvailing new mysteries God warns men to doubt their own lights, for the day will come when *the science of the most learned will be put to confusion.* Have you not every day examples of bodies animated by a movement capable of overcoming the force of gravity ? Does not the bullet, shot into the air, momentarily overcome this force ? Poor men, who think yourselves so learned, and whose silly vanity is every instant disconcerted, know that you are still very small."

75. These explanations are clear, categorical, and without ambiguity ; from them results this capital point : that the universal fluid, in which dwells the principle of life, is the principal agent of the manifestations, and that this agent receives its impulse from the spirit, whether incarnated or wandering. This fluid

condensed constitutes the *périsprit*, or semi-material
envelope of the spirit.   In the state of incarnation, the
périsprit is united to the matter of the body ; in the
wandering state it is free.   When the spirit is incarnate, the substance of the *périsprit* is more or less
bound, more or less adherent, if we may so express it.
With certain persons there is a kind of emanation of
this fluid from their organization ; and it is this, properly speaking, that constitutes mediums for physical
manifestations.   The emission of the animalized fluid
may be more or less abundant, its combination more
or less easy, from whence mediums more or less powerful ; it is not permanent, which explains the intermittence of the power.

76. Let us cite a comparison.   When one has the
will to act materially on a given point at a distance, it
is the thought that wills ; but the thought alone cannot
go to strike the point ; an intermediary is necessary,
which it directs — a stick, a projectile, a current of air,
&c.   Remark, too, the thought does not act directly
on the stick, for if it is not touched it will not act
alone.   The thought, which is but the incarnated spirit
within us, is united to the body by the *périsprit ;* but
it can no more act on the body without the *périsprit*,
than it can act on the stick without the body ; it acts
on the *périsprit* because it is the substance with which
it has the greatest affinity ; the *périsprit* acts on the
muscles, the muscles grasp the stick, and the stick
strikes its aim.   When the spirit is not incarnate, a
foreign auxiliary is necessary ; this auxiliary is the
fluid by which he fits the object to follow the impulse
of his will.

77. Thus, when an object is put in motion, raised or
thrown into the air, the spirit does not grasp, push, or

raise it, as we should, with the hand ; he *saturates* it, so to say, with his fluid, combined with that of the medium, and the object, thus momentarily vivified, acts like a living being, with this difference, that, having no will of its own, it follows the impulse of the will of the spirit.

Since the vital fluid emitted in some way by the spirit, gives a factitious and momentary life to inert bodies ; since the *périsprit* is but this same vital fluid, it follows that when the spirit is incarnate, it is he who gives life to the body, by means of his *périsprit ;* he remains united to it as long as the organization permits ; when he withdraws, the body dies. Now, if, instead of a table, a statue of wood were made, and acted on as is the table, we will have a statue that will move, will strike, will answer by its movements and by its blows ; in a word, we shall have a statue momentarily animated by an artificial life ; we say talking tables, we could also say talking statues. What a light this theory throws on a crowd of phenomena hitherto without solution ! How many allegories and mysterious effects does it not explain?

78. But the incredulous object that the fact of raising tables without a support is impossible, because it is contrary to the law of gravity. We will answer them, firstly, that their denial is not a proof ; secondly, that if the fact exists, it may well be contrary to all the known laws ; that would prove one thing, that it must rest on unknown law, and that those who deny cannot pretend to know all the laws of nature. We have just explained this law, but it is no reason that it may be accepted by them, precisely because it is given by spirits who have left their terrestrial clothing instead of being by spirits who still have it, and have

seats in the Academy. In such a manner that if the spirit of Arago living had given this law, they would have accepted it with their eyes shut; but given by the spirit of Arago dead, it is a Utopia; and why so? because they believe that, Arago being dead, everything in him is dead. We have not the pretension to dissuade them; yet, as this objection might embarrass some people, we shall try to answer it, putting ourselves at their stand-point, that is to say, by making abstract for an instant of the theory of factitious animation.

79. When the space under the bell of the pneumatic machine is emptied, this bell adheres with such force that it is impossible to raise it, on account of the weight of the column of air that rests upon it. Let the air enter, and the bell rises with the utmost facility, because the air below counterbalances the air above; at the same time, left to itself, it will remain on the platform by virtue of the force of gravity. Now, let the air below be compressed till it have a density greater than that above, the bell will be raised in spite of gravity; if the current of air is rapid and violent it could be sustained in space without *visible* support, in the manner of those toys that are made to flutter in a waterfall. The universal fluid, then, *which is the element of all matter*, being accumulated around the table, why should it not have the property to diminish or increase its specific relative weight, as the air for the bell of the pneumatic machine, as hydrogen gas for balloons, without its being considered against the law of gravity? Do you know all the properties and all the power of this fluid? No: well, do not deny a fact because you cannot explain it.

80. Let us return to the theory of the movement of

the table. If, by the means indicated, the spirit can raise a table, he can raise anything else ; an easy-chair, for instance. If he can raise an easy-chair, he can, with a sufficient force, raise at the same time a person seated on it. This is the explanation of this phenomenon, which Mr. Home has produced a hundred times, on himself and other persons ; he renewed it during a voyage to London, and in order to prove that the spectators were not the sport of an optical illusion, he made a mark on the wall with a pencil, and persons passed beneath him. It is said Mr. Home is a powerful medium for physical effects ; he was in this case the efficient cause and the object.

We spoke of the possible augmentation of weight ; it is, in fact, a phenomenon sometimes produced, and which has nothing more anomalous than the prodigious resistance of the bell under the atmospheric column. Under the influence of some mediums, objects as light have been known to offer the same resistance, then suddenly yield to the slightest effort. In the experiment mentioned above, the bell in reality weighs neither more nor less by itself, but it appears heavier from the effect of the exterior cause that acts upon it ; it is probably the same here. The table has always the same intrinsic weight, for the mass is not augmented, but a foreign force is opposed to its movement ; and this cause may be in the ambient fluids that penetrate it, as that which augments or diminishes the apparent weight of the bell is in the air. Make the experiment of the pneumatic bell before an ignorant peasant ; not understanding that it is the air he does not see that acts, it will not be difficult to persuade him it is the devil. It may be said, perhaps, that, this fluid being imponderable, its accumulation cannot augment the weight of an object. Agreed; but remark that if we used the word *accumulation*, it is by comparison, and not from absolute assimilation to the air. It is imponderable; so be it: at the same time nothing proves that it is so; its inmost nature is unknown to us, and we are far from being acquainted with all its properties.

Before having experimented on the weight of the air, no one suspected the effects of this same weight. Electricity is also ranked among the imponderable fluids; yet a body may be held back by an electric current, and offer a strong resistance to one who would raise it: it has in appearance increased in weight. It would be very illogical to conclude that no support exists, because we cannot see it. The spirit, then, may have levers that are unknown to us; Nature proves to us daily that her power does not stop at the evidence of our senses.

We can explain only by a similar cause the singular phenomenon, of which there have been several examples, of a young person, feeble and delicate, raising with two fingers, without effort and as a feather, a strong, robust man, with the chair on which he is seated. This proves a cause foreign to the person; it is an intermitting of the faculty.

CHAPTER V.

SPONTANEOUS PHYSICAL MANIFESTA-
TIONS.

Noises, Racket, and Disturbance. — Objects thrown, &c.

82. THE phenomena of which we have spoken are induced, but it sometimes happens that they take place spontaneously, without participation of the will; far from it, since they often become very importunate. The thought that they may be an effect of the imagination, over-excited by spirit ideas, is utterly excluded by the fact that they are produced among persons who never heard of spirit ideas, and at a moment they least expect them. These phenomena, which may be called practical natural Spiritism, are very important; for they cannot be suspected of connivance; this is why we ask persons who are engaged in spirit phenomena to gather all the facts of this nature which come to their knowledge, but, above all, to verify with care their reality, by a minute study of the circumstances, that they may be assured that they are not the sport of illusion or mystification.

83. Of all the spirit manifestations, the simplest and most frequent are sounds and rappings; here, especially, we must fear an illusion, for a crowd of natural causes might produce them — the wind whistling or moving an object, a body we ourselves move without perceiving it, an acoustic effect, a hidden animal, an

99

insect, &c.; nay, even the pranks of evil jesters.
Spirit noises have always a peculiar character, an intensity of sound and very varied tone, which render
them easily recognizable, and do not allow them to be
confounded with the cracking of the wood, the snap-
ping of the fire, or the monotonous tic-tac of the pen-
dulum : they are dry blows, sometimes hollow, feeble,
and light, sometimes clear, distinct, and noisy, which
change from place to place, and are repeated with
mechanical regularity. Of all the means for making
sure, the most efficacious, that which leaves no doubt
of their origin, is their obedience to the will. If the
blows come from a designated place, if they answer to
the thought by their number or intensity, an intelligent cause for them cannot be disavowed ; but the
want of obedience in them is not always a contrary
proof.

84. Let us admit, now, that, by a minute verification, the certainty is acquired that the noises or other
effects are real manifestations ; is it rational to be afraid
of them ? No, assuredly ; for in any case there could
not be the least danger in them : persons who have
been persuaded it is the devil, alone could be affected
by them in a grievous manner, — as children are afraid
of the *loup-garou*, man-wolf, or of *Croque-mitaine.*

It must be admitted that these manifestations acquire, under certain circumstances, a persistence and
proportion very disagreeable, creating a very natural
desire to be relieved of them. An explanation is
unnecessary to this subject.

85. We have said that the physical manifestations
have for their motive to call our attention to something, and to convince us of the presence of a power
superior to man. We have said, also, that the elevated

spirits are not engaged in these kinds of manifestations ; they employ inferior spirits to produce them, as we employ servants for coarse work, and that with the motive we have indicated. This end once attained, the material manifestation ceases, because it is no longer necessary. One or two examples will make this thing better understood.

86. Several years ago, at the beginning of my studies on Spiritism, being one evening engaged in a work on that matter, rappings were heard around me for four consecutive hours ; it was the first time that a similar thing had happened to me. I satisfied myself that it was from no accidental cause, but, at the moment, knew nothing more. I had, at this time, occasion frequently to see an excellent writing medium. The next day I questioned the spirit, who communicated by this medium, as to the cause of the rappings. " It is," he answered, " your familiar spirit, who wants to speak to you." " And what does he want to say to me ? " " You may ask him yourself, for he is there."

Having then interrogated that spirit, he made himself known under an allegorical name (I have since known, from other spirits, that he belongs to a very elevated order, and has played a very important part in the world) ; he pointed out errors in my work, indicating to me the lines where they would be found, gave me useful and wise advice, and would come at my call whenever I wished to interrogate him. Since then, in fact, this spirit has never left me. He has given me many proofs of great superiority, and his benevolent and efficacious intervention has been manifested for me in the affairs of material life, especially on those bearing on metaphysics. But from our first conversation, the rappings ceased. What did he desire to effect? To enter into a regular communication with me ; for that he must warn me. The warning given, then explained, regular relations established, the rappings became useless : this is why they ceased. The drum is no longer beaten to awaken the soldiers when once they are up.

A fact almost similar happened to one of our friends. For some time his room resounded with various noises, which became very annoying. Occasions being presented of interrogating the spirit of his father, by a writing medium, he ascertained what was wanted, did what he recommended, and after that nothing more was heard. It is to be remarked, that persons who have a regular and easy means of communication with the spirits are much more rarely subject to manifestations of this kind, which may be readily conceived.

87. Spontaneous manifestations are not always limited to noises and rappings ; they sometimes degenerate into real racket and disturbances ; furniture and various objects overthrown, projectiles of all kinds thrown from without, doors and windows opened and shut by invisible hands, tiles broken,— which cannot be placed to the account of illusion. The overthrowing is often very effective, but often there is only the appearance. An uproar is heard, a sound of something falling and breaking with a crash, blocks of wood roll over the floor : running to the spot, everything is found tranquil and in order ; then scarcely outside, when the tumult recommences.

88. Manifestations of this kind are neither rare nor new ; scarcely any local chronicle that does not possess some history of the kind. Fear has, doubtless, exaggerated the facts, which have been made to take

proportions ridiculously gigantic, in passing from mouth to mouth; superstition aiding, the houses where they have happened have been reputed as haunted by the devil, and hence all the marvelous or terrible stories of ghosts. On its part, knavery has not let slip so excellent an occasion for working upon credulity, and that often to the profit of its own personal interests. Besides, it may be readily imagined what impression facts of this kind, even reduced to the reality, might have on weak characters, predisposed by education to superstitious ideas. The surest means of remedying the possible inconveniences, since they cannot be prevented, is to make known the truth. The simplest things are terrifying when their cause is unknown. When people shall have become familiarized with spirits, and when those to whom they are manifested no longer believe they have a legion of demons at their heels, they will no longer fear. In the "*Revue Spirite*" may be seen stated many authentic facts of this kind, among others, the history of the rapping spirit of Bergzabern, whose evil tricks lasted more than eight years (Nos. of May, June, and July, 1858); that of Dibbelsdorf (August, 1860); that of Noyers Street, Paris (August, 1860); that of the spirit of Castelmaudary, under the title of *History of an Infernal* (February, 1860); that of the manufacturer of St. Petersburg (April, 1860); and many others.

89. Transactions of this nature have often the character of a real persecution. We know six sisters living together, who, for several years, found, every morning, their dresses dispersed, hidden under the roof, torn, and cut in pieces, whatever precautions they might take to put them under lock and key. It has often happened that persons in bed, and *perfectly awake,*

have seen their curtains shaken, their coverings and pillows violently torn from them, have been raised up on their mattresses, and sometimes even thrown out of the bed. These doings are more frequent than is believed ; but the most of the time, those who are the victims dare not speak of them, for fear of ridicule. To our own knowledge, certain individuals have been subjected to treatment for insanity, in order to cure them of what they supposed to be hallucinations, and thus have been made really crazy. Medicine cannot comprehend these things, because it admits as cause only the material element ; from whence often result most fatal mistakes. History, some day, will tell of certain modes of treatment of the nineteenth century, as now it recounts certain processes of the middle ages. We entirely admit that some things are the work of malice or malevolence ; but if, after every investigation, it is proved that it is not the work of man, it must be conceded that it is, as some will say, of the devil ; we shall say, of spirits ; but of what spirits ?

90. Superior spirits no more amuse themselves with *charivaris* than grave and serious men do here. We have often made some of them come, that we might inquire into their motive in thus disturbing people. Most of them have had no other than amusement ; these are light rather than wicked spirits, who laugh at the fears they occasion, and the useless researches that are made to discover the cause of the tumult. Often they set upon an individual whom they are pleased to vex, and pursue him from dwelling to dwelling ; at other times they attach themselves to a locality, with no other motive than caprice. Sometimes, also, it is a vengeance they exercise, as we shall have

occasion to show. In some cases their intention is more praiseworthy ; they wish to call attention and be put *en rapport*, either to give some warning useful to the person, or to ask something for themselves. We have often known some of them to ask prayers, others to solicit the accomplishment, in their name, of a vow they had not been able to fulfill, others wishing to repair an evil they had committed while in this life. In general it is wrong to be afraid ; their presence may be inopportune, but not dangerous. Of course there is a strong desire to be relieved from it, and usually what is done for that purpose has the directly contrary effect. If they are spirits who are amusing themselves, the more seriously the thing is taken, the more they persist in it, like mischievous children, who torment the more those who they see are impatient, and like to make cowards afraid. If one would be wise enough to laugh at their ill turns, they would grow weary and leave. We know a person who, far from being irritated, excited them, defying them to do such and such a thing, so that, at the end of a few days, they came no more. But, as we have said, there are those whose motive is less frivolous. For this reason it is always useful to know what they want. If they ask something, it is certain their visits will cease as soon as their desire can be satisfied. The best means to be informed in this respect, is to invoke the spirit by the intermediary of a good writing medium ; by his answers we shall at once see with whom we have to do, and can act accordingly. If it be an unhappy spirit, charity will urge us to treat him with the respect he deserves ; if it be an idle jester, we can act toward him without ceremony ; if he is malevolent, we can pray God to make him better. In every case, prayer will always have a good result. But the gravity of the forms of exorcism make them laugh, and they care nothing about them. If we can enter into communication with them, we must distrust the burlesque or terrifying qualities they sometimes assume to play upon a person's credulity.

We shall return to treat this subject more in detail, and to speak of the causes that sometimes render prayer inefficacious, in the chapters on *Haunted Places and Obsession.*

91. These phenomena, though executed by inferior spirits, are often prompted by spirits of a more elevated order, for the purpose of convincing people of the existence of incorporeal beings of a power superior to man. The report that follows, even the terror it causes, call attention, and end by opening the eyes of the most skeptical. These find it easiest to place these phenomena to the score of imagination — a very convenient explanation, and one that dispenses with the necessity of making others ; yet when objects are turned upside down, or thrown at your head, it requires a very complacent imagination to suppose such things are, when they are not. An effect of some kind is seen ; this effect has, necessarily, a cause : if a *cool and calm* observation shows us that this effect is independent of all human will and all material cause, — if, further, it gives us *evident* signs of intelligence and free will, *which is the most characteristic sign,* — we are forced to attribute it to an unknown intelligence. What are these mysterious beings ? This is what the spiritist studies teach us in the least contestable manner, by the means they give us to communicate with them. These studies teach us, above all, to separate what is real from the false or exaggerated in the phe-

nomena we cannot explain. If an isolated effect be produced, — noise, movement, or apparition even, — the first thought should be that it is owing to an entirely natural cause, which is the most probable: then this cause must be sought for with the utmost care, and the intervention of spirits admitted only in good earnest: this is the way not to be deceived. For instance, he who, without any person being near him, receives a box on the ear, or blows of a stick on his back, as has been known, cannot doubt the presence of an invisible being.

One should guard not only against recitals that may be more or less exaggerated, but against his own impressions, and not attribute everything he cannot understand to an occult origin. An infinity of very simple and very natural causes may produce effects strange at first sight, and it would be truly superstitious to fancy spirits always busy upsetting the furniture, breaking dishes, instigating the thousand and one household vexations, which it is most rational to place to the account of carelessness.

92. The explanations given of the movement of inert bodies naturally apply to all the spontaneous effects. The noises, though stronger than the table rappings, have the same cause; objects are thrown or displaced by the same force that raises any object soever. A circumstance comes in here to the support of this theory. It might be asked, Where is the medium in this case? The spirits have told us that, in such cases, there is always some one whose power is exercised against his will. Spontaneous manifestations are very rarely produced in isolated places; they almost always take place in inhabited houses, and through the presence of certain persons who exercise

an influence without desiring it; these persons are real mediums, who themselves are ignorant of it, and whom, for that reason, we call *natural mediums;* they are to other mediums what natural somnambulists are to magnetic somnambulists, and quite as curious to observe.

93. The voluntary or involuntary intervention of a person endowed with a special aptitude for the production of these phenomena, appears to be necessary in most cases, though there are cases in which the spirit appears to act alone; but then it might be that he could draw the animalized fluid elsewhere, and not from a person present. This explains why spirits, who surround us constantly, do not every moment produce disturbances. It is first necessary that the spirit should desire it; that he should have an end, a motive; without that he does nothing. Then, too, he must often find, exactly in the place where he desires to act, a suitable person to second him — a rare coincidence. Such a person coming unexpectedly, he profits by it. Notwithstanding the meeting of all those favorable circumstances, he might be prevented by a superior will, which does not permit him to act as he pleases. He might be permitted to act only within certain limits, and in a case where these manifestations would be considered useful, either as a means of conviction or trial, for the person who is the object of them.

94. On this subject we will cite only the conversation in regard to the manifestations in June, 1860, in Noyers Street, in Paris. The details may be found in the *Revue Spirite* of August, 1860.

1. *To St. Louis.* "Will you please tell us if the

incidents said to have occurred in Noyers Street are real ? As to the possibility, we do not doubt."

"Yes, these incidents are true ; only men's imaginations exaggerate them, either from fear or irony ; but, I repeat, they are true. These manifestations are brought about by a spirit who is amusing himself a little at the expense of those who live in the place."

2. "Is there any person in the house who may be the cause of these manifestations ?"

"They are always caused by the presence of the person whom they attack ; either the attacking spirit has a grudge against the person living in the place where he is, and wants to play tricks on him, or, perhaps, even seeks to drive him away."

3. "We ask, if, among the persons in the house, there is one who may be the cause of these phenomena, by a spontaneous and involuntary medianimic influence."

"It must be so ; without that the thing could not have occurred.

"A spirit lives in a place he likes ; he remains inactive so long as a suitable nature is not present in the place ; when the person comes, then he amuses himself as much as he can."

4. "Is the presence of the person in the very place indispensable ?"

"Ordinarily so, and it is in this instance ; that is why I said without that the incident could not have occurred ; but I did not mean to generalize ; there are cases in which immediate presence is not necessary."

5. "As these spirits are always of an inferior order, is it an unfavorable sign for the person that he is fit to serve them as an auxiliary ? Would it show a sympathy with beings of that nature ?"

"No, not precisely ; for this suitability arises from a physical disposition ; at the same time, it very often shows a material tendency which it would be preferable not to have ; for the higher one is morally, the more one attracts good spirits, who necessarily keep away bad ones."

6. "From whence does the spirit take the projectiles he uses ?"

"These things are most often taken on the place, or in the vicinity ; a force coming from a spirit projects them, and they fall in the spot designated by that spirit."

7. "Since spontaneous manifestations are often permitted, or even excited, for the purpose of convincing, it seems to us that if certain skeptical people were personally the object of them, they would be obliged to yield to such evidence. They sometimes complain that they never witness conclusive facts ; would it not depend on the spirits to give them some sensible proofs ?"

"Are not atheists and materialists every moment witnesses of the effects of the power of God and of thought ? That does not prevent them from denying God and the soul. Did the miracles of Jesus convert all his contemporaries ? Did not the Pharisees, who said to him, 'Master, show us a sign,' resemble those who, in our time, ask you to make them see manifestations ? If they are not convinced by the wonders of creation, they would no more be convinced even if spirits should appear to them in the most unequivocal manner, because their pride makes them like restive horses. The occasions of seeing would not be wanting if they should seek in sincerity. God does not see fit to do for them more than for those who sincerely seek instruction, for the reward is only to the willing. Their skepticism will not prevent the will of God from being accomplished ; you see plainly it has not hindered the spread of the doctrine.

"Cease to be disquieted by their opposition, which is to the doctrine what shade is to the picture ; it gives it a stronger light. What merit would they have in being convinced by force ? God will leave them to all the responsibility of their obstinacy, and that responsibility will be more terrible than you think. 'Blessed are those who have not seen, and yet have believed,' as Jesus said, because they do not doubt God's power."

8. "Do you think it would be of use to invoke that spirit, to ask some explanations of him ?"

"Invoke him if you wish, but it is an inferior spirit, who will give you only very insignificant answers.

95. *Conversation with the disturbing spirit of Noyers Street.*

1. Invocation.

"Why have you called me ? Do you want to be struck with stones ? Then we should see a fine run away, in spite of your brave air."

2. "If you should bring stones here, it would not frighten us ; we actually ask if you can bring them here."

"Here I could not, perhaps ; you have a guardian who watches over you."

3. "In Noyers Street was there a person who served as your auxiliary to help in the malicious tricks you have played on the people in the house ?"

"Certainly ; I found a good instrument, and no learned, wise, and prudent spirit to hinder me. I am gay. I love to amuse myself."

4. " Who was the person who served as your instrument ? "

" A servant."

5. " Was it against her will she served you ? "

" O, yes ; the poor girl! she was the most frightened."

6. " Did you act in this way from a hostile motive ? "

" I had no hostile motive ; but the men who seize upon everything will make it turn to their advantage."

7. " What do you mean by that ? We don't understand you."

" I was trying to amuse myself ; but you will study the thing, and will have one more fact to show that we exist."

8. " You say you had no hostile motive, and yet you have broken all the windows in the house ; you have thus caused a real loss."

" That is but a detail."

9. " Where did you procure the objects you threw ? "

" They are very common. I found them in the court-yard, and in the next gardens."

10. " Did you find them *all*, or did you make some of them ? " (See Chapter VIII.)

" I made nothing, composed nothing."

11. " If you had not found them, could you have made them ? "

" It would have been more difficult ; but to tell the truth, matters can be mixed, and make something."

12. " Now tell us how you threw them."

" Ah, that is harder to tell. I was helped by the electrical nature of that girl, joined to mine, less material ; so between us we transported the different matters."

13. " You would like, I think, to tell us something

about yourself. Tell us, then, if it is long since you died."

" Long enough ; more than fifty years."

14. " What were you when you were living ? "

" Not much good ; I picked rags around here, and sometimes they scolded me because I loved Goodman Noe's red wine too much ; so I would have liked to drive them all away."

15. " Is it of yourself, and of your own free will, that you have answered our questions ? "

" I had an instructor."

16. " Who is your instructor ? "

" Your good King Louis."

Remark. This question was propounded on account of certain answers which seemed beyond the capacity of this spirit, in the depth of the ideas, and even in the form of the language. It is not at all astonishing that he should have been aided by a more enlightened spirit, who desired to profit by this occasion to give us some instruction. This is a very ordinary occurrence, but a remarkable particularity in this circumstance is, that the influence of the other spirit made itself felt even in the writing ; that of the answers, when he intervened, is more regular, more flowing ; that of the rag-picker is angular, coarse, irregular, often scarcely legible, and bears an entirely different character.

17. " What do you do now ; does the thought of your future occupy you ? "

" Not yet ; I am wandering. They think so little of me in the world, that nobody prays for me ; as I am not helped, I don't work."

Remark. We shall see, by and by, how much we

can contribute to the advancement and consolation of the inferior spirits by prayers and advice.

18. "What was your name when you were living?"
"Jeannet."

19. "Well, Jeannet, we will pray for you. Tell us if our invocation has given you pleasure, or annoyed you?"

"Pleasure rather, for you are good fellows; gay livers, though a little severe; all the same, you have listened to me. I am satisfied.

"JEANNET."

Phenomenon of Materialization.

96. This phenomenon differs from those of which we have spoken only in the kind intention of the spirit who is their author, in the nature of the objects, almost always of a gracious character, and by the sweet and almost delicate manner in which they are brought. It consists in the spontaneous bringing of objects which are not in the place where you are; these are most often flowers, sometimes fruits, confectionery, jewels, &c.

97. Let us first say that this phenomenon is one of those most easily imitated, and consequently of which we must be on our guard against imposture. We know how far sleight of hand can go in such matters; but without having to do with a person of this profession, we might easily be the dupe of a skillful maneuver. The best of all guarantees is in the *character, the known honor, the absolute disinterestedness* of the person who obtains the effects; in the second place, in the attentive examination of all the circumstances under which they are produced; finally,

in the enlightened knowledge of Spiritism, which alone can enable us to discover what is to be suspected.

98. The theory of the phenomenon of materialization, and of physical manifestations in general, is summed up in a remarkable manner in the following dissertation, by a spirit whose communications bear an incontestable seal of profundity and logic. Several of them will be found in the course of this work. He made himself known under the name of *Erastus*, a disciple of St. Paul, and as the spirit protector of the medium who served him as an interpreter.

"To obtain these phenomena, there must necessarily be mediums whom I will call *sensitive;* that is to say, endowed in the highest degree with the medianimic faculties of expansion and penetrability ; because the easily excitable nervous system of some of these mediums permits them, by means of certain vibrations, to project round them with profusion their animalized fluid.

"Impressionable natures, persons whose natures vibrate to the least sentiment, to the smallest sensation, whom moral or physical influence, internal or external, easily affects, are subjects very apt to become excellent mediums for the physical effects of tangibility and materialization. In fact, their nervous system, almost entirely deprived of the refractory envelope which isolates this system among most incarnated beings, makes them suitable for the development of these various phenomena.

"Consequently, with subjects of this nature, whose other faculties are not adverse to medianimization, the phenomena of tangibility will be more easily obtained ; rappings in the walls and in the furniture, *intelligent* movements, and even the suspension in space of the heaviest, inert matter. *A fortiori*, these results will be obtained if, instead of one medium, there are at hand several, equally well endowed.

"But from the production of these phenomena to the obtaining of that of materializations, there is a whole world; for, in this case, not only is the labor of the spirit more complex, more difficult, but, more than this, the spirit can operate only by means of one medium; that is, several mediums could not simultaneously concur in the production of the same phenomenon. On the contrary, it sometimes happens that the presence of persons antipathetic to the spirit who operates, radically fetters his operation. To these motives, which, as you see, do not lack importance, add that the materialization always necessitates a greater concentration, and, at the same time, a greater diffusion of certain fluids which can be obtained only from the best endowed mediums, those, in a word, whose *electro-medianimic* machinery is the best conditioned.

"In general, these effects are, and will remain, exceedingly rare. I do not need to prove to you why they are, and will be, less frequent than the other tangible effects; from what I have said, you will yourself make that deduction. Besides, these phenomena are of such a nature, that not only all mediums are not suitable, but even all spirits cannot produce them. In fact, there must exist between the spirit and the medium influenced a certain affinity, a certain analogy, in a word, a certain resemblance, which permits the expansible part of the perispritaltic (Note 5) fluid of the incarnated to be mingled, united, combined with that of the spirit who desires to produce the effect.

This fusion should be such that the resulting force becomes, so to say, *one;* as the electric current acting on the coal produces one flame, one single brightness. Do you say, Why this union? why this fusion? It is that for the production of these phenomena it is necessary that the essential properties of the operating spirit be augmented by some of those of the mediumized; it is that the vital fluid, indispensable to the production of all the medianimic phenomena, is the *exclusive* appanage of the incarnated ; and that, consequently, the spirit operator is obliged to be impregnated with it. It is thus only that he can, by means of certain properties of your ambient fluid, unknown to you, isolate, render invisible, and cause to move, certain material objects, and even the incarnated themselves.

"It is not permitted me, at this moment, to unvail to you these special laws that rule the gases and fluids that surround you ; but before many years shall have elapsed, before one generation of man be accomplished, the explanation of these laws and of these phenomena will be revealed to you, and you will see a new order of mediums arise, who will fall into a peculiar state as soon as they shall be medianimized.

"You see with how many difficulties the production of these phenomena is surrounded ; you can conclude from this, very logically, that phenomena of this kind are exceedingly rare, as I have said, and with still greater reason, that the spirits seldom lend themselves to their production, because it requires on their part a quasi-material labor, which is for them an ennui and a fatigue. On the other hand there is this : it is that very often, in spite of their energy and will, the state of the medium himself opposes an impassable barrier.

"It is thus evident, and doubtless your reasoning sanctions it, that the tangible facts of rappings, movements, suspensions, are simple phenomena, which are operated by the concentration and dilatation of certain fluids, and which may be elicited and obtained by the will and the work of mediums who are suited thereto, when they are seconded by friendly and kind spirits ; while the facts of materialization are multiple, complex, require a concourse of special circumstances, can be operated only by a single spirit and a single medium, and necessitate, over and above the wants of tangibility, a very especial combination of circumstances to isolate and render invisible the object or objects subject to the materialization.

"All you spiritists comprehend my explanations, and you can perfectly understand the reason for this concentration of special fluids for the locomotion and tangibility of inert matter ; you believe in it as you believe in the phenomena of electricity and magnetism, with which the medianimic facts are full of analogy, and are, so to say, its consecration and development. As to the skeptics, — and the scientists, worse than the skeptics, — I have nothing to do with convincing them ; I do not trouble myself about them : they will, some day, be convinced by the force of evidence, for they must necessarily bow before the unanimous testimony of spiritist facts, as they have been forced to do before other facts they have at first rejected.

"To recapitulate : while the facts of tangibility are frequent, the facts of materialization are very rare, because their conditions are very difficult ; consequently no medium can say, "At such an hour, at such a

moment, I will obtain a materialization ; for often the
spirit himself finds a hindrance to his work. I must
add that these phenomena are doubly difficult in public, for there almost always are met energetically refractory elements, which paralyze the efforts of the
spirit, and, with still greater reason, the action of the
medium. On the contrary, be certain that these phenomena are almost always produced in private, spontaneously, most often unknown to the mediums, and
without premeditation, and very rarely when these
have foretold them ; from whence you may conclude
that there is a legitimate motive of suspicion whenever
a medium flatters himself he can obtain them at will ;
in other words, that he can command spirits as servants, which is simply absurd. Again, take as a general rule, that these spirit phenomena are not given in
the way of a show, and to amuse the curious. If some
spirits lend themselves to such things, it can be only
for simple phenomena, and not for those which, like
materialization and others similar, exact exceptional
conditions.

"Remember, spiritists, that if it is absurd to reject
systematically all the phenomena from beyond the
tomb, neither is it wise to accept them all blindly.
When a phenomenon of tangibility, of apparition, of
visibility, or of materialization is manifested spontaneously, and, as it were, instantaneously, accept it : but I
cannot repeat to you too often, accept nothing blindly ;
let each action be subjected to an examination, minute,
searching, severe ; for, believe me, Spiritism, so rich in
sublime and grand phenomena, has nothing to gain
from those small manifestations which skillful jugglers
can imitate.

"I know very well what you will say to me, — that

these phenomena are useful to convince the skeptical; but know this, that if you had no other means of conviction, you would not have, to-day, the hundredth part of the spiritists that you have. Speak to the heart; it is by that you will make the most serious conversions. If, for certain persons, you consider it useful to act by material facts, at least present them under such circumstances that there can be no false interpretation, and, above all, do not go aside from the normal condition of these facts; for facts presented under bad conditions furnish arguments to the skeptical, instead of convincing them.   ERASTUS."

99. This phenomenon offers a very striking peculiarity, which is, that certain mediums obtain it only in a somnambulic state. This is easily explained: there is with a somnambulist a natural disengagement, a kind of isolation of the spirit and of the *périsprit*, which must facilitate the combination of the necessary fluids. Such is the case with the materializations we have witnessed. The following questions were addressed to the spirit who produced them, but his answers being unsatisfactory, we submitted them to the spirit *Erastus*, much more enlightened on the theory, and who completed them by very judicious remarks. One is the workman, the other the scientist; and the comparison of these two intelligences is an instructive study, for it proves that simply being a spirit is not sufficient to make one comprehend everything.

1. "Will you please tell us why the materializations you made were produced only during the magnetic sleep of the medium?"

"That depends on the nature of the medium; the

effects I produced with mine asleep, I could have produced equally well with another medium in a waking
state."

2. "Why did you make us wait so long? and why
excite the covetousness of the medium, irritating his
desire to obtain the promised object?"

"Time is necessary for me to prepare the fluids that
serve for the materialization ; as to the excitation, it is
often only to amuse those present, as well as the somnambulist."

Remark by Erastus. "The spirit who answered
knew no better ; he does not reason on the motive of
this covetousness, which he instinctively incites without
understanding its effect ; he thinks to amuse, while
in reality he undoubtedly provokes a greater emission
of fluid ; it is the consequence of the difficulty the
phenomenon presents ; a difficulty always greater
when it is not spontaneous, especially with certain
mediums."

3. "Does the production of the phenomena pertain
to the special nature of the medium? and could it be
produced with other mediums with more facility and
promptitude?"

"The production pertains to the nature of the medium, and can be produced only with corresponding
natures ; as to promptitude, our custom of corresponding often with the same medium is a great help to
us."

4. "Does the influence of the persons present count
for anything?"

"When there is skepticism, opposition, we can be
greatly annoyed : we like better to give our proofs with
believers, and persons versed in Spiritism ; but I do

not mean by that to say that ill will could completely
paralyze us."

5. " From whence did you take the flowers and *bonbons* you brought ? "

" The flowers I took from the gardens, wherever it
pleased me."

6. " And the *bonbons ?* Surely the confectioner would
miss them."

" I took them from wherever it pleased me ; the
merchant did not miss them at all, for I put others in
their place."

Remark of Erastus. " I think this is explained in
a very unsatisfactory manner, because of the incapa-
city of the spirit who answered. Thus, he may have
caused a real wrong ; but the spirit does not wish to
pass for one who would wrong any person whatever.
An object can be replaced only by an identical object
of the same form, same value ; consequently, if a spirit
had the faculty to substitute an object similar to that
he takes, he would have no reason for taking it, and
might give that which served him in replacing."

7. " Is it possible to bring flowers from another
planet ? "

" No ; it is not possible to me."

(*To Erastus.*) " Could other spirits have the power? "

" No ; that is not possible, on account of the difference in the surrounding atmospheres."

8. " Could you bring flowers from another hemi-
sphere, — the tropics, for instance ? "

" From any part of the earth I can."

9. " Could you make the objects you have brought
disappear, and carry them back ? "

" Just as well as I made them come. I can take
them as I will."

10. "Does the production of this phenomenon cause you any trouble — any annoyance?"

"It causes us no trouble, when we have permission; it might cause us a great deal, if we wished to produce effects without being authorized to do so."

Remarks of Erastus. "He does not wish to acknowledge his trouble, though it may be very real, as he is obliged to effect what might be called a material operation."

11. "What are the difficulties you encounter?"

"No other than bad fluidic dispositions, which might oppose us."

12. "How do you bring the object? Do you hold it in your hands?"

"No; we envelop it in ourselves."

Remark of Erastus. "He does not clearly explain his operation, for he does not envelop the object with his own personality; but as his personal fluid is dilatable, penetrable, and expansible, he combines a part of this fluid with a part of the animalized fluid of the medium, and it is in that combination that he hides and transports the object subject to the materialization. It is not, thus, right to say that he envelops it in himself."

13. "Could you, with the same facility, bring an object of considerable weight, of fifty kilometres, for instance?"

"Weight is nothing to us; we bring flowers because that may be more agreeable than a great weight."

Remark of Erastus. "That is true; he could bring one or two hundred kilometres of objects; for the weight that exists for you is annulled for him; but here again he does not give the reason for what happens. The mass of the combined fluids is proportionate to the mass of the objects; in a word, the force should be in proportion to the resistance; from whence it follows, that if the spirit brings only a flower, or a light object, it is often because he does not find, either in the medium or in himself, the elements necessary for a greater effort."

14. " Are there sometimes disappearances of objects when the cause is unknown, which may be the work of spirits ? "

" That happens very often ; more often than you think ; and it could be remedied by begging the spirit to bring back the object that disappeared."

Remark of Erastus. " That is true ; but sometimes what is carried off is well carried off; for such objects, when we cannot find them at home, are often carried very far away. At the same time, as the carrying away objects requires nearly the same conditions as bringing them, it can take place only with the aid of mediums endowed with special faculties : this is why, when anything disappears, it is probably more your own stupidity than that of the spirits."

15. " Are there effects regarded as natural phenomena which are due to the action of spirits ? "

" Your days are full of such effects, which you do not understand, because you have not thought of them, and which a little reflection would make you see clearly."

Remark of Erastus. "Do not attribute to the spirits what is the work of humanity, but believe in their secret constant influence, which brings to life around you a thousand circumstances, a thousand incidents, necessary to the accomplishment of your actions, your existence."

16. " Among the objects brought, are there not some that may have been fabricated by spirits ; that is, pro-

duced spontaneously by the modifications to which the spirits can subject the fluid, or the universal element."

"Not by me, for I have not permission to do it ; an elevated spirit alone can do it."

17. "How did you introduce those objects the other day ? for the room was shut."

"I made them enter with me, enveloped, so to say, in my substance ; as to telling you more at length, it is not possible."

18. "How did you manage to render visible what was, a moment before, invisible ? "

"I took away the matter that enveloped them."

Remark by Erastus. "It is not matter, properly so called, that envelops them, but a fluid, drawn partly from the *périsprit* of the medium, partly from that of the operating spirit."

19. (*To Erastus.*) "Can an object be brought into a place perfectly closed ? in a word, can the spirit spiritualize a material object, so that it may penetrate matter ? "

"This question is complex. The spirit can render the objects brought invisible, but not penetrable ; he cannot break the aggregation of matter, which would be the destruction of the object. This object, made invisible, he can bring when he pleases, and disengage it at the proper moment, to make it appear. It is otherwise for those we compose ; as we introduce only the elements of matter, and as these elements are essentially penetrable, as we ourselves penetrate and pass through the most condensed bodies with as much facility as the solar rays pass through the panes of glass, we can truly say, we have introduced the object into a place, however tightly shut it may be; but only in this case can we say it."

NOTE. — See afterward, for the theory of the spontaneous formation of objects, the chapter entitled, *Laboratory of the Spiritual World.*

Chapter VI.

VISUAL MANIFESTATIONS.

Questions on Apparitions. — Theoretic Essay on Apparitions. — Globular Spirits. — Theory of Hallucinations.

100. Of all the spirit manifestations the most interesting are, undoubtedly, those by which spirits can render themselves visible. It will be seen, by the explanation of this phenomenon, that it is no more supernatural than the others. We first give the answers of the spirits to questions on this subject.

1. "Can spirits make themselves visible?"

"Yes; especially during sleep: at the same time some persons see them as well waking; but this is more rare."

Remark. While the body rests, the spirit is disengaged from its material ties; it is more free, and can more easily see other spirits with whom it enters into communication. Dreams are but the remembrances of this state; when nothing is remembered, it is said there has been no dreaming; but the soul has none the less seen and enjoyed its liberty. We treat more especially here of apparitions in the waking state.

2. "Do the spirits who manifest themselves to the sight belong more to one class than another?"

"No; they may belong to all classes, — to the most elevated as to the most inferior."

3. " Is it given to all spirits to manifest themselves visibly ? "

" All can ; but they have not always the permission, nor the will."

4. " What is the motive of spirits who make themselves visible ? "

" That depends upon circumstances ; according to their nature, the motive may be good or bad."

5. " How could this permission be given if the motive were bad ? "

" It is then to try those to whom they appear.   The intention of the spirit may be evil, but the result may be good."

6. " What can be the motive of the spirits who have evil intentions, in showing themselves ? "

" To terrify, and often to avenge."

" What is that of the spirits who come with a good intention ? "

" To console those who regret them, to prove that they exist and are near you, to give advice, and to claim assistance for themselves."

7. " What inconvenience could there be if the possibility of seeing spirits were permanent and general ? Would it not be a means of relieving the doubts of the most skeptical ? "

" Man being constantly surrounded by spirits, their incessant sight would trouble him, would hamper him in his actions, would destroy his initiative in most cases ; while believing himself alone, he acts more freely. As for the skeptical, they have plenty of means of being convinced if they would profit by them, and were not blinded by pride. You know very well that there are persons who have seen, and who believe none the more for that, since they say it is an illusion.

Do not disquiet yourself for those people. God sees to them."

Remark. There would be as great inconvenience in seeing spirits always with us, as in seeing the air that surrounds us, or the myriads of microscopic animals that flutter around us and on us. From whence we should conclude that what God has done is well done, and that he knows better than we what is suited to us.

8. "If the sight of spirits has inconveniences why is it permitted in certain cases?"

"It is to give a proof that all does not die with the body, that the soul preserves its individuality after death. This temporary sight suffices to give this proof, and attests to the presence of your friends near you, but it has not the inconveniences of permanence."

9. "In more advanced worlds than ours, is the sight of spirits more frequent?"

"The nearer man is brought to the spiritual nature, the more easily he enters into relations with spirits: it is the grossness of your envelope that makes the perception of ethereal beings most difficult and most rare."

10. "Is it rational to be terrified at the apparition of a spirit?"

"He who reflects ought to understand that a spirit, whatever he may be, is less dangerous than a living person. Besides, spirits go everywhere, and there is no need to see them to know that they may be beside us. The spirit that would do harm can do it without showing himself, and even more surely; he is not dangerous because he is a spirit, but because of the influence he can exert in the thought, turning it away from good and toward evil."

Remark. Persons who are afraid in solitude or in darkness rarely consider the cause of their terror; they could not say what they fear, but assuredly they should more fear to meet men than spirits; for a wrong-doer is more dangerous living than after death. A lady of our acquaintance had, one evening, in her room, an apparition so distinct, she thought it a person, and her first movement was that of fright. Having assured herself that no one was there, she said to herself, "It appears *it is only a spirit*. I may sleep in peace."

11. "Can the person to whom a spirit appears engage in conversation with him?"

"Perfectly well; and that is what should always be done in such cases, — asking the spirit who he is and what he wants, and how we may be useful to him. If the spirit is unhappy and suffering, our commiseration soothes him; if it is a benevolent spirit, he may come with the intention of giving us good advice."

"How, in this case, can the spirit answer?"

"He does it sometimes by articulate sounds, like a person living; most often by transmission of thought."

12. "Do the spirits who appear with wings really have them, or are those wings but symbolical appearances?"

"Spirits have not wings; they do not need them; for they can, as spirits, transport themselves everywhere. They appear according to the way in which they desire to affect the person to whom they show themselves: some appear in ordinary costume, others enveloped in draperies; some with wings, as attributes of the category of spirits they represent."

13. "Are the persons we see in dreams always those they seem to be?"

" It is almost always those persons themselves whom your spirit goes to find, or who come to find you."

14. " Could not mocking spirits take the appearance of persons who are dear to us, to lead us into error ? "

" They take fantastic appearances only to amuse themselves at your expense ; but there are things with which they are not permitted to sport."

15. Thought being a kind of invocation, it is easily understood that it evokes the presence of the spirit ; but how is it that often the persons of whom we think most, — whom we ardently desire to see, — do not come in dreams, while we see people who are indifferent to us, and those of whom we never think ? "

" There is not always the possibility of spirits manifesting themselves to the sight, even in dreams, and in spite of the desire there may be to see them : causes independent of their will may prevent them. It is, also, often a trial which the most ardent desire cannot overpass. As to indifferent persons, if you do not think of them, it is possible they may think of you. Besides, you can have no idea of the relations of the world of spirits ; you meet there a crowd of intimate acquaintances, old and new, of whom you have no idea in the waking state."

Remark. When there is no means of controlling the visions or apparitions, they can undoubtedly be looked upon as hallucinations ; but when they are confirmed by events, they cannot be attributed to the imagination ; such are, for instance, the apparitions at the moment of their death, either in dream or in a waking state, of persons of whom we do not think, and who, by various signs, reveal the wholly unexpected circumstances attending their death. Horses have often been known to rear, and refuse to go forward, in presence of the apparitions that terrified their drivers. If imagination counts for something with men, surely it cannot with animals. Besides, if the images seen in dreams were always an effect of waking perceptions, nothing could explain why it often happens that we never dream of those things most often in our thoughts.

16. " Why are some visions more frequent in sickness ? "

" They occur the same in a state of perfect health, but in sickness the material ties are relaxed ; the weakness of the body leaves more liberty to the spirit, which enters more easily into communication with other spirits."

17. "Spontaneous apparitions appear to be more frequent in certain countries. Is it that certain people are better endowed than others to have this kind of manifestations ? "

" Are you acquainted with the details of each apparition ? Apparitions, noises, all the manifestations, indeed, are equally spread over the whole world ; but they present distinctive characters, according to the people among whom they take place. For instance, among those who have little knowledge of writing, there are no writing mediums ; among others they abound : elsewhere there are more often noises and movements than intelligent communications, because these are less esteemed there and less sought after."

18. " Why do apparitions prefer the night ? May it not be an effect of silence and obscurity on the imagination ? "

" It is for the same reason that you see the stars in the night, which you cannot see in the daylight. The great brightness may efface a light apparition ; but it is an error to believe that the night has anything to do with it. Question those who have seen them, and you will see that the majority have taken place by day."

Remark. Apparitions are much more frequent and general than is believed; but many persons do not confess it, from fear of ridicule; others attribute them to illusion. If they appear more numerous among certain people, that is because there they more carefully preserve traditions, either true or false, almost always exaggerated by the love of the marvelous; credulity makes them see the supernatural in the most common phenomena; the silence of solitary places, the depths of ravines, the groanings of the forest, the screamings of the tempest, the echo of the mountains, the fantastic form of the clouds, the shadows, the mirage, all assist the illusion of simple and artless imaginations, and they tell with the utmost sincerity what they have seen, or what they think they have seen. But beside this fiction there is the reality; the serious study of Spiritism tends to free it from all the absurd accessories of superstition."

19. "Is the sight of spirits produced in a normal state, or only in an ecstatic state?"

"It can take place in perfectly normal conditions; at the same time the persons who see them are quite often in a peculiar state, bordering on ecstasy, which gives them a kind of double sight." (*Book on Spirits*, No. 447.)

20. "Do those who see spirits see them with their eyes?"

"They believe they do; but in reality it is the soul that sees, and what proves it is, that they can see them with their eyes shut."

21. " How can the spirit make itself visible ? "

" The principle is the same as that of all manifestations ; it comes from the properties of the *périsprit*, which can undergo various modifications at the will of the spirit."

22. " Can the spirit itself be made visible, or can it make itself visible only by the aid of the *périsprit ?* "

" In your material state spirits can manifest themselves only by the aid of their semi-material envelope ; it is the intermediary by which they act on your senses. It is under this envelope that they appear sometimes with a human form, sometimes otherwise, either in dreams or in a state of waking."

23. " Might it be said that it is by the condensation of the fluid of the *périsprit* that the spirit becomes visible ? "

" Condensation is not the word ; it is rather a comparison which may help you to understand the phenomenon, for there is not really condensation. By the combination of the fluids, there is produced in the *périsprit* a peculiar disposition, that has no analogy for you, and which renders it perceptible."

24. " Are the spirits that appear always intangible, and inaccessible to the touch ? "

" Intangible, as in a dream, in their normal state ; at the same time they can make an impression on the touch, and leave traces of their presence, and even in some cases momentarily become tangible, which proves that between them and you there is matter."

25. " Is every one capable of seeing spirits ? "

" In sleep, yes, but not in a waking state. In sleep the soul sees without intermediary ; when awake it is always more or less influenced by the organs ; this is why the conditions are not altogether the same."

26. "In what consists the faculty of seeing spirits during the waking hours?"

"This faculty depends upon the organization; it depends upon the greater or less facility which the fluid of the seer has for combining with that of the spirit. Thus it does not suffice to the spirit to wish to show himself; it is necessary that he find in the person to whom he desires to show himself the · necessary aptitude."

"Can this faculty be developed by exercise?"

"It can, like all the other faculties; but it is one of those of which it is better to await the natural development than to hasten it, for fear of exciting the imagination. The general and permanent sight of spirits is exceptional, and is not a normal condition of man."

27. "Can the apparition of spirits be called forth?"

"It may be sometimes, but very rarely; it is almost always spontaneous; and for that it is necessary to be endowed with a special faculty."

28. "Can spirits make themselves visible under any other than a human form?"

"The human form is the normal form; the spirit can vary its appearance, but it is always the human type."

"Can they show themselves under the form of flame?"

"They can produce flames, lights, as well as all other effects to attest their presence; but this is not the spirit itself. Flame is often only a mirage, or an emanation from the *périsprit;* it is, in all cases, only a part; the *périsprit* appears entire only in visions."

29. "What do you think of the belief that attributes the *ignis fatuus* to the presence of souls or spirits?"

"Superstition produced by ignorance. The real cause of the *ignis fatuus* is well known."

"The blue flame said to have appeared on the head of Servius Tullius when a child, is it a fable or a reality?"

"It was real; it was produced by the familiar spirit who wanted to warn the mother. This mother — a seeing medium — saw a ray of the protecting spirit of her child. All seeing mediums do not see in the same degree, the same as your writing mediums do not all write the same thing. Where this mother saw only a flame, another medium would have seen the whole body even of the spirit."

30. "Could spirits present themselves under the form of animals?"

"That might happen, but it is always only very inferior spirits who take these appearances. It can, in all cases, be only a momentary appearance, for it would be absurd to believe that any animal whatever could be the incarnation of a spirit. Animals are always only animals, and nothing more."

Remark. Superstition alone can produce the belief that some animals are animated by spirits; it must be a very obliging or a very vivid imagination to see anything supernatural in everything a little out of the way; but fear often makes one see what does not exist. Yet fear is not always the source of this idea; we knew a lady, very intelligent in other matters, who loved beyond measure a great black cat because she believed its nature was above the animal; had she known anything of Spiritism, it would have shown her the absurdity of the cause of her predilection, by proving to her the impossibility of such a metamorphosis.

Theoretical Essay on Apparitions.

101. The most ordinary apparent manifestations take place during sleep, by dreams ; these are visions.   It does not enter into our plan to examine all the particularities that dreams may present ; we sum up by saying they may be an actual vision of things present or absent ; a retrospective vision of the past ; and, in some exceptional cases, a presentiment of the future. Often, also, they are allegorical pictures which the spirits cause to pass before our eyes, to give us useful warnings or salutary advice, if they are good spirits ; or to lead us into error, or to flatter our passions, if they are imperfect spirits.   The following theory applies to dreams as to all other cases of apparitions. (See *Book on Spirits*, Nos. 400 and following.)

We should consider it an insult to the good sense of our readers to refute all the absurdities of what is commonly called the interpretation of dreams.

102. Apparitions proper take place in a waking state, during the full and entire liberty of the faculties. They are usually presented under a vaporous and diaphanous form, sometimes vague and indistinct ; it is often at first a white light whose outline is gradually developed.   At other times the forms are perfectly defined, and the smallest features can be distinguished, so that an exact description of them could be given. The manner, the aspect, are the same as were those of the spirit when living.

Being able to take all appearances, the spirit presents himself under that by which he could be most readily recognized, if such is his desire.   Thus, although, as a spirit, he has no corporeal infirmity, he will show himself disabled, lame, humpbacked, wounded, with scars, if that is necessary to establish his identity. Æsop, for example, as a spirit, is not deformed; but if he is evoked as Æsop, even should he since have had many existences, he will appear ugly and humpbacked, with the traditional costume. One remarkable thing is that, except in some particular instances, the least defined parts are the inferior members, while the head, the trunk, the arms, the hands, are always perfectly shown; also they are rarely seen to walk, but glide like shadows. As to the costume, it is ordinarily composed of a drapery ending in long, floating folds, or with hair in flowing, graceful curls, the appearance of spirits who have preserved nothing of terrestrial things; but the common spirits, those whom one has known, usually wear the costume of the latter part of their life. They have often the attributes characteristic of their elevation, as an aureole, or wings for those who may be considered as angels, while others have those which recall their terrestrial occupations; thus a warrior might appear in his armor, a savant with his books, an assassin with a poniard, &c. The superior spirits have a beautiful countenance, noble and serene; the more inferior something ferocious and brutal, and sometimes still bear the traces of the crimes they have committed or the punishments they have endured. The question of costume and of all these accessory objects is, perhaps, what most astonishes. We shall return to it in a special chapter, because it is united to other very important facts.

103. We have said that an apparition has a vaporous appearance; in some cases it might be compared to the image reflected in a glass without foil, and which, despite its clearness, does not prevent the objects behind the glass from being seen through the reflected

image. It is usually thus that the seeing mediums distinguish them ; they see them go and come, enter a room or leave it, circulate among the crowd of the living, having the air—at least the ordinary spirits—of taking an active part in all that is going on around them, of interesting themselves in it, of listening to what is said. They often see them approach a person and whisper ideas, influence, console if they are good, jeer if they are malicious, seeming sad or contented with the results they obtain ; in a word, it is the double of the corporeal world. Such is this secret world that surrounds us, in the midst of which we live unknowingly, as unthinkingly as we live in the midst of the myriads of the microscopic world. The microscope has revealed to us the world of infinity of small things which we had not suspected ; Spiritism, aided by seeing mediums, has revealed to us the world of spirits, which also is one of the active forces of nature. With the aid of seeing mediums we have been able to study the invisible world, become initiated into its customs, as blind people could study the visible world with the help of men who enjoy sight. (See, further, the chapter on *Mediums*, article concerning *seeing mediums.*)

104. The spirit who wishes to appear, or can appear, assumes sometimes a still more perfect form, having all the appearance of a solid body to the extent of producing a complete illusion, making a person think that a corporeal being stands before him. In some cases, also, and under certain circumstances, the tangible may become real ; that is to say, we can touch, handle, feel the same resistance, the same warmth, as in a living body, which does not prevent him from vanishing with the rapidity of lightning. It is, then, no longer

by the eyes their presence is verified, but by the touch. If the simply visual apparition might be attributed to illusion, or a kind of fascination, the doubt is not permitted when you can grasp it, handle it, when it seizes you and holds you fast. The facts of tangible apparitions are the rarest; but those that have happened in these last days by the influence of some powerful mediums (Mr. Home among others), and which have all the authenticity of unexceptionable witnesses, prove and explain those related in history of persons seen after death with all the appearances of reality. Yet, as we have already said, however extraordinary these phenomena may be, all the marvelous disappears when we know the manner in which they are produced, and comprehend that, far from being a derogation of Nature's laws, they are only a new application of them.

105. By its nature and in its normal state, the *périsprit* is invisible, and it has that property in common with many fluids which we know exist, and yet which we have never seen; but it can also, the same as some other fluids, undergo modifications that render it perceptible to the sight, whether by a sort of condensation or by a change in the molecular disposition: it then appears to us under a vaporous form. Condensation (this word must not be taken in its exact meaning; we use it only for want of another, and by comparison), — condensation, let us say, may be such that the *périsprit* acquires the properties of a solid and tangible body; but it can instantaneously resume its ethereal and invisible state. We can understand this state by that of vapor which can pass from invisibility to a state of fog, then liquid, then solid, and *vice versa*. These different states of the

périsprit are the result of the will of the spirit, and not an exterior physical cause, as in our gases. When the spirit appears to us, he puts his *périsprit* into the state necessary to render him visible ; but for that his will alone is not sufficient, for the modification of the *périsprit* is effected by his combination with the fluid of the medium ; but this combination is not always possible, which explains why the visibility of spirits is not general. It is not enough that the spirit desires to be seen ; it is not enough that a person desires to see him ; it is necessary that the two fluids may combine, that there should be between them a kind of affinity ; perhaps, also, that the emission of the person's fluid should be sufficiently abundant to effect the transformation of the *périsprit ;* and probably still other conditions, to us unknown ; it is also necessary that the spirit should have permission to make himself visible to the person, which is not always granted, or granted only under certain conditions, for reasons we cannot always appreciate.

106. Another property of the *périsprit*, and which pertains to its ethereal nature, is penetrability. Matter is no obstacle; it passes through everything as the light passes through transparent bodies. This is why no closing can shut out spirits ; they visit the prisoner in his cell as easily as the man in the open fields.

107. Apparitions in a waking state are neither rare nor new ; they have occurred in every age ; history relates very many ; but without going so far, they are frequent in our own day, and many persons have had what, at first sight, they have taken for what it is considered proper to call *hallucinations.* They are, especially, frequent in the case of the death of absent persons who visit their relations or friends ; often they

seem to have no particular motive; but it may be said that, in general, the spirits who appear are attracted by sympathy. If every one would search his memory, he would see that there are few persons without a knowledge of some facts of this kind, whose authenticity cannot be doubted.

108. We will add to the preceding considerations the examination of some optical effects which have given rise to the singular system of *globular spirits.*

The air is not always of an absolute limpidity, and there are condrtions under which the currents of aeriform molecules and their agitation produced by the heat are perfectly visible. Some persons have taken that for masses of spirits moving around in space; the mere mention of this opinion is all that is necessary to refute it; but there is another species of illusion, no less absurd, against which it is equally well to be forewarned.

The aqueous humor of the eye offers points, scarcely perceptible, that have lost their transparency. These points are like opaque bodies in suspension in the liquid, and whose movements they follow. They produce in the air, and at a distance, from the effects of enlargement and refraction, the appearance of small disks varying from one to ten millimetres in diameter, and which seem to swim in the atmosphere. We have seen persons take these disks for spirits, who follow and accompany them everywhere, and in their enthusiasm take for figures the shades of irisation, which is almost as rational as to see a figure in the moon. A simple observation, furnished by these people themselves, would bring them to the land of reality.

These disks, or medallions, they say, not only accompany them, but follow all their movements; they go to the right, to the left, up, down, or stop, according to the movement of the head: that is not astonishing, since the seat of the appearance is in the globe of the eye ; it should follow all its movements. If they were spirits, it must be admitted that they would be confined to entirely too mechanical a part for free and intelligent beings — a very tedious part, even for inferior spirits, and certainly entirely incompatible with our ideas of superior spirits. Some, it is true, think the black points bad spirits. These disks, the same as the black spots, have an undulatory movement which never varies from a certain angle, and their not rigidly following the line of vision adds to the illusion. The reason is very simple. The opaque points of the aqueous humor, primary cause of the phenomenon, are, as we have said, held, as it were, in suspension, and have always a tendency to descend ; when they ascend, it is in consequence of the movement of the eye from low to high ; but, after reaching a certain distance, if the eye is fixed, the disks descend of themselves, then stop. Their mobility is extreme, for an imperceptible movement of the eye is sufficient to make them change their direction and traverse rapidly the whole extent of the arc in the space where the object is produced. So long as it is not proved that an image possesses a spontaneous and intelligent movement of its own, there can be seen in it but a simple optical or physiological phenomenon. It is the same with the sparks, which are sometimes produced in sheafs and bundles, more or less compact, by the contraction of the muscles of the eye, and which are, probably, owing to the phosphorescent electricity of the iris, as they are usually limited to the circumference of the disk of that organ. Similar illusions can only

be the result of incomplete observation.   Whoever
may have seriously studied the nature of spirits by all
the means practical science gives, will understand their
puerility.   While we combat the theories by which the
manifestations are attacked, when these theories are
based on ignorance of facts, we should also seek to
destroy the false ideas which exhibit more enthusiasm
than reflection, and which, in that very way, do more
harm than good with the skeptical, already so disposed
to look for the ridiculous.

109. The *périsprit*, as may be seen, is the principle
of all the manifestations ; its knowledge has given the
key to a crowd of phenomena ; it has been the means
of making an immense step in the science of Spiritism,
and has caused it to enter a new path by taking from
it all marvelous character.   We have found it by the
spirits themselves, for, remember carefully, it is they
who have given us the explanation of the action of
spirit on matter, of the movement of inert bodies,
noises and apparitions.   We shall yet find in it that
of several other phenomena which remain for us to examine before passing to the study of the communications proper.   They will be as much better understood
as the reason for the first causes shall be better.   If
this principle has been thoroughly comprehended, each
one may for himself easily make the application of the
various facts which may be presented to the observer.

110. We are far from regarding the theory we give
as absolute, and as being the last word ; it will, doubtless, be completed or rectified by new studies ; but however incomplete or imperfect it may be to day, it can
at least assist in showing the possibility of the facts by
causes which have nothing in them of the supernatural : if it be a hypothesis, the merit of rationality and

probability cannot be altogether refused to it; and it is worth more than all the explanations given by those who try to prove that in the spirit phenomena all is but illusion, phantasmagoria, and subterfuge.

Theory of Hallucination.

111. Those who do not admit the incorporeal and invisible world, think to explain everything by the word hallucination. The definition of this word is well known; it is an error, an illusion of a person who thinks he has perceptions which he has not really (from the Latin *hallucinari*, to err, made of *ad lucem*); but the scientists have not yet, that we know, given the physiological reason.

Optics and physiology appear to have no further secrets from them; how, then, is it that they have failed to explain the nature and the source of the images presented to the mind under certain circumstances?

They wish to explain everything by the laws of matter: be it so; let them give, then, by those laws a theory of hallucination; good or bad, it will, at any rate, be an explanation.

112. The cause of dreams has never been explained by science; it attributes them to an effect of the imagination, but it does not tell us what is imagination, nor how it produces these so clear and perfect images that sometimes appear to us; it is explaining an unknown thing by another equally unknown; the question remains untouched. It is, they say, a remembrance of the preoccupations of our waking state; but admitting this solution, which is not one, it would still remain to show what this magic mirror is that so preserves the impression of things; how, above all, explain those visions of things real which have never been

seen, or even thought of, in a waking state? Spiritism
alone can give us the key to this strange phenomenon,
which passes unperceived because of its very common-
ness, like all the wonders of nature we trample under
foot.

Scientists have disdained to investigate hallucination; whether it be real or not, it is not the less a phenomenon which physiology should be able to explain
under pain of confessing its insufficiency. If some
day a savant should undertake to give of it, not a
definition, be it understood, but a physiological explanation, we should see if his theory solves all the
cases; if they do not omit, especially the facts, so common, of apparitions of persons at the moment of their
death, let them say from whence comes the coincidence
of the apparition with the death of the person. If it
were an isolated fact, it might be attributed to chance;
but it is very frequent; chance has none of these re-
newals. If he who sees the apparition has had his
imagination struck with the idea that the person would
die, so be it; but the one that appears is most often
the one he has least thought of; then the imagination
counts for naught. Still less can the circumstances
of the death, of which there has been no idea, be explained by imagination. Will the hallucinationists say
that the soul (if they so much as admit a soul) has moments of over-excitement, when its faculties are exalted?
We agree with them; but when what is seen is real, it
is not illusion. If, in its exaltation, the soul sees a
thing that is not present, it is because it is transported;
but if our soul can be transported toward an absent
person, why should not the soul of the absent person
be transported toward us? In their theory of hallucination, let them take especial account of these facts,

and not forget that a theory to which contrary facts may be opposed is necessarily false or incomplete.

While waiting their explanation, we shall endeavor to put forth some ideas on this subject.

113. Facts prove that there are veritable apparitions, of which the spirit theory can give a perfect reason, and which those alone can deny who admit nothing outside of the organism; but by the side of the real visions are there hallucinations in the sense attached to this word? That is not doubtful. What is their source? The spirits will put us in the way of knowing, for the explanation seems to us complete in the answers made to the following questions : —

" Are visions always real, and are they not sometimes the effect of hallucination? When we see, in dreams and otherwise, the devil, for instance, or other fantastic things that do not exist, is it not produced by imagination?"

" Yes, sometimes : when persons are struck by what they have read, or impressed by stories of deviltries, they remember them, and think they see what does not exist. But we have also said, that the spirit under his semi-material envelope can take all kinds of forms to manifest himself. A mocking spirit thus can appear with horns or claws if it so please him, to sport with credulity, as a good spirit can show himself with wings and a radiant countenance."

" May the figures and other images that often present themselves in a half sleep, or simply when the eyes are shut, be considered as apparitions?"

" As soon as the senses grow dull, the spirit is freed, and can see, far off or near, what he could not see with the eyes. These images are very often visions ; but they may, also, be an effect of the impressions which

the sight of certain objects has left in the brain,
which preserves its traces as it preserves those of
sounds. The freed spirit sees, then, in his own brain,
these imprints, which are fixed there as on the plate of
a daguerreotype. Their variety and their blending
form strange and fugitive wholes, which are almost
immediately effaced, in spite of the efforts made to
retain them. To a similar cause must be attributed
certain fantastic apparitions, which have nothing real
about them, often produced in a state of sickness."

It is certain that memory is the result of impressions
preserved in the brain ; but what strange phenomenon
prevents the confounding together of these impressions, so varied, so multiple? That is an impenetra-
ble mystery, but not more strange than that of the
sonorous undulations that cross each other in the air,
and remain none the less distinct. In a healthy and
well-organized brain these impressions are clear and
precise : in a less favorable state they are effaced and
confused ; from thence loss of memory or confusion
of ideas. That appears still less extraordinary if it be
admitted, as in phrenology, a special destination to
each part, and even to each fibre of the brain. The
images reaching the brain through the eyes leave
there an impression which brings to remembrance a
picture as if it were before one ; but this is not merely
an affair of memory, for it is not seen ; but in a certain state of emancipation, the soul sees into the brain,
and there finds again these images, especially those
most deeply seated, according to the nature of the
preoccupations or the dispositions of the mind. Thus
it finds the impressions of scenes religious, diabolic,
dramatic, worldly ; figures of strange animals seen at
some other epoch, in painting or in story ; for recitals,

also, leave impressions. Thus the soul really sees but sees only an image daguerreotyped in the brain. In the normal state, these images are fugitive and ephemeral, because all the cerebral parts act freely ; but in a state of disease the brain is always more or less enfeebled, the equilibrium no longer exists between all the organs ; some alone preserve their activity, while others are in some sort paralyzed ; from thence the permanence of certain images, which are not, as in the normal state, effaced by the preoccupations of the exterior life. That is the real hallucination, and the primary cause of fixed ideas.

As may be seen, we have given a reason for this anomaly by a well-known and thoroughly physiological law — that of cerebral impressions ; but we have always been obliged to bring in the soul ; and if materialists have not yet given a satisfactory solution of this phenomenon, it is because they will not admit soul : so they may say our solution is good for nothing, because we rest on a contested principle. Contested by whom ? By them, but admitted by the immense majority since there have been men on the earth ; and the denial of some cannot make law.

Is our explanation good ? We give it for what it is worth, in default of others, and, if you please, by way of simple hypothesis, while awaiting a better. Such as it is, does it account for all the cases of vision ? Certainly not ; and we defy all the physiologists to give a single one, exclusively from their point of view, that does solve them all ; for when they have pronounced their cabalistic words of over-excitement and exaltation, they have said nothing. Then, if all the theories of hallucination are insufficient to explain all the facts, it must be that there is something else besides hallucination. Our theory would be false if we should apply it to all cases of visions, because there is still something that would contradict it. It may be correct if confined to certain facts.

CHAPTER VII.

BI-CORPOREITY AND TRANSFIGURATION.

Apparitions of the Spirit of the Living. — Double Men. — St. Alphonse de Liguori and St. Antoine de Padua. — Vespasian. — Transfiguration. — Invisibility.

114. THESE two phenomena are varieties of the phenomenon of visual manifestation, and however marvelous they may appear at first sight, it will be easily perceived, by the explanation that can be given of them, that they are not out of the order of natural phenomena. They both rest on this principle — that all that has been said of the properties of the *périsprit* after death applies to the *périsprit* of the living. We know that during sleep the spirit partly recovers its liberty ; that is, it is isolated from the body ; and it is in this state that we have, many times, had occasion to observe it. But the spirit, be the man dead or living, has always its semi-material envelope, which, for the same causes that we have described, can acquire visibility and tangibility. Very positive facts leave no doubt of this ; we will cite some examples of our own personal knowledge, whose truth we can guarantee ; every one can, no doubt, remember analogous ones, by searching his memory.

115. The wife of one of our friends several times saw a fruit merchant of the neighborhood, whom she

knew by sight, but to whom she had never spoken,
enter her room in the night, whether she had a light
or not.   This apparition caused her great terror, greater because at that time she had no knowledge of Spiritism, and the phenomenon happened very often.   But
the merchant was perfectly alive, and probably sleeping at that hour : while his material body was at
home, his spirit and his fluidic body was with this
lady ; with what motive ?   No one knows.   In such
case a spiritist, initiated in such things, would have
asked him ; but she had no idea of it.   Each time the
apparition vanished without her knowing how, and
each time, also, after its disappearance, she went to the
doors to assure herself that they were perfectly shut,
and that nobody could have been introduced into her
room.   This precaution proved to her that she was
perfectly awake, and not the sport of a dream.   At
other times she saw, in the same way, a man she did
not know ; but one day she saw her brother, who was
then in California.   He had so much the appearance
of a real person, that, at the first moment, she thought
he had returned, and was going to speak to him ; but
he disappeared without giving her time.   A letter,
afterwards received, proved that he was not dead.
This lady was what was called a natural seeing medium, but at that time, as we have said, she had never
heard of mediums.

116. Another lady, who lives in the country, being
very seriously ill, saw, about ten o'clock one evening,
an aged gentleman, living in the same town, whom
she had sometimes met in society, but of no intimate
acquaintance.   This gentleman was seated in an arm-
chair, at the foot of her bed, and from time to time
took snuff; he seemed to be watching.   Surprised at

such a visit at such an hour, she wished to ask the cause of it; but he signed to her not to speak, but to go to sleep: several times she was about to address him, but each time with the same result. She ended by going to sleep. Some days after, being convalescent, she received a visit from this same gentleman, but at a more suitable hour; and this time it was himself: he was dressed the same, had the same snuff-box, the same manners. Persuaded that he had come during her illness, she thanked him for the trouble he had taken. The gentleman, much surprised, said he had not had the pleasure of seeing her for a very long time. The lady, who understood spirit phenomena, saw at once what it was, but not wishing to explain it to him, contented herself with telling him she had probably dreamed it. "Very probably," will say the skeptical, the strong-minded, for them the synonym of men of mind; but it is certain she slept not at all, no more than the preceding. Then she dreamed awake; in other words, she had a hallucination. That is the great word, the universal explanation of everything that is not understood. As we have already refuted this objection, we will continue, addressing ourselves to those who can understand us.

117. Here is another and more characteristic fact, and we should be curious to see how it can be explained by the play of the imagination. A gentleman, living in the country, had never wished to marry, in spite of the importunity of his family. They had constantly insisted in favor of a person living in a neighboring town, and whom he had never seen. One day, being in his room, he was astonished to find himself in the presence of a young girl, dressed in white, her head crowned with flowers. She told him she was his

betrothed, held out her hand to him, which he took in his, and on which he saw a ring. In a few moments she disappeared. Surprised at this apparition, and being sure that he was fully awake, he asked if any one had come during the day, but was answered no person had been seen. A year after, yielding to the renewed solicitations of a relative, he decided to go and see the person proposed to him. He arrived the day of the *Fête-Dieu* (festival of Corpus Christi day). They returned from the procession, and one of the first persons he saw, on entering the house, was a young girl, whom he recognized as the one who had appeared to him, dressed in the same manner: for the day of the apparition was also that of the *Fête Dieu*. He remained speechless, and the young girl uttered a cry of surprise, and fainted. Restored to her senses, she said she had already seen this gentleman, the same day in the preceding year. The marriage was concluded. This was about 1835 ; at that time there was no question about spirits, and besides, both were persons of extreme positivism, and imagination the least exalted possible.

It may be said, perhaps, that both had their minds occupied with the idea of the proposed union, and that this preoccupation brought about a hallucination ; but it must not be forgotten, that the husband was so indifferent that he was a year without going to see his intended. Admitting even this hypothesis, the double apparition remains to be explained, the coincidence of the costume with the day of the *Fête-Dieu*, and then the physical recognition between persons who had never seen each other — circumstances that could not be the effect of imagination.

118. Before going further, we should answer imme-

diately a question that will not fail to be asked ; this is, to know how the body can live while the soul is absent. We can say that the body can live with the organic life, which is independent of the presence of the spirit, and the proof of this is, that plants live, and have no spirit ; but we would add that during life the spirit is never completely detached from the body. Spirits, as also some seeing mediums, recognize the spirit of a living person by a luminous train joined to its body, a phenomenon that never occurs when the body is dead, for then the separation is complete. Thus, the body can never die during the absence of the spirit, and it can never happen that the spirit on its arrival finds the door shut, as some romancers have said, in their fairy histories. (*Book on Spirits*, Nos. 400 and following.)

119. To return to our subject. The spirit of a living person isolated from the body can appear the same as that of a dead person, and have all the appearance of reality ; and further, for the same causes that we have explained, it can acquire a momentary tangibility. It is this phenomenon called *bi-corporeity* that has given foundation to the stories of double men, that is to say, individuals whose simultaneous presence has been verified in two different places. Here are two examples, drawn not from our popular legends, but from ecclesiastical history.

St. Alphonse de Liguori was canonized before the usual time, for having been seen simultaneously in two different places, which passed for a miracle.

St. Antoine de Padua was in Spain, and at the time he was preaching, his father, who was in Padua, was going to the torture, accused of murder. At this moment St. Antoine appeared, showed the innocence of his father, and pointed out the true criminal, who was afterward punished. It was proved that St. Antoine had not left Spain.

St. Alphonse, having been invoked and interrogated by us on this fact, gave us the following answers : —

1. " Can you give us the explanation of this phenomenon ? "

" Yes ; man, when he is completely dematerialized by his virtue, when he has elevated his soul toward God, can appear in two places at once, and in this way. The incarnated spirit, feeling sleep come, can ask God to transport him to some especial place. His spirit, or his soul, as you would call it, then leaves his body, followed by a *part* of *his périsprit*, and leaves the unclean matter in a state bordering on death. I say, *bordering* on death, because there remains in the body a tie which attaches the *périsprit* and the soul to the matter, and this tie cannot be defined. The body appears then in the place desired. I believe this is all you wish to know."

2. " This does not give us the explanation of the visibility and tangibility of the *périsprit*."

" The spirit, finding himself freed from matter, can, according to his degree of elevation, make matter tangible."

3. " Is the sleep of the body indispensable to the spirit appearing in other places ? "

" The soul can divide itself, when it feels itself taken to a different place from where the body is. It may happen that the body does not sleep, though that is very rare ; but then the body is not in a perfectly normal condition ; it is always in a state more or less ecstatic."

Remark. The soul does not divide itself in the

literal sense of the word ; it radiates on different sides, and thus can be manifested on several points without being divided ; the same as a light, which can be reflected simultaneously in several glasses.

4. "A man being asleep while his spirit appears elsewhere, what would happen were he awakened suddenly ? "

"That could not happen, because, if any one had such an intention, the spirit would reënter the body, and foresee the intention, for the spirit reads the thought."

This identical explanation has been given to us several times, by the spirit of persons dead or living. St. Alphonse explains the fact of this double presence, but does not give the theory of its visibility and tangibility.

120. Tacitus relates an analogous fact. During the months that Vespasian passed in Alexandria to await the periodical return of the spring winds, and the season when the sea should become safe, several prodigies took place, showing the favor of the heavens, and the interest which the gods seemed to take in this prince.

These prodigies redoubled in Vespasian the desire of visiting the sacred dwelling-place of the god, to consult him about the empire. He ordered that the temple should be closed to every one, entered himself, and just as the oracle was about to be pronounced, he perceived behind him one of the principal Egyptians, named Basilide, who, he knew, had been left sick several days' journey from Alexandria. He inquired of the priests if Basilide had come that day to the temple, and asked of the passers-by if he had been seen in the city ; finally, he sent some men on horseback, and was assured that, at that moment, he was eighty miles distant. Then he no longer doubted that the vision was supernatural, and the name of Basilide was to him instead of an oracle. (TACITUS, Histories, Book IV., Chap. 81, 82. *Translation of Burnouf.*)

121. The individual who is seen in two different places simultaneously has, then, two bodies, but only one of them is real; the other is but an appearance; we might say the first has the organic life, the second the life of the soul; at the awakening, the two bodies reunite, and the life of the soul reënters the material body. It does not appear possible, at least we have no example of it, and reason seems to show it, that in the state of separation the two bodies can enjoy, simultaneously, and to the same degree, active and intelligent life. It shows, moreover, what we have said — that the real body could not die if the apparent body remained visible; the approach of death always recalling the spirit into the body, were it but for an instant. It equally results that the apparent body could not be killed, because it is not organic, and is not formed of flesh and bones; it would disappear the moment a person might desire to kill it.

122. We pass to the second phenomenon, that of *transfiguration.* It consists in a change of aspect of a living body. In this connection is a fact whose perfect authenticity we can guarantee, and which happened in the years 1858 and 1859. In the suburbs of St. Etienne, a young girl of fifteen years of age enjoyed the singular faculty of being transfigured, that is to say, of taking, at given moments, all the appearances of certain persons dead; the illusion was so complete, that people would suppose the person before them, so like were the features, the expression, the

sound of the voice, and even the speech. This phenomenon was renewed hundreds of times, the will of
the young girl counting for nothing. Several times
she took the appearance of her brother, dead some
years before ; she had not only his face, but the height
and size of his body. A doctor of the country was
many times witness of these strange effects, and wishing to be assured that he was not the sport of an
illusion, made the following experiment.

We have the facts from himself, from the father of
the young girl, and from several other honorable and
trustworthy eye-witnesses. He conceived the idea of
weighing her in her normal state, then in that of the
transfiguration, when she had the appearance of her
brother, more than twenty years old, and much larger
and stronger. Well, it was found that in this last
the weight was nearly doubled. The experiment was
conclusive, and it was impossible to attribute the
appearance to a simple optical illusion. Let us try to
explain this fact, which, at one time, would have been
called a miracle, and which we call a simple phenomenon.

123. Transfiguration, in some cases, may be caused
by a simple muscular contraction which can give to
the countenance an entirely different expression, so as
to render the person unrecognizable. We have often
seen it with somnambulists, but in such cases the
transformation was not radical ; a woman could appear
young or old, beautiful or ugly, but it would be always
a woman ; and her weight neither augmented nor
diminished. In the case we are considering it is very
evident it is something more : the theory of the *périsprit* will put us on the right road.

It is admitted that the spirit can give every appearance to his *périsprit;* that by a modification of the molecular disposition he can give it visibility, tangibility, and consequently *opacity;* that the *périsprit* of a living person, isolated from the body, can undergo the same transformations ; that this change of state is effected by the combination of fluids. Imagine, now, the *périsprit* of a living person, not isolated, but radiating around the body in such a way as to envelop it like a vapor : in this state it could undergo the same modifications as if it were separated ; if it lose its transparency, the body can disappear, become invisible, and be vailed, as if it were plunged in a fog. It could even change its aspect, become brilliant, if such be the will or the power of the spirit. Another spirit, combining his own fluid with the first, can substitute his own appearance, in such a way that the real body could disappear under an exterior fluidic envelope, whose appearance could vary at the will of the spirit. Such appears to be the cause of the phenomenon, strange and rare, it must be said, of transfiguration. As to the difference in weight, it is explained in the same manner as for inert bodies. The intrinsic weight of the body does not vary, because the quantity of matter has not augmented ; it is under the influence of an exterior agent, who can increase or diminish relative weight, as we have explained above, Nos. 78 and following. It is thus probable that if the transfiguration had taken place under the form of a small child, the weight would have diminished in proportion.

124. It may be imagined that the body can take an appearance larger or of the same dimension, but how take one smaller, that of a small child, as we have said ? In such case, would not the real body exceed the apparent body ? But we have not said that the effect

can be produced ; we have simply desired to show, in reverting to the theory of specific weight, that the apparent weight would have diminished. As to the phenomenon in itself, we affirm neither its possibility nor its impossibility ; but in the case where it has taken place, no satisfactory solution having been given does not invalidate the thing ; it must not be forgotten that we are at the beginning of science, that it is far from having said its last word on this point, as on many others. Besides, the parts in excess could perfectly well be made invisible.

The theory of the phenomenon of invisibility comes very naturally within the preceding explanation, and those given on materialization, Nos. 96 and following.

125. It remains to speak of the singular phenomenon of *agénères*, which, extraordinary as it may appear at first sight, is no more supernatural than the others. But as we have explained in the *Revue Spirite* (February 1859), we consider it useless to reproduce the details in this work ; we will only say, it is a variety of the tangible apparition ; it is the state of some spirits who can momentarily assume the form of a living person, so as to create a complete illusion. (From the Greek *a* privative, and *géine, géinomai*, to engender; which has not been engendered.)

CHAPTER. VIII

LABORATORY OF THE INVISIBLE WORLD.

Clothing of Spirits. — Spontaneous Formation of Tangible Objects. — Modification of the Properties of Matter. — Magnetic Curative Action.

126. WE have said that the spirits present themselves clothed in tunics, with draperies, or even with their ordinary dress. Draperies appear to be a general costume in the spirit world; but it is asked, Where do they find the garments exactly like those they wore while living, with all the accessories of the toilet? It is very certain they did not carry these things with them, since the real objects are there under our very eyes; then whence come those they wear in the other world? This question has been often asked; but with many it is a simple affair of curiosity; nevertheless it confirmed a principle of great importance; for its solution has put us in the way of a general law, which finds its application in our corporeal world. Many facts have come to complicate it, and show the insufficiency of the theories that have been tried.

Up to a certain point, a reason could be given for the costume, because it might be considered as making, in some sort, a part of the individual; it is not the same with the accessories, as for instance, the snuff-box of the sick lady of whom we spoke, No. 117. Let us remark on this subject that there is no question here of one dead, but of one living, and that this gentleman, when he came again in person, had a snuff-box perfectly similar. Where, then, did his spirit find the one he had at the foot of the sick lady's bed? We could cite a great many cases where the spirits of the dead or living have appeared with various objects, such as canes, arms, pipes, lanterns, books, &c.

There came to us a thought that inert bodies have their ethereal analogies in the invisible world ; that the condensed matter that forms the objects might have a very refined part escaping our senses. This theory was not without probability, but it was powerless to give a reason for all the facts. It seemed as if it must baffle all interpretations. Up to this time there had been question only of images or appearances : we have seen that the *périsprit* can acquire the properties of matter and become tangible, but this tangibility is only momentary, and the solid body vanishes like a shade. This is a very extraordinary phenomenon, but far beyond it is to see solid, persistent matter produced, as numerous authentic facts prove, and notably that of direct writing, of which we shall speak in detail in a special chapter. Yet as this phenomenon is intimately connected with the subject before us, and is one of its most positive applications, we will anticipate the order in which it should come.

127. Direct writing, or *pneumatography*, is that which is produced spontaneously without the help of a medium's hand or pencil. It is sufficient to take a sheet of white paper, which may be done with all necessary precautions, so as to feel assured of not being the dupe of treachery, fold and deposit it somewhere, in a drawer, or even on a table ; and, if the conditions are favorable,

at the end of a longer or shorter time there will be found, traced on the paper, characters, various signs, words, phrases, even discourses, most often with a gray substance of the appearance of lead, at other times with red pencil, ordinary ink, or even printing ink. There is the fact in all its simplicity; and though not very common, it is still not very rare, for there are persons who easily obtain it. If a pencil were put with the paper it might be supposed the spirit had used it to write; but when the paper is entirely alone, it is evident the writing is formed by a deposited matter; where does the spirit obtain this matter? Such is the question to whose solution we have been conducted by the snuff-box already mentioned.

128. The spirit of St. Louis has given us the solution in the following answers:—

1. "We have cited the case of an apparition of a living person. This spirit had a snuff-box and took snuff. Did he experience the sensation of snuff-taking?"

"No."

2. ' This snuff-box had the form that he ordinarily used, and which was at home. What was this one in his hands?"

"An appearance; it was in order that the circumstance should be remarked as it was, and that the apparition should not be taken for a hallucination produced by the person's state of health. The spirit desired that this lady should believe in the reality of his presence; he took all the appearances of reality."

3. "You say it is an appearance; but an appearance is not real; it is like an optical illusion: we should like to know if this snuff-box was only an image without reality, or if it possessed something of material?"

"Certainly, it is by the aid of this material principle

that the *périsprit* takes the appearance of clothes, like those the spirit wore while living."

Remark. It is evident that the word appearance must here be understood in the sense of aspect, imitation. The real snuff-box was not there; that which the spirit held was only its representation ; it was thus an appearance compared to the original, though formed of a material principle.

Experience teaches us that we must not always take literally certain expressions employed by the spirits ; in interpreting them according to our ideas, we are exposed to great mistakes : this is why we must study deeply the sense of their words every time they present the least ambiguity ; it is a recommendation constantly given to us by the spirits themselves. Without the explanation we have called forth, the word appearance, constantly reproduced in analogous cases, might lead to a false interpretation.

4. "Could inert matter be duplicated ? Is there in the invisible world an essential matter which could clothe the form of the objects we see ? In a word, could these objects have their ethereal double in the invisible world, as men are represented there by spirits ? "

" That is not the way of it : the spirit has over the elements, spread everywhere throughout your atmosphere, a power you are far from suspecting. He can, at will, concentrate these elements, and give them the apparent form proper to his designs."

Remark. This question, as may be seen, was the translation of our thought ; that is, of the idea we had formed of the nature of these objects. If the answers were, as some pretend, the reflection of the thought, we should have obtained the confirmation of our theory, instead of a contrary one.

5. "I ask the question anew in a categorical manner, in order to avoid all equivocation : are the clothes with which the spirits are covered something ? "

"It seems to me that my preceding answer solves that question. Do you not know that the *périsprit* itself is something ? "

6. "It results from this explanation that spirits make ethereal matter undergo transformations at their will, and that thus, for instance, the spirit did not find the snuff-box ready made, but made it himself for the moment he had need of it, by an act of his will, and that he could unmake it : it must be the same with all the other objects, such as clothing, jewels, &c."

"Evidently so."

7. "The snuff-box was perfectly visible to this lady ; could the spirit have made it tangible for her ? "

"He could."

8. "The case so happening, could this lady have taken it into her hands, believing she held a real snuff-box ? "

"Yes."

9. "If she had opened it, she would probably have found snuff in it ; if she had taken this snuff, would it have made her sneeze ? "

"Yes."

10. "The spirit, then, could give not only the form but the special properties ? "

"If he wishes : it is only by virtue of this principle I have answered affirmatively the preceding questions. You will have proofs of the powerful action spirit exercises over matter, and which you are far from suspecting, as I told you."

11. "Suppose, then, that he had desired to make a venomous substance, and that a person had taken it; would he have been poisoned?"

"He could have done so, but he did not; that would not have been permitted."

12. "Would he have had the power to make a salutary substance, suitable to cure in case of sickness, and is it ever done?"

"Yes, very often."

13. "He could, then, as well make an alimentary substance: suppose he had made a fruit, a dish of any kind; could a person have eaten of it and had his hunger appeased?"

"Yes, yes; but do not seek so hard to find out what is so easy to understand. Even a ray of the sun can render perceptible to your gross organs those material particles that fill the space in the midst of which you live; do you not know that the air contains the vapors of water? Condense them, you restore them to the normal condition; deprive them of heat, and these impalpable and invisible molecules become a solid, a very solid body, and many other substances from which your chemists draw still more astonishing wonders, only the spirit possesses instruments more nearly perfect than yours — will and God's permission."

Remark. The question of satisfaction is here very important. How and in what way can a substance that has only temporary existence and properties satisfy hunger? This substance, by its contact with the stomach, produces *the sensation* of satisfaction, but not the satisfaction resulting from fullness. If such a substance can act on the economy and modify a morbid state, it can quite as well act on the stomach and produce the feeling of satisfaction. At the same time we beg the druggists and restaurateurs not to become jealous, nor believe that the spirits will destroy their trade : these cases are rare, exceptional, and never depend on the will ; otherwise people could be nourished and cured too cheaply.

14. " Could objects, rendered tangible by the will of the spirit, have a character of permanence and stability, and become useful ? "

" It could be, *but it is not done;* it is beyond the laws."

15. " Have all spirits the same degree of power to render objects tangible ? "

" It is certain that the more elevated the spirit is, the more easily he obtains this result ; but still that depends on circumstances ; inferior spirits could have the power."

16. " Does the spirit always know exactly how he produces his clothing, or other objects, whose appearance he gives ? "

" No ; he often assists in their formation by an instinctive act which he does not, himself, comprehend, if he be not sufficiently enlightened for it."

17. " If the spirit can draw from the universal element the materials to make all these things, to give to these things, with their properties, a temporary reality, he can as well draw from it what is necessary for writing ; and consequently this would appear to give us the key to the phenomenon of direct writing."

" There you are at last ! "

Remark. It was there, in fact, we wished to come by all our preliminary questions ; the answer proves that the spirit read our thought.

18. " If the matter used by the spirit has no persis-

tence, how does it happen that the traces of the writing do not disappear?

"Do not epiloguize the words. In the first place I did not say, never; there it was of a voluminous material object; here it is of signs traced which it is useful to have preserved, and they are preserved. I meant that the objects thus composed by the spirits could not become objects to use, for they do not, in reality, possess aggregation of matter like your solid bodies."

129. The above theory may be thus summed up; the spirit acts on matter; he draws from the universal cosmic matter the elements necessary to form, at his will, objects having the appearance of various bodies which exist on the earth. He can equally well, by his will, effect on elementary matter an intimate transformation, which gives it certain properties. This faculty is inherent in the nature of the spirit, who often, when necessary, exercises it without thinking, as an instinctive act. The objects formed by the spirit have a temporary existence, subordinated to his will or to necessity; he can make and unmake them at will. These objects can, in some cases, have to the eyes of living persons all the appearances of reality, that is to say, become momentarily visible, and even tangible. There is formation, but not creation; the spirit can draw nothing from the void.

130. The existence of one single elementary matter is now almost generally admitted by science, and confirmed, as we have seen, by the spirits. This matter gives birth to all the bodies of nature: by the transformations it undergoes, it produces also the various properties of these same bodies; it is in this way a salutary substance can become venomous by a simple modification; chemistry affords us numerous examples. Every-

body knows that two innocent substances, combined in certain proportions, can produce a deleterious one. One part oxygen and two of hydrogen, both inoffensive, form water ; add an atom of oxygen, and you have a corrosive liquid. Without changing the proportions, often a simple change in the method of molecular aggregation can change the properties ; thus an opaque body can become transparent, and *vice versa.* Since the spirit has by his sole will so powerful an action on elementary matter, it may be conceived that he can not only form substances, but can denaturalize their properties, will having herein the effect of a reactive.

131. This theory gives us the solution of a fact in magnetism, well known, but hitherto unexplained — that of the change of the properties of water by the will. The acting spirit is that of the magnetizer, most frequently assisted by a foreign spirit ; he effects a transmutation by the aid of the magnetic fluid, which, as has been said, is the substance most nearly approaching cosmic matter, or the universal element. If he can effect a modification in the properties of water, he can as well produce an analogous phenomenon on the fluids of the organism, and from thence the curative effect of the magnetic action properly directed.

We know the great part played by the will in all the phenomena of magnetism ; but how explain the material action of so subtile an agent ? The will is not a being, a substance ; it is not even a property of the most ethereal matter ; the will is the essential attribute of the mind, that is to say, of the thinking being. By the aid of this lever he acts on elementary matter, and, by a consecutive action, he reacts on its compounds, whose intimate properties can thus be transformed.

Will is the attribute of the incarnate as well as of

the wandering spirit; from thence the power of the magnetizer, a power which we know to be in proportion to the strength of the will. The incarnate spirit, being able to act on elementary matter, can, then, as well vary its properties in certain limits : here we have explained the faculty of curing by laying on of hands — a faculty possessed by some to a greater or less degree. (See chapter on *Mediums*, article relating to *Healing Mediums*. See also the *Revue Spirite*, July, 1859, pages. 184 and 189.)

CHAPTER IX.

HAUNTED PLACES.

132. THE spontaneous manifestations that have been produced in all times, and the persistence of some spirits in giving ostensible marks of their presence in certain localities, are the source of the belief in haunted places. The following answers have been made to questions on this subject:—

1. "Do spirits attach themselves solely to persons, or do they also attach themselves to things?"

"That depends upon their elevation. Some spirits can be attached to terrestrial objects; misers, for instance, who have hidden their treasures, and who are not sufficiently dematerialized, can still watch over and guard them."

2. "Do wandering spirits prefer particular places?"

"Still the same principle. Spirits who are no longer on the earth go where they find anything to love; they are attracted by persons rather than by material objects; yet they might, momentarily, have a preference for certain places; but these are always inferior spirits."

3. "Since the attachment of spirits for a locality is a sign of inferiority, is it equally a proof that they are bad spirits?"

"Certainly not. A spirit may be but little advanced, yet not be bad for all that; is it not the same among men?"

4. "Has the belief that spirits frequent ruins from preference any foundation ? "

"No ; spirits go in these places as they go everywhere else ; but the imagination is struck by the somber aspect of these places, and attributes to their presence what is, most often, but a very natural effect. How many times has not fear taken the shadow of a tree for a phantom, the cry of an animal, or the breath of the wind, for a ghost ! Spirits love the presence of men ; so they seek rather inhabited places than those that are isolated."

"Yet, from what we know of the diversity of character among spirits, there may be among them misanthropes who prefer solitude."

"Did I not answer in an absolute manner to the question ? I said, They can go into deserted places, as everywhere else, and it is very evident that those who go there go because they please ; but that is not a reason why ruins should be places of predilection for them ; for, indeed, there are many more in towns and in palaces than in the midst of woods."

5. " Popular beliefs have usually a foundation of truth, which may be the source of that of haunted places."

"The foundation of truth is the manifestation of spirits, in which man has believed at all times, by instinct ; but, as I have said, the aspect of these melancholy places strikes his imagination, and he naturally connects them with the beings he looks upon as supernatural. This superstitious belief is kept alive by the recitals of poets, and the fantastic tales that have cradled his infancy."

6. " Have spirits who gather together, certain days and hours for so doing ? "

"No ; days and hours belong to time, for the use of

men, and for corporeal life; but of which the spirits have no need, and about which they do not trouble themselves."

7. "What is the origin of the idea that spirits, by preference, come in the night?"

"The impression produced on the imagination by silence and obscurity. All these beliefs are superstitions, which the rational knowledge of Spiritism must destroy. It is the same with the days and hours they believe to be most propitious to them; believe that the influence of midnight has never existed save in stories."

"If it be so, why do certain spirits announce their arrival and manifestations for that hour, and for certain days, like Friday, for instance?"

"There are spirits who take advantage of credulity, and amuse themselves with it. For the same reason, some pretend to be the devil, or give themselves infernal names. Show them that you are not their dupes, and they will not return."

8. "Do spirits return, by preference, near the tomb where their bodies rest."

"The body is but a covering; they care no more for the envelope that has made them suffer, than the prisoner for his chains. The remembrance of the persons dear to them is the only thing they value."

"Are the prayers made at their graves more agreeable, and do they attract them rather than otherwise."

"Prayer is an invocation that attracts spirits, you very well know. Prayer has greater action inasmuch as it is fervent and sincere; before a venerated tomb the thought is more concentrated: the preservation of relics is a testimony of affection for the spirit, to which he is always sensible. It is always the thought that acts on the spirit, and not the material object; these objects have more influence on him who prays, by fixing his attention, than on the spirit."

9. " According to that, the belief in haunted places would not appear to be absolutely false ? "

" We have said that some spirits can be attracted by material things; they can be so by certain places, where they seem to choose their dwelling, till the circumstances that led them there are at an end."

" What are the circumstances that might lead them there ? "

"Their sympathy for some of the persons there, or their desire to communicate with them. Yet their intentions are not always so praiseworthy : when they are bad spirits, they may wish to execute vengeance on certain persons of whom they have cause of complaint. The sojourn in an especial place may be for some a punishment inflicted on them, — especially if they have committed a crime there, — in order that they may have this crime constantly before their eyes."

10. " Are places always haunted by their former inhabitants ? "

"Sometimes, but not always; for if the former inhabitant is an elevated spirit, he cares no more for his terrestrial dwelling than for his body. The spirits who haunt certain places have often no other motive than caprice; at least, if they are not attracted thither by their sympathy for certain persons."

" Can they remain there to protect a person, or his family ? "

" Assuredly, if they are good spirits; but in this case, they never manifest their presence by disagreeable things."

11. "Is there anything real in the history of the 'White Lady'?"

"It is a tale drawn from a thousand facts that are true."

12. "Is it rational to fear places haunted by spirits?"

"No; the spirits who haunt certain places, and make a racket there, seek rather to amuse themselves at the expense of credulity and cowardice than to do evil. Besides, remember, there are spirits everywhere, and wherever you may be, you have them constantly at your side, even in the most peaceable houses. They appear to haunt certain houses only because they find an occasion to manifest their presence."

13. "Is there any means of expelling them?"

"Yes; but most often the means used attract, instead of removing, them. The best means to drive away bad spirits is to attract the good. Draw good spirits to you by doing as much good as possible, and the bad will go away; for the good and the bad are incompatible. Be always good, and you will always have good spirits at your side."

"Yet there are many good persons subject to the torments of bad spirits."

"If these persons are really good, it may be only a trial to exercise their patience, and make them still better: but, believe me, it is not those who talk most of virtue who have most of it. He who possesses real qualities is often ignorant of them himself, or does not speak of them."

14. "What must be believed with regard to the efficacy of exorcism to drive away bad spirits from haunted places?"

"Have you ever seen this means succeed? Have you not, on the contrary, seen the racket redoubled after the ceremony of exorcism! They are amused at being taken for the devil."

" Spirits who do not come with an evil intention may also manifest their presence by noise, and even by making themselves visible, but they never make a troublesome racket. They are often suffering spirits, whom you can soothe by praying for them; at other times they are benevolent spirits, who wish to prove to you that they are near you; or they may be light, frolicsome spirits. As the noisy, troublesome spirits are almost always those who are amusing themselves, the best thing to do is to laugh at them: they will become tired if they see they can neither terrify nor annoy you. (See Chapter V., *Spontaneous Physical Manifestations*.)

The above explanations show that there are spirits who are attached to certain localities, and remain there from preference, but that they do not need to manifest their presence by obvious effects. Any place whatever may be the abiding-place, either forced or from predilection, of a spirit, even a bad one, without his ever producing any manifestation.

The spirits who are attached to localities, or to material things, are never superior spirits, but, without being superior, they may neither be wicked nor have any evil intention; they are even, sometimes, companions more useful than injurious, for if they are interested in persons, they can protect them.

Chapter X.

NATURE OF COMMUNICATIONS.

Gross, Frivolous, Serious, or Instructive Communications.

133. WE have said that every effect that reveals in its cause an act of free will, however insignificant the act may be, gives assurance by that of an intelligent cause. Thus a simple movement of a table, answering our thought, or showing an intentional character, may be considered an intelligent manifestation. If the result were limited to that, it would always be something to give proof that there is, in these phenomena, more than a purely material action; but its practical utility would be, for us, null, or at least very restricted; it is quite otherwise when this intelligence acquires a development which permits a regular exchange and connection of thoughts; no longer, then, simple manifestations, but veritable *communications.* By the means now used, they can be obtained as extended, as explicit, and as rapid as those we maintain with men.

If the infinite variety existing among spirits, under the double view of intelligence and morality, has been thoroughly considered, according to the spirit scale (*Livre des Esprits,* No. 100), the difference that must exist in their communications may be readily conceived; they must reflect the elevation or the lowness of their ideas, their knowledge and their ignorance, their vices and their virtues; in a word, they should no more resemble each other than those of men, from the savage to the most enlightened European. All the shades they present may be grouped in four principal categories, according to their most prominent characteristics; they are, *gross*, *frivolous*, *serious*, or *instructive.*

134. The *gross communications* are those given in expressions that shock decency. They can emanate only from spirits of a low state, still soiled with the impurities of matter, and differ in nothing from those that might be given by vicious and gross men. They are repugnant to every person who has the least delicacy of sentiment; for they are according to the character of the spirits — trivial, dirty, obscene, insolent, arrogant, malevolent, and even impious.

135. *Frivolous communications* emanate from light, mocking, mischievous spirits, more roguish than wicked, and who attach no importance to what they say. As there is nothing unseemly about them, they please some persons who are amused with them, and find pleasure in their fruitless conversations, where many words are used to say nothing. These spirits often make sudden witty, sarcastic sallies, and, in the midst of common facetiousness, often say hard truths, which almost always go straight to the mark.

These light spirits multiply around us, and seize every occasion to mingle in the communications; truth is the least of their care: this · is why they take a roguish pleasure in mystifying those who are weak, and who sometimes presume to believe their word. Persons who take pleasure in such communications naturally give access to light and deceiving spirits ; serious spirits remove from them, as, among us, serious men withdraw from the society of the giddy.

136. *Serious communications* are grave as to the subject and the manner in which they are made. Every communication which excludes frivolity and grossness, and which has a useful end, be it even of private interest, is serious, but is not, for all that, always exempt from error. The serious spirits are not always equally enlightened ; there are many things of which they are ignorant, and in which they may be deceived in all sincerity : this is why the spirits truly superior constantly recommend us to submit all communications to the scrutiny of reason and the severest logic.

It is, then, necessary to distinguish the *true-serious* from the *false-serious* communications, and it is not always easy ; for even under cover of the gravity of the language certain spirits, presumptuous or false scientists, seek to give prevalence to the falsest ideas and the most absurd systems ; and to obtain greater credit and importance, they do not hesitate to use the most respectable and even the most venerated names. That is one of the greatest dangers in the practical science ; we shall return to it later, with all the developments so important a subject requires ; at the same time we shall show the means of providing against the danger of false communications.

137. *Instructive communications* are the serious, which have for their principal object instruction of some kind given by the spirits on the sciences, morals, or philosophy, &c. They are more or less profound according to the degree of elevation and dematerialization of the spirit. To draw a real advantage from

these communications, they must be regular, and followed up with perseverance. Serious spirits attach themselves to those who desire to be instructed, and they second them, while they leave to light spirits the care of amusing those who see in these manifestations only a passing distraction. It is only by the regularity and frequency of the communications that we can appreciate the moral and intellectual value of the spirits with whom we converse, and the degree of confidence they merit. If experience is necessary to judge men, it is still more so to judge spirits.

In giving to these communications the qualification of instructive, we suppose them *true;* for a thing not *true* would not be *instructive*, were it said in the most imposing language. We cannot, then, rank in this category certain teachings which have naught serious but the form, often bombastic and emphatic, by the aid of which the spirits, more presumptuous than learned, who dictate them, hope to create delusion; but these spirits, being unable to supply the groundwork lacking in them, cannot long sustain their part; they soon betray their weak side; for few of their communications have a sequel, or can be pressed to their extreme limits.

138. The means of communicating are very varied. The spirits, acting on our organs and on our senses, can manifest themselves to the sight as apparitions, to the touch by tangible impressions, hidden or visible, to the hearing by sounds, to the smelling by odors, without known cause. This last method of manifestation, though very real, is, without contradiction, the most uncertain, from the numerous causes that may lead to error; so we will stop here. What we ought

to examine with care are the various means of obtaining communications ; that is to say, an exchange, regular and followed by thoughts. These means are, rappings, talking, and writing. We shall develop them in special chapters.

Chapter XI.

SEMATOLOGY AND TYPTOLOGY.

Language of Signs and Rappings. — Alphabetic Typtology.

139. The first intelligent manifestations were obtained by rappings, or typtology. This primitive means, which came in the infancy of the art, offered but very limited resources, and with it communications were confined to monosyllabic answers, Yes or No, by the aid of a designated number of raps. It was afterward perfected, as we have said.

The rappings were obtained in two ways, by special mediums ; and a certain aptitude for physical manifestations was usually necessary for this mode of operation. The first, which might be called *swinging typtology*, consists in the movements of the table, which raises itself on one side, then falls, striking its foot. For this, it is sufficient for the medium to rest the hands on the edge of the table : if he wishes to converse with any special spirit, he must make an' invocation ; in a contrary case, it is the first comer who is presented, or he who is in the habit of coming.

Having agreed, for instance, one rap for Yes, and two for No, — this is indifferent, — the questions they wish to ask are addressed to the spirit. We shall see, later, those from which it is proper to abstain. The difference is in the brevity of the responses, and the difficulty in so formulating the question that it may be answered by Yes or No. Suppose we ask the spirit, "What do you want?" He can answer only by one phrase; so we must say, "Do you want some thing?" "No." "Some other?" "Yes;" — and so on.

140. It is to be remarked that, in the use of this means, the spirit often joins a kind of pantomime, that is, he expresses the energy of his affirmation, or negation, by the force of the raps. He also expresses the nature of the sentiments that animate him, — violence, by the rudeness of his movements; anger and impatience, in striking reiterated blows with force, as a person strikes with the foot with rage, sometimes throwing the table to the ground. If he is kind and polite, at the beginning and end of the sitting he inclines the table in salutation; if he desires to address himself to one person in the circle, he inclines the table toward him with gentleness or violence, according as he desires to express affection or antipathy. This is, properly speaking, sematology, or the language of signs, as typtology is the language of rappings.

The following is a remarkable example of the spontaneous employment of sematology: A gentleman of our acquaintance was in his parlor one day, where several persons were engaged with manifestations, when he received a letter from us. While he was reading it, the stand which served for experimenting suddenly came toward him. Having finished reading the letter, he went to put it on a table at the other end of the room; the stand followed him, and inclined itself toward the table on which he had laid the letter. Surprised at this coincidence, he thought there must be some relation between this movement and the letter. He interrogated the spirit, who answered that he was our familiar spirit. This gentleman having informed us of the circumstance, we, in our turn, asked the spirit to tell us the motive of the visit he had made; he answered, "It is natural that I should go to see persons with whom you are in relation, in order to be able, at need, to give you, as well as them, the necessary warnings."

It is thus evident that the spirit had wished to call his attention, and had sought an occasion to let him know that he was there. A dumb person could not have done better.

141. Typtology was not slow in being perfected and enriched with a more complete means of communication — that of *alphabetic typtology*. It consists in designating the letters of the alphabet by means of raps; words, phrases, and even whole discourses, could thus be obtained. Following a rule, the table rapped a certain number of times to indicate each letter; that is, one for *a*, two for *b*, &c.: during this time, a person writes the letters as they are designated. When the spirit has finished, he lets them know it by some sign agreed upon.

This mode of proceeding, as may be seen, is very long, and requires an enormous time for communications of any length; yet there are persons who have had the patience to use it for the dictation of several pages; but practice brought about the discovery of abbreviative means, which allowed greater rapidity. The one most in use consists in having an alphabet written out, also a series of figures, marking the units; while the medium is at the table another person goes successively through the alphabet, if a word is in question, or of the figures, if a number; the necessary letter reached, the table raps of itself, and the person writes the letter; then begins again, for the second, the third, and so on. If a letter has been mistaken, the spirit warns by several raps, or by a movement of the table, and they begin again. With practice it is quite rapid, but it is much abridged by divining the end of the word begun, which is known by the sense of the phrase: if there is any uncertainty, the spirit is asked if he meant such or such a word, and he answers Yes, or No.

142. All the above-mentioned effects can be obtained in a still more simple manner, by raps in the very wood itself of the table, without any movement, and which we have described in the chapter on *Physical Manifestations,* No. 64.

This is *interior typtology.* All mediums are not equally suited to this last mode of communication; for there are many who obtain only rappings by swinging; yet, with practice, most of them may attain it, and this manner has the double advantage of being more rapid, and less open to suspicion, than the other, which may be attributed to voluntary pressure. It is true that the inward raps could be imitated by an insincere medium. The best things can be counterfeited, which proves nothing against them. (See, at the end of volume, chapter entitled *Frauds and Deceptions.*) However perfected this method may become, it can never attain the rapidity and facility of writing, and it is now very little employed; yet it is sometimes very interesting as a phenomenon, principally for novices, and it has the advantage of proving, in a peremptory manner, its absolute independence of the medium's thought. In this way answers have been obtained so unforeseen, so strikingly to the purpose, that it must be a person very obstinate in his opinion not to yield to the evidence : thus it is for many persons a powerful means of conviction. But no more by this means than by any other do the spirits like to lend themselves to the caprices of those who desire to put them to the proof by misplaced questions.

143. In order the better to assure its independence of the medium's thought, various instruments have been devised, consisting of dials on which letters are traced, in the manner of the dials of the electric telegraph. A needle, moved by the influence of the medium, by the aid of a conducting thread and a pulley, indicates the letters. As we know these instruments only by drawings and descriptions published in America, we cannot pronounce upon their merit ; but we think their very complication would be an inconvenience ; that the independence from the medium's thought is quite as well attested by the inward raps, and still more by the unforeseen nature of the responses, than by all the material means. On the other side, the skeptical, who are always disposed to see everywhere snares and preparations, are much more apt to suppose them in a special mechanism than in taking the first table at hand, deprived of all accessories.

144. A more simple machinery, but which insincerity might easily abuse, as we shall see in the chapter on *Frauds*, is one we shall describe under the name of *Table Girardin*, in memory of the use Madame Emile de Girardin made of it in the many communications she obtained as medium ; for Madame de Girardin, intellectual as she was, had the weakness to believe in spirits and their manifestations. This instrument consists of an upper movable stand, of from thirty to forty centimetres in diameter, turning freely and easily on

its axis, in the manner of a roulette. On the surface, and at the circumference, are traced, as on a dial, letters, figures, and the words *yes* and *no*. In the centre is a fixed needle.

The medium resting his fingers on the edge of the table, this turns and stops when the desired letter is under the needle. Notice is taken of the letters indicated, and thus words and phrases are rapidly formed. It must be remarked that the table does not slide under the fingers, but the fingers, remaining on it, follow the movements of the table. Perhaps a powerful medium might obtain an independent movement; we think it possible, but have never witnessed it. If the experiment could be made in this way, it would be infinitely more conclusive, because it would remove a possibility of deceit.

145. It remains now for us to destroy a somewhat widely-spread error, which consists in confounding all spirits that communicate by raps, with rapping spirits. Typtology is a means of communicating, like any other, and not more unworthy of elevated spirits than writing or speaking. All spirits, good or bad, may use it, the same as the other methods. It is the elevation of the thoughts that characterizes superior spirits, and not the instrument they use to transmit them; doubtless they prefer the most convenient, and, above all, the most rapid means, but, in default of pencil and paper, they do not disdain to use the ordinary talking table; and the proof is, that some of the most sublime things have been obtained in this way. We ourselves do not use it; not that we despise it, but simply because, as a phenomenon, it has taught us all we can know; it can add nothing to our convictions,

and the extent of the communications we receive re-quires a rapidity incompatible with typtology.

Thus all spirits who rap are not rapping spirits; the name should be reserved for those who may be called rappers by profession, and who, by the aid of this means, are pleased in amusing a circle, or vexing them by their importunity. On their part, spiritual things may sometimes be received, but never anything very profound; it would be a waste of time to ask them any scientific or philosophic questions; their ignorance and inferiority have justly won for them the title given to them by other spirits — that of the clowns or moun-tebanks of the world of spirits. Let us add, that, while they very often act on their own account, they are also often used by superior spirits, when these desire to produce material effects.

CHAPTER XII.

PNEUMATOGRAPHY, OR DIRECT WRITING.
— PNEUMATOPHONY.

Direct Writing.

146. *Pneumatography* is the writing produced directly by the spirit, without a medium ; it differs from psychography in that this last is the transmission of the thought of the spirit by means of writing by the hand of a medium.

The phenomenon of direct writing is, without contradiction, one of the most extraordinary in Spiritism ; but however anomalous it may appear at first sight, it is now a proved and incontestable fact. If theory is necessary to give a reason for spirit phenomena in general, it is still more so, perhaps, in this case, certainly one of the strangest yet presented, but which ceases to appear supernatural as the principle is understood.

At the first revelation of this phenomenon, the predominant idea was that of doubt ; the idea of deception instantly entered the mind ; in fact, everybody knew the action of so-called sympathetic inks, whose traces, at first completely invisible, could appear at the end of a certain time. It was very easy to abuse credulity, and we do not affirm that it has never been done ; we are even convinced that some persons, whether from a mercenary motive or simply from self-love and a desire to make others believe in their power, have employed these subterfuges. (See the chapter on *Deceptions*.)

But, because a thing can be imitated, it would be absurd to conclude that the thing does not exist. Has there not been found, in these latter days, the way to imitate the lucidity of the somnambulist, so as to produce a perfect illusion? And because this jugglery has been exhibited at all the fairs, must we conclude that there are no real somnambulists? Because some merchants sell adulterated wine, is that a reason there should be no pure wine? It is the same with direct writing; besides, the precautions to insure its reality were very simple and easy, and, thanks to these precautions, it can no longer be the object of doubt.

147. Since the possibility of writing without a medium is one of the attributes of the spirit, and since spirits have always existed, and have also always produced the various phenomena we know, they could as well have produced direct writing in olden times as to-day; and thus may be explained the apparition of the three words in the palace of Belshazzar. The middle ages, so fertile in prodigies, but which were stifled at the stake, must have known direct writing, and perhaps in the theory of the modifications which spirits can effect in matter, which we have developed in Chapter VIII., may be found the principle of the belief of the transmutation of metals.

Whatever may be the results obtained at various times, it is only since the manifestations have become common that there has been anything said of direct writing. The first who appears to have made it known in these latter days is Baron de Guldenstubbe, at Paris, who has published a very interesting work on this sub-

ject, containing a great many *fac-similes* of writings he
has obtained. (Note 7.)   The phenomenon had already
been known in America for some time.   The social
position of Baron Guldenstubbe, his independence, the
consideration he enjoys in the highest society, incon-
testably remove all suspicion of voluntary fraud, for
he could have no interested motive.

It could more easily be believed that he was himself
the subject of an illusion ; but to that, one fact answers
peremptorily : the same phenomenon has been obtained
by others, surrounding themselves with all the precautions necessary to avoid all deception, and every cause
of error.

148. Direct writing is obtained, like most of the *non-
spontaneous* spirit manifestations, by concentration of
thought, prayer, and invocation.   It has often been
obtained in church, in tombs, at the foot of the statues
or images of the persons called ; but it is evident that
the locality has no other influence than to produce a
greater degree of reflection, and a more profound concentration of thought ; for it is proved that it can be
quite as well obtained without these accessories, and
in the most common places, on a simple piece of do-
mestic furniture, if the requisite moral conditions are
found, and the necessary medianimic faculty enjoyed.

In the beginning, it was thought necessary to put a
pencil with the paper ; the fact could then, up to a certain point, be explained.   It is known that spirits effect
the movement and displacement of objects, that they
sometimes take and throw them to a distance ; they
could as well, then, take the pencil and use it to write ;
as they give it the impulse, in the hand of the medium,
of a planchette, &c., they could just as well do it in a
direct manner.   But it was soon found that a pencil was

not necessary; a simple piece of paper, folded or not, was sufficient, on which, after a few minutes, writing would be found. This completely changes the aspect of the phenomenon, and gives us an entirely new order of things ; the characters were traced with some kind of substance ; since none was furnished to the spirit, he must have made it, composed it himself ; where did he get it ?

That was the problem.

Turn back to the explanation given in Chapter VIII., Nos. 127 and 128, and there the complete theory of this phenomenon will be found. In this writing the spirit uses neither our substance nor our instruments ; he himself makes the matter and the instrument he needs, gathering his materials in the universal primitive element, which he, by his will, causes to undergo the modifications necessary to the effect he wishes to produce.

Of course he can as well make red pencils, printer's ink, or ordinary ink, as black pencil ; nay, even type solid enough to make a raised impression, as we have seen. The daughter of a gentleman whom we know — a child of twelve or thirteen years — has obtained whole pages written with a substance like crayon.

149. Such is the result to which the phenomenon of the snuff-box, reported in Chapter VII., No. 116, has conducted us, and on which we dwelt to some extent, because we saw in it an occasion to search into one of the gravest laws of Spiritism — a law whose knowledge can clear up more than one mystery, even in the visible world.

It is thus that a fact, common in appearance, can bring out the light ; all that is necessary is to observe with care, and that any one can do as well as we, when they do not limit themselves to seeing effects without searching out their causes. If our faith is strengthened day by day, it is because we understand; then make people understand, if you would make serious proselytes.

The knowledge of causes has another effect; it traces a line of demarcation between truth and superstition.

If we look at direct writing in regard to the advantages it can offer, we shall say that, until now, its principal utility has been the material verification of a grave fact: the intervention of a hidden power, which finds, in that way, a means of manifesting itself. But the communications thus obtained are rarely of any extent; they are usually spontaneous, and limited to words, sentences, often unintelligible signs; they have been obtained in all languages — Greek, Latin, Syriac, hieroglyphics, &c.; but they have not yet been given to those sustained and rapid conversations that psychography, or writing by mediums, permits.

Pneumatophony.

150. Spirits, being able to produce noises and rappings, can as well make any sound of nature, vocal sounds imitating the human voice, beside us, or in the air: this phenomenon we call *pneumatophony*.

From what we know of the nature of spirits, it may be believed that some of them of an inferior order delude themselves, and believe they speak as when alive. (See *Revue Spirite*, February, 1858: *History of the Ghost of Mlle. Clarion.*)

It is necessary to guard against taking for spirit voices all sounds that have no known cause, or simple ringing in the ears, and, above all, thinking there is the least truth in the common belief that the ringing in the ears warns us that some one is talking of us. These ringings, whose cause is purely physiological, have, besides, no sense, while the pneumatophonic sounds express thoughts; and it is by that alone we can recognize them as due to an intelligent, and not to an accidental, cause. We may rely on the principle that the *manifestly intelligent* effects only are those which attest the intervention of spirits; as to the others, there are, at least, a hundred chances to one that they are due to accidental causes.

151. It happens frequently that in half sleep we hear words, names, sometimes even entire phrases distinctly pronounced, and that, too, loudly enough to waken us with a start. Though this may, in some cases, be really a manifestation, there is nothing in it sufficiently positive to prevent it being attributed to a cause analogous to that we have developed in the theory of hallucination, Chapter VI., Nos. 111, &c. What is heard in this way has, besides, no continuation; it is not the same as when entirely awake, for then, if it is a spirit who is making himself heard, there can almost always be an exchange of thought and a regular conversation.

Spirit or pneumatophonic sounds have two very distinct methods of being produced; sometimes it is a voice which resounds in the soul; but while the words may be clear and distinct, there is nothing material in them; at other times they are exterior, and as distinctly articulated as if they came from a person at our side. In whatever manner they may be produced, the phenomenon of pneumatophony is almost always spontaneous, and can be but very rarely induced.

Chapter XIII.

PSYCHOGRAPHY.

Indirect Psychography.—Baskets and Planchettes.—
Direct or Manual Psychography.

152. SPIRIT science has progressed like all other sciences, but more rapidly than the others ; for but a few years separate us from those primitive and incomplete means which were triflingly called talking tables ; and already communication can be had with spirits as easily and as rapidly as people have with each other, and by the same means — writing and speaking. Writing has the advantage of showing more materially the intervention of an unseen power, and of leaving traces we can preserve as we do our own correspondence. The first means employed was that of planchettes, or baskets armed with a pencil.

153. We have said that a person endowed with a special aptitude can impress a movement of rotation to a table or any other object whatever ; take now, instead of a table, a little basket (either of wood or of willow ; no matter which, the substance is indifferent). If a pencil is passed through the bottom of it and solidly fastened, the point outward, then, holding the whole squarely on the point of the pencil placed on a sheet of paper, resting the fingers on the edge of the basket, it will begin to move ; but instead of

turning, it will carry the pencil in various ways over the paper, whether in insignificant characters or in writing. If a spirit is invoked, and he desires to communicate, he will answer, not by rappings, as in typtology, but by written words. The motion of the basket is no longer automatic, as in the turning tables ; it becomes intelligent. In this way, when the pencil reaches the end of the line, it does not return to begin another ; it continues circularly, so that the lines of writing form a spiral, and the paper has to be turned several times to read what is written. The writing thus obtained is not very legible, the words not being separated ; but the medium, by a sort of intuition, easily deciphers it. For economy, a slate and slate pencil can be substituted for the ordinary paper and pencil. We call this basket *corbeille-toupie.* For this basket is sometimes substituted a card, the pencil forming the axis of the teetotum.

154. Other ways have been thought of to secure the same end. The most convenient is that we shall call *corbeille-à-bec* (basket with a beak), which consists in adapting to the basket an inclined piece of wood in the position of the bowsprit of a vessel. Through a hole pierced in the end of this stick or beak a pencil is passed, long enough for the point to rest on the paper. The medium having his fingers on the edge of the basket, the whole machine is moved, and the pencil writes as in the above case, with this difference, that the writing is, in general, more legible, the words separated, and the lines are not so spiral, the medium easily taking the pencil from one line to another. Dissertations of several pages are obtained in this way as rapidly as with the hand.

155. The intelligence that acts is often manifested

by other unequivocal signs. Having reached the end
of the page, the pencil makes a spontaneous movement
to turn ; if he wish to refer to a preceding passage
in the same page, or in another, he seeks it with the
point of the pencil, as with the finger, then underlines
it. Should the spirit wish to address one of the assistants, the end of the beak of wood is directed toward
him. To abridge, he often expresses the words *yes*
and *no* by the sign of affirmation and negation, as we
do with the head ; if he wish to express anger or impatience, he strikes forcibly with the point of the
pencil, often breaking it.

156. Instead of a basket, some persons use a kind
of little table made for the purpose, with three feet,
one of which carries a pencil ; the other two are
rounded, or furnished with a little ivory ball, to make it
glide smoothly over the paper. Others use a simple
planchette, triangular, oblong, or oval ; on one edge is
an *oblique* hole for the pencil ; placed to write, it is
inclined, and rests by one side on the paper ; this side
is sometimes finished with two little rollers to facilitate
the movement. It may be readily imagined that there
is nothing absolute in any of these arrangements ; the
most convenient is the best.

With all these machines, two persons are almost
always necessary ; but it is not necessary that the second person should be endowed with the medianimic
faculty : it is only to maintain the equilibrium, and
diminish the fatigue of the medium.

157. We call the writing thus obtained *indirect
psychography*, in opposition to *direct* or *manual psychography*, obtained by the medium's self. To understand the last, it is necessary to notice what happens
in this operation. The spirit who is communicating

acts on the medium, who, under this influence, directs his arm and hand to write, without having (at least in ordinary cases) the least consciousness of what he writes ; the hand acts on the basket, and the basket on the pencil. Thus, *it is not the basket that becomes intelligent ;* it is an instrument directed by an intelligence ; it is, in reality, but a pencil-holder, an appendage to the hand, an intermediary between the hand and the pencil ; suppress this intermediary, and hold the pencil in the hand, and you will have the same result, with a mechanism much more simple, since the medium writes as he does in normal conditions, so every one who writes with the aid of a basket, planchette, or other object, could write directly.

Of all the means of communication, *writing with the hand* — called by some *involuntary* writing — is, without contradiction, the most simple, the easiest, and the most convenient, because it requires no preparation, and because, as in ordinary writing, it can be used for the most extended development. We shall return to this in speaking of mediums.

158. In the beginning of the manifestation, when there were less exact ideas on this subject, several writings were published, headed *Communications of a Basket, of a Planchette, of a Table,* &c. All that is insufficient and erroneous in these expressions is now understood as a not sufficiently serious view of their character. In fact, as has been seen, tables, planchettes, and baskets are only unintelligent instruments, though momentarily animated with a factitious life, which can communicate nothing of themselves ; it is taking the effect for the cause, the instrument for the principal ; as well might an author add to the title of

his work that it was written with a steel pen or a goose quill.

Besides, these instruments are not absolute; we know one person who, instead of the basket we have described, used a funnel with a neck, through which he put the pencil. It might have been said communications of a funnel, or of a stewpan, or a salad dish. If they were given by rappings, and these rappings were made by a chair or cane, it is no longer a talking table, but a talking chair or cane. What is necessary to know is, not the nature of the instrument, but the method of obtaining. If the communications take place by writing, let the pencil-holder be what it may, for us it is psychography; if by rappings, it is typtology. Spiritism, having taken the proportions of a science, requires a scientific language.

CHAPTER XIV.

OF MEDIUMS.

Mediums for Physical Effects. — Electrical Persons. — Sensitive or Impressible Mediums. — Hearing Mediums. — Speaking Mediums. — Seeing Mediums. — Somnambulic Mediums. — Healing Mediums. — Pneumatographic Mediums.

159. EVERY person who feels, in any degree whatever, the influence of the spirits, is a medium. This faculty is inherent in man, and consequently not an exclusive privilege ; so there are few in whom are not found some rudiments of it.

It might thus be said that very nearly every one is a medium. Usually, this qualification is applied only to those in whom the medianimic faculty is clearly characterized, and shown by visible effects of a certain intensity, which depends on an organization more or less sensitive. It must be remarked that this faculty is not revealed in the same manner with all ; mediums, usually, have a special aptitude for such or such order of phenomena, which makes as many varieties as there are kinds of manifestations. The principal are, *mediums for physical effects ; sensitive or impressible mediums ; auditive ; speaking ; seeing ; somnambulistic ; healing ; pneumatographic ; writing or psychographic.*

1. *Mediums for Physical Effects.*

160. *Mediums for Physical Effects* are more espe
cially fit to produce material phenomena, such as move·
ments of inert bodies, noises, &c. They may be divided
into *optional mediums and involuntary mediums.* (See
Part II., Chapters II. and IV.)

Optional Mediums are those who have a consciousness of their power, and who produce the spirit phenomena by the power of their will. This faculty,
though, as we have said, inherent in the human species, is far from existing in all in the same degree ; yet,
if there are few persons with whom it is absolutely null,
those who are capable of producing great effects, such
as the suspension of heavy bodies in space, aerial translation, and, above all, apparitions, are still more rare.
The most simple effects are those of rotation of an object,
rapping by the raising of the object, or even within its
substance. Without attaching primary importance to
these phenomena, we engage not to neglect them ; they
may give occasion to interesting observations and aid
conviction. But it is to be remarked that the faculty of
producing physical effects rarely exists with those who
have more perfect means of communication, as writing
and speaking. Generally, the faculty diminishes in one
sense in proportion as it develops in another.

161. *Involuntary* or *natural* mediums are those in
whom the influence is exercised without their will.
They have no consciousness of their power, and often
the abnormal occurrences around them seem to them
nothing extraordinary ; it is a part of themselves,
absolutely like persons endowed with second sight,
and who never suspect it. These subjects are very
worthy of observation ; and collecting and studying

facts of this kind that may come to our knowledge should not be neglected ; they show themselves at all ages, even with very young children. (See, in Chap. V., *Spontaneous Manifestations*.)

This faculty is not, by itself, the indication of a pathological state, for it is not incompatible with perfect health. If the one who possesses it is suffering, that proceeds from a foreign cause ; also therapeutic means are powerless to end it. It may, in some cases, be consecutive with a certain organic weakness, but it is never the efficient cause. No inquietude, then, can be reasonably felt in a hygienic point of view ; it could produce inconvenience only if the subject, having become an optional medium, should abuse its use, because in that case there might be enfeebling of the organs, from too abundant emission of the vital fluid.

162. Reason revolts at the idea of the tortures, moral and corporeal, to which science has sometimes subjected weak and delicate beings, to ascertain if there were treachery on their part ; these *experimentations*, most often made through malice, are always injurious to sensitive organizations ; there might result from them serious disorders in the economy ; to make such trials is to sport with life. The sincere observer needs not these means ; besides, a person familiar with these phenomena knows that they belong more to the moral than to the physical order, and that their solution will be vainly sought in our exact sciences. For the very reason that these phenomena belong to the moral order, everything that can over-excite the imagination should be avoided with the most scrupulous care. We know what accidents fear can occasion, and persons would be less imprudent if they knew all the cases of insanity and epilepsy that have their origin in the

stories of the *were wolf* and Croquemitanie ; what will
it be, then, if persuaded it is the *devil ?*

Those who accredit such ideas know not the responsibility they assume ; *they might kill.* But the
danger is not alone for the subject, but for those
around him, who might be frightened at the thought
of their house being a haunt of demons. It is this
fatal belief that has caused so many acts of atrocity in
times of ignorance. At the same time, with a little
more discernment, they would know that, in burning
the body supposed to be possessed by the devil, they
could not burn the devil. Since they wish to get rid
of the devil, it is he they should kill: the spirit doctrine, by enlightening us on the true cause of all these
phenomena, gives him the death-blow. *Thus, far
from encouraging this idea, we should, as a duty of
morality and humanity, combat it where it exists.*

What should be done when such a faculty is spontaneously developed in an individual, is to leave the
phenomenon to take its natural course. Nature is
more prudent than man : besides, Providence has His
views, and the smallest can be an instrument of the
greatest designs. But it must be conceded that this
phenomenon sometimes acquires fatiguing and importunate proportions for every one (Note 8) ; here is
what, in all cases, should be done. In Chapter V., on
Spontaneous Physical Manifestations, we have already
given some advice on this subject, saying that it is
necessary to try to come into relations with the spirit,
to know from him what he wants. The following
method is also founded on observation. The invisible
beings who reveal their presence by effects, are, in
general, of an inferior order of spirits, who can be

governed by moral ascendency ; it is this ascendency we must endeavor to acquire.

To obtain it, the subject must be made to pass from the state of *natural* to that of *optional* medium. Then there is produced an effect analogous to that which takes place in somnambulism. It is known that natural somnambulism generally ceases when it is replaced by magnetic somnambulism. The emancipative faculty of the soul is not stopped, but is turned into another course. It is the same with the medianimic faculty. Then, instead of arresting the phenomena, which is rarely successful, and not always without danger, the medium must be incited to produce them at will, by overawing the spirit ; by this means he may be able to master him, and from a somewhat tyrannical ruler he makes of him a subordinate, and often very docile being. A fact worthy of remark, and justified by experience, is, that in such cases a child has as much, and often more, authority than an adult ; new proof in support of this main point in the doctrine that the spirit is a child only by the body, and that he has, by himself, a development necessarily anterior to his actual incarnation — a development that can give him the ascendency over spirits who are his inferiors.

The moralization of the spirit by the counsels of a third influential and experienced person, if the medium is not in a state to do it, is often a very efficacious means : we shall return to it later.

163. In this category of mediums seem to belong the persons endowed with natural electricity — veritable *human torpedoes*, producing, by simple contact, all the effects of attraction and repulsion. It would be wrong, however, to regard them as *mediums*, for

true mediumship supposes the direct intervention of a spirit; but in the case of which we speak, conclusive experiments have proved that electricity is the only agent of these phenomena.

This strange faculty, which might almost be called an infirmity, may sometimes be allied to mediumship, as may be seen in the history of the *rapping Spirit of Bergzabern;* but often it is completely independent. So, as we have said, the sole proof of the intervention of spirits is the intelligent character of the manifestations; wherever this character does not exist, there is the right to attribute them to a purely physical cause.

The question is, to know if *electric persons* would possess a greater aptitude for becoming *mediums for physical effects;* we think so, but this would be the result of experience.

2. *Sensitive or Impressible Mediums.*

164. Persons capable of perceiving the presence of spirits by a vague impression, a kind of feeling throughout the whole body, for which they can give no reason, are thus designated. This variety has no very decided character; all mediums are necessarily impressible: impressionability is rather a general than a particular quality; it is the rudimentary faculty indispensable to the development of all the others; it differs from purely physical and nervous impressionability, with which it must not be confounded; for there are persons who have not delicate nerves, and who yet feel, more or less, the presence of spirits; and others, very irritable, who have not the slightest perception of them. This faculty is developed by habit, and may acquire such a subtilty that the person endowed with

it recognizes, by the impression he feels, not only the good or bad nature of the spirit at his side, but even his individuality, as a blind person recognizes, by a certain unknown sense, the approach of this or that person ; he becomes, in relation to spirits, a veritable sensitive plant. A good spirit always makes a gentle and agreeable impression ; that of a bad spirit, on the contrary, is painful, anxious, and disagreeable ; there is, as it were, a scent of impurity.

3. *Hearing Mediums.*

165. They hear the voice of the spirits : it is, as we have said, in speaking of pneumatophony, sometimes an interior voice, which makes itself heard in the soul ; at other times it is an exterior voice, clear and distinct as that of a living person. An auditive medium can enter into conversation with the spirits. When they are accustomed to communicate with certain spirits, they immediately recognize the character of the voice. When a person is not himself endowed with this faculty, he can communicate with a spirit by means of an auditive medium, who fills the office of interpreter.

This faculty is very agreeable when the medium hears only good spirits, or only those he calls ; but it is not the same when a bad spirit is always after him, making him hear at every moment the most disagreeable, and often the most improper things. It then becomes necessary to get rid of him by the means we indicate in the chapter on *Obsession.*

4. *Talking Mediums.*

166. Hearing mediums, who transmit only what they hear, are not, properly speaking, *talking mediums;* these last very often hear nothing ; with them the

spirit acts on the organs of speech, as he acts on the hand of writing mediums. The spirit wishing to communicate acts on the organ he finds most flexible; of one the hand, of another the speech, of another the hearing. The talking medium usually expresses himself without having a consciousness of what he says, and often says things completely beyond his customary ideas, his knowledge, or even the height of his intelligence.

Though he may be perfectly awake, and in a normal state, he rarely preserves the remembrance of what he has spoken; in a word, speech is, with him, the instrument the spirit uses, and through which another person can enter into communication, as can be done by the interposition of the hearing medium.

The passivity of the hearing medium is not always so complete; there are some who have the intuition of what they say at the moment of pronouncing the words. We shall return to this variety when we treat of intuitive mediums.

5. *Seeing Mediums.*

167. Seeing mediums are endowed with the faculty of seeing spirits. There are some who enjoy this faculty in the normal state; then they are perfectly awake, and preserve an exact remembrance of it; others have it only in a somnambulic state, or one bordering on somnambulism. This faculty is rarely permanent; it is almost always the effect of a momentary and fleeting crisis. All persons endowed with second sight may be placed in the category of seeing mediums. The possibility of seeing spirits in dreams most certainly results from a kind of mediumship, but does not, properly speaking, constitute seeing mediums.

We have explained this phenomenon in Chapter VI., on *Visual Manifestations*.

The seeing medium thinks he sees with his eyes, as also those who have double sight ; but in reality it is the soul that sees, because he sees as well with his eyes shut as with them open ; from whence it follows that a blind person can see spirits as well as one who has the use of his eyes. This last point might give an interesting subject for study, to know if this faculty is more frequent with the blind. Spirits who have been blind have told us that, while living, they had, by the soul, a perception of certain objects, and that they were not plunged in *black* obscurity.

168. A distinction must be made between incidental and spontaneous apparitions, and the faculty proper of seeing spirits. The former are frequent, particularly at the moment of the death of persons loved or known, and who come to warn us they are no longer in the world. There are numerous examples of facts of this kind, without reckoning visions during sleep. At other times, relatives or friends, who, though a longer or shorter time dead, appear either to warn us of a danger, or to give advice, or to ask a service. The service a spirit can claim consists usually in the accomplishment of a thing he could not do while living, or in the help of prayers. These apparitions are isolated facts, which have always an individual and personal character, and do not constitute a faculty proper. The faculty consists in the possibility, if not permanent, at least very frequent, of seeing any spirit, even that of an entire stranger. It is this faculty that, properly speaking, constitutes seeing mediums.

Among seeing mediums there are those who see only those whom they call, and whom they describe with a perfect minuteness ; they tell, to the smallest detail, their gestures, their expression of countenance, their features, costume, and even the sentiments by which they are animated. With others this faculty is still more general ; they see all the surrounding spirit population go, come, and, as one might say, attend to their affairs.

169. One evening we were at a representation of the opera of Oberon, with a very good seeing medium. There were in the house quite a number of seats vacant, but many of which were occupied by spirits, who seemed to be taking their share in the scene ; some went near certain of the spectators, and appeared to listen to their conversation. On the stage another scene was passing ; behind the actors several humorous, jovial spirits amused themselves in mimicking them, imitating their gestures in a grotesque manner ; others, more serious, seemed to inspire the singers, and make efforts to give them energy. One of them was constantly near one of the principal female singers ; we thought his intentions a little light. Having called him, after the fall of the curtain, he came to us, and reproached us with some severity for our rash judgment. " I am not what you think," said he ; " I am her guide and spirit protector ; it is I who am charged to direct her." After some moments of very serious conversation, he left us, saying, " Adieu ! she is at home. I must go watch over her."

We afterward called the spirit of Weber, the author of the opera, and asked him what he thought of the execution of his work. " It is not so very bad," said he ; " but it is tame ; the actors sing — that is all ; there is no inspiration. Wait!" added he ; " I will try to give them a little of the sacred fire." Then we saw him on the stage, hovering above the actors : a breath seemed to part from him, and spread over them, and a very visible increase of energy took place among them.

170. Here is another fact which proves the influence spirits exercise at their will on man. We were, as before, at a theatrical representation with another seeing medium. Having engaged in conversation with a *spirit spectator*, he said to us, " Do you see those two ladies alone in that private box ? Well, I warrant you I will make them leave the theater."

So said, he was soon in the box, talking to the two ladies ; suddenly, from having been very attentive to the play, they looked at each other, consulted together, and finally went out, and did not return. The spirit made us a comical gesture, to show that he had kept his word, but did not return, that we might ask further explanations.

We have thus been many times witness of the part spirits play among the living : we have seen them at many reunions, — ball, concert, church, funerals, weddings, &c., — and everywhere we have found them exciting the evil passions, stirring up discord, inciting brawls, and rejoicing in their prowess ; others, on the contrary, combated this pernicious influence, though but rarely listened to.

171. The faculty of seeing spirits can, without doubt, be developed, but it is one of which it is best to await the natural development, without trying to call it out, if one would not wish to become the dupe of his imagination. When the germ of a faculty exists, it will be manifested of itself ; from principle, we must be contented with those God has granted to us, without seeking the impossible ; for then, in wishing to have

too much, we risk losing what we have. When we said spontaneous apparitions are frequent, we did not intend to say that they are very common ; as to seeing mediums, properly so called, they are still more rare, and we should be very careful of those who pretend to enjoy this faculty ; it is prudent not to trust them except upon positive proofs. We do not mean those who are given to the ridiculous illusion of globu‧lar spirits, which we described No. 108, but of those who pretend to see spirits in a rational manner. Some persons may, doubtless, be deceived in all sincerity, but others may simulate this faculty from self-love or interest. In this case, particular account must be taken of the character, of the morality and habitual sincerity ; but it is especially in the details the most certain test can be found, for they can be such as to leave no doubt ; as, for instance, the exactness of the description of spirits whom the medium has never known living. The following fact is of this category : —

A widowed lady, whose husband frequently communicated with her, found herself one day with a seeing medium, who did not know her nor her family : the medium said to her, " I see a spirit near you."

"Ah !" said the lady, " it is, doubtless, my husband, who seldom leaves me."

" No," answered the medium ; " it is an elderly lady ; her head-dress is very singular ; she has a white band across her forehead."

From this particular and other descriptive details, the lady unmistakably recognized her grandmother, of whom she was not thinking. ‧ If the medium had wished to simulate the faculty, it was easy to follow the thought of the lady, whereas, instead of the husband, of whom she was thinking, he sees a woman with a peculiarity of head-dress, of which nothing had given him the idea. This fact proves another thing, —that the sight, with the medium, was not the reflection of any person's thought. (See No. 102.)

6. *Somnambulic Mediums.*

172. Somnambulism may be considered as a variety of the medianimic faculty, or, rather, they are two orders of phenomena very often found combined. The somnambulist acts under the influence of his own spirit ; it is his soul, which, in moments of emancipation, sees, hears, and perceives, outside the limit of the senses ; what he expresses, he draws from himself ; his ideas are, in general, more just than in the normal state, his knowledge more extended, because his soul is free ; in a word, he lives, by anticipation, the life of spirits.

The medium, on the contrary, is the instrument of a foreign intelligence ; he is passive, and what he says comes not from himself. To recapitulate : the somnambulist expresses his own thought, the medium that of another. But the spirit who communicates to an ordinary medium could also as well to a somnambulist ; often the state of emancipation of the soul renders this communication more easy. Many somnambulists see spirits perfectly, and describe them with as much precision as the seeing mediums ; they can talk with them, and transmit their thought to us ; what they say beyond the circle of their own knowledge is often suggested to them by other spirits. Here is a remarkable example, where the double action of the spirit of the somnambulist and of the foreign spirit reveals itself in the most unequivocal manner.

173. One of our friends had for a somnambulist a young boy of fourteen or fifteen years of age, of very ordinary intelligence, and extremely limited instruction. Nevertheless, in somnambulism he gave proofs of extraordinary lucidity and great perspicacity. He excelled especially in the treatment of diseases, and made a great many cures regarded as impossible. One day he gave a consultation to a sick person, whose malady he described exactly.

"That is not all," said they; "now you must indicate the remedy." "I cannot," he answered. "*My angel doctor is not here.*" "What do you mean by your angel doctor?" "He who dictates to me." "It is not you, then, who see the remedies?" "Why, no; don't I tell you my angel doctor dictates them to me?"

Thus, with this somnambulist, the action of seeing the disease was that of his own spirit, who for that needed no assistance, but the indication of the remedies was given by another; this other not being there, he could say nothing. Alone, he was only a somnambulist; assisted by what he called his angel doctor, he was a *somnambulistic medium.*

174. Somnambulistic lucidity is a faculty that pertains to the organism, and which is entirely independent of the elevation, of the advancement, and even of the moral state of the subject. A somnambulist may, then, be very clear, and be incapable of solving certain questions, if his spirit be but little advanced. He who talks by himself may say good or bad, true or false things; put more or less delicacy or fastidiousness into his proceedings, according to the degree of elevation or inferiority of his own spirit; then the assistance of a foreign spirit may supply his insufficiency;

but a somnambulist may be assisted by a lying, or trifling, or even a bad spirit, as well as mediums ; it is here, above all, that the moral qualities have a great influence to attract good spirits. (See *Book on Spirits*, *Somnambulism*, No. 425; and in this, the chapter on the *Moral Influence of the Medium*.)

7. *Healing Mediums*.

175. We shall here give but a glance at this variety of mediums, because this subject requires too extended developments for our outline ; we know, besides, that a doctor, one of our friends, proposes to treat it in a special work on intuitive healing. We shall say only that this kind of mediumship consists principally in the gift possessed by some persons of healing by the simple touch, by the look, even by the gesture, without the help of any medication. It will, doubtless, be said, that it is nothing but magnetism. It is evident the magnetic fluid here plays a great part ; but when this phenomenon is carefully examined, it is easily seen that there is something more. Ordinary magnetization is a real treatment, continuous, regular, and methodical ; in it things happen very differently. Nearly all magnetizers are capable of curing, if they know how properly to undertake it ; but with healing mediums the faculty is spontaneous, and some even possess it without ever having heard of magnetism. The intervention of a hidden power, which constitutes mediumship, becomes evident under certain circumstances : it is so, particularly, when it is considered that most persons, whom we can reasonably qualify as healing mediums, have recourse to prayer, which is a real invocation. (See No. 131.)

176. Here are the answers to the following questions addressed to the spirits on this subject : —

1. " Can persons endowed with magnetic power be considered as forming a variety of mediums ? "

" You cannot doubt it."

2. " Yet the medium is an intermediary between the spirits and man ; but the magnetizer, drawing his strength from within himself, seems not to be the intermediary of any foreign power."

" It is an error : the magnetic power resides, doubtless, in the man ; but it is augmented by the action of the spirits he calls to his aid. If you magnetize with a view to healing, for instance, and you invoke a good spirit, who interests himself in you and your patient, he augments your strength and your will ; he directs your fluid, and gives it the necessary qualities."

3. " But there are very good magnetizers who do not believe in spirits."

" Do you think that spirits act only on those who believe in them ? Those who magnetize for good purposes are seconded by good spirits. Every man who has a desire to do good undoubtedly calls them ; the same as by the desire of evil, and evil intentions, he calls the evil."

4. " Would he who has the power act more efficaciously, should he believe in the intervention of spirits ? "

" He would do things you would look upon as miracles."

5. " Have some persons truly the gift of healing by the simple touch, without employing magnetic passes ? "

" Assuredly ; have you not numerous examples of it ? "

6. "In this case is there magnetic action, or only influence of spirits?"

"Both; these persons are veritable mediums, because they act under the influence of spirits; but that is not to say they would be writing mediums, as you would understand it."

7. "Can this power be transmitted?"

"The power, no; but the knowledge of the things necessary to its exercise where it is possessed. A person would not suspect that he has this power if he did not believe it has been transmitted to him."

8. "Can cures be made by prayer alone?"

"Yes, sometimes, if God permits; but perhaps the good of the sick person is that he should suffer, and then you believe that your prayers are not heard."

9. "Are there some forms of prayer more efficacious for that than others?"

"Superstition alone can attach a virtue to certain words, and ignorant or lying spirits alone can entertain such ideas in prescribing forms. Yet it may happen that, for persons not much enlightened, and incapable of understanding things purely spiritual, the employment of a formula helps to give them confidence; in this case it is not the form that is efficacious, but the faith that is increased by the idea attached to the use of the form."

8. *Pneumatographic Mediums.*

177. This name is given to mediums suitable to the obtaining of direct writing, which is not given to all writing mediums. This faculty is, as yet, extremely rare; it is, probably, developed by exercise; but, as we have said, its practical utility is limited to the patent verification of the intervention of an occult

power in the manifestations. Experience alone can prove its possession : a person can try, and also ask it of a protecting spirit, through other means of communication. According to the degree of power possessed by the medium, simple marks, signs, letters, words, phrases, and even whole pages are obtained. It suffices, ordinarily, to fold a piece of paper, put it in some place designated by the spirit, for ten minutes, or a quarter of an hour, or sometimes longer. Prayer and concentration of thought are essential conditions ; this is why it may be looked upon as impossible to obtain anything in a reunion of persons but little serious, or who might not be animated by sympathetic and benevolent sentiments. (See *Theory of Direct Writing*, Chapter VIII., *Laboratory of the Invisible World*, No. 127, &c., and Chapter XII., *Pneumatography*.)

We shall treat, in a special manner, of writing mediums in the following chapters.

CHAPTER XV.

WRITING OR PSYCHOGRAPHIC MEDIUMS.

Mechanical.—Intuitive.—Semi-Mechanical.—Inspired or Involuntary Mediums.—Mediums for Presentiments.

178. Of all the means of communication, manual writing is the most simple, the most convenient, and the most complete. It is to that all efforts should tend, for it permits us to establish with the spirits as continuous and regular relations as among ourselves. We should cling to it the more, because it is that by which the spirits best reveal their nature, and the degree of their perfection or inferiority. By the ease with which they express themselves, they let us know their secret thoughts, and allow us, at the same time, to judge and appreciate them at their value. The faculty of writing, for a medium, is especially the one that is most susceptible of development by exercise.

Mechanical Mediums.

179. If certain effects produced in the movements of the table, of the basket, or of the planchette that writes, be examined, an action exercised directly by the spirit on these objects cannot be doubted.

The basket is, at times, shaken with so much violence, that it escapes from the hands of the medium;

sometimes, even, it is directed toward certain persons in the circle, to strike them ; at other times, its movements testify an affectionate sentiment.

The same thing occurs when the pencil is in the hand ; often it is thrown forcibly to a distance, or the hand, like the basket, is convulsively shaken, and strikes the table with anger even when the medium is perfectly calm, and astonished not to be master of himself. Let us observe, in passing, that these effects always denote the presence of imperfect spirits ; those really superior are constantly calm, dignified, and benevolent ; if they are not listened to properly, they retire, and others take their place. Thus the spirit can express his thought directly, either by the movement of an object in the hand of the medium, or by his action on the hand itself.

When the spirit acts directly on the hand, he gives to it an impulse completely independent of the will. It goes on without interruption, and in spite of the medium, as long as the spirit has anything to say, and stops when he has finished.

What characterizes the phenomenon in this case is, that the medium has no consciousness of what he writes ; absolute unconsciousness constitutes *passive or mechanical mediums*. This faculty is precious, as it can leave no doubt of its independence of the thought of him who writes.

Intuitive Mediums.

180. The transmission of thought takes place by the intervention of the medium's spirit, or, rather, of his soul ; for by this name we designate the incarnated spirit. The foreign spirit, in this case, does not act on the hand to make it write ; he does not hold it,

does not guide it ; he acts on the soul with which he is identified. The soul, under this impulse, directs the hand, and the hand directs the pencil.

Let us remark here one important thing to know ; it is, that the foreign spirit is not substituted for the soul, for he cannot displace it : he controls it at his will, he impresses his will upon it. The part of the soul is not absolutely a passive one ; it receives the thought of the foreign spirit, and transmits it. In this case the medium is conscious what he writes, though it is not his own thought ; this is what is called *intuitive medium.*

If this be so, it may be said, nothing proves that it is any more the thought of a foreign spirit than of the medium. The distinction is, in fact, sometimes quite difficult to make, but it may happen that this will be of little consequence. The suggested thought can always be recognized, in that it is never preconceived ; it is born as it is written, and often is contrary to the idea previously formed ; it may even be beyond the knowledge and capacity of the medium.

The part of the mechanical medium is that of a machine, the intuitive medium acts as an interpreter. In fact, to transmit the thought, he should understand it ; appropriate it in some sort, in order to translate it faithfully ; yet this thought is not his — it but passes through his brain. Such is exactly the part of the intuitive medium.

Semi-Mechanical Mediums.

181. In the purely mechanical medium, the movement of the hand is independent of the will ; in the intuitive medium, the movement is voluntary and optional.

The semi-mechanical medium partakes of both natures; he feels an impulse given to his hand in spite of himself, but, at the same time, has a consciousness of the words as rapidly as they are formed. With the first, the thought follows the act of writing; with the second, it precedes it; with the third, it accompanies it. These last mediums are the most numerous.

Inspired Mediums.

182. Every person who, whether in the normal state or in a state of ecstasy, receives, by the thought, communications foreign to his preconceived ideas, may be ranked in the category of inspired mediums; which is, as may be seen, a variety of intuitive mediumship, with this difference, that the intervention of an occult power is still less apparent; for, with the inspired, it is more difficult to distinguish between the thought proper and that which is suggested. What peculiarly characterizes this is its spontaneity. Inspiration comes to us from spirits who influence us for good or evil, but it is more especially from those who wish us well, and whose advice we too often wrongly avoid following. It applies to every circumstance in life, in the resolutions we make; as far as this goes, we might say every one in the world is a medium, for there is no person who has not his spirit protectors and familiars, who make every effort to suggest salutary thoughts to their wards.

If every one were thoroughly convinced of this truth, there would be more frequent recourse to the guardian angel in moments when one knows not what to say or do. Let us, then, invoke him with *fervor and confidence* in cases of necessity, and we shall be more often astonished by the ideas that will come as by enchantment, whether we may have something to decide or something to compose. If no idea comes, it is because it is necessary for us to wait.

The proof that the idea that comes unexpectedly is one foreign to us, is, that if it had been in us we should always have been master of it, and there would be no reason it could not have manifested itself at will. He who is not blind has only to open his eyes to see when he pleases ; so, the same, he who has ideas of his own always has them at his disposal ; if they do not come at will, it is because he is obliged to draw them from other sources.

In this category may also be classed persons who, without being endowed with an extraordinary intelligence, and without leaving the normal state, have flashes of intellectual lucidity which gives them temporarily an unaccustomed facility of conception and elocution, and, in some cases, a presentiment of the future. In these moments, justly called, of inspiration, ideas abound, are continuous, carry us along, as it were of themselves, by an involuntary and almost feverish impulse ; it seems to us that a superior intelligence comes to our aid, and that our mind is relieved of a load.

183. Men of genius of all kinds — artists, scientists, men of letters — are doubtless advanced spirits, capable oy themselves of understanding and conceiving great things ; but it is precisely because they are considered capable that the spirits who desire the accomplishment of certain work suggest to them the necessary ideas ; and thus they are most frequently *mediums without knowing it.* Yet they have a vague intuition of a foreign assistance ; for he who appeals to inspiration makes but an invocation ; if he did not hope to be

heard, why should he so often cry, "Aid me, my good genius!"

The following answers confirm this assertion:—

"What is the primary cause of inspiration?"

"Spirits who communicate by the thought."

"Has not inspiration the revelation of great things for its object?"

"No; it often has relation to the most ordinary occurrences of life. For example, you wish to go somewhere a secret voice tells you not to do so, for there is danger for you; or it tells you to do a thing you had not thought of; that is inspiration. There are very few persons who have not been more or less inspired at certain moments."

"An author, a painter, a musician, for instance, could they, in moments of inspiration, be considered mediums?"

"Yes, for in these moments the soul is freer and more withdrawn from matter; it recovers a portion of its faculties as spirit, and more easily receives the communications of other spirits who inspire it."

Presentiment Mediums.

184. Presentiment is a vague intuition of future things. Some persons have this faculty more or less developed; they may owe it to a kind of double sight, which permits them to foresee the consequences of present things and the thread of events; but often, also, it proceeds from occult communications, and, in this case, to those thus endowed may be given this name of *presentiment mediums*, which is a variety of *inspired mediums*.

CHAPTER XVI.

SPECIAL MEDIUMS.

Special Aptitudes of Mediums.—Synoptical List of the different Varieties of Mediums.

185. BESIDES the categories of mediums we have enumerated, mediumship presents an infinite variety of shades which constitute what are called special mediums, who possess peculiar aptitudes not yet defined, according to the qualities and knowledge of the manifesting spirit.

The nature of the communication always sustains a relation to the nature of the spirit, and bears the seal of his elevation or inferiority, his knowledge or ignorance ; but, merit being equal in a hierarchical point of view, he has undoubtedly a propensity to engage in one thing rather than another ; the rapping spirits, for instance, never depart from physical manifestations ; and among those who give intelligent manifestations are spirit poets, musicians, painters, moralists, scientists, physicians, &c. We speak of spirits of a middle order, for, once arrived at a certain degree, the aptitudes are blended in the unity of perfection. But, besides the aptitude of the spirit, there is that of the medium, who is an instrument for him, more or less suitable, more or less flexible, and in whom he discovers special qualities that we cannot appreciate.

Let us make a comparison : a very skillful musician has in his hands several violins, which, to the ordinary eye, will all be very good instruments, but between which the consummate artist distinguishes a great difference ; he perceives therein shades of exceeding delicacy, which make him choose some and reject others, shades which he comprehends rather by intuition than by anything he can define in them. It is the same with respect to mediums ; with equal qualities in the medianimic power, the spirit will give the preference to one or to the other, according to the kind of communication he desires to make. Thus, for instance, persons, as mediums, write admirable poems, though in the ordinary conditions they never knew how, nor could compose two verses ; others, on the contrary, who are poets, and who, as mediums, have been able to write only prose, in spite of their desire.

The same with drawing, music, &c.

There are those who, without having, by themselves, any scientific knowledge, have a more special aptitude for receiving scientific communications ; others are for historical studies ; others serve more easily as interpreters for spirit moralists ; in a word, whatever may be the flexibility of the medium, the communications he receives with most facility have, generally, a special seal ; there are even those who never emerge from a certain circle of ideas, and when they are taken from that, they have but incomplete, laconic, and often false, communications. Aside from the causes of aptitude, the spirits communicate more or less willingly by such or such an intermediary, according to their sympathies ; so, all other things being equal, the same spirit will be much more explicit with certain mediums, solely because they suit him better.

186. It would then be an error, if, having at hand a good medium, even one who writes with the utmost facility, we should from that alone expect to obtain good communications of all kinds. The primary condition certainly is, to be assured of the source where they emanate, that is, of the qualities of the spirit who transmits them ; but it is not the less necessary to be careful of the qualities of the instrument given to the spirit : we must, then, study the nature of the medium, as we study the nature of the spirit, for these are the two essential elements for obtaining a satisfactory result. There is a third, that plays an equally important part — the intention, the secret thought, the more or less praiseworthy sentiment of the interrogator ; and so it may be said, *To obtain a good communication, it must emanate from a good spirit ; that this good spirit may be able to transmit it, he must have a good instrument ; that he may desire to transmit it, the motive must suit him.*

The spirit, who reads in the thought, judges if the question proposed merits a serious answer, and if the person who addresses him is worthy to receive it : in a contrary case, he does not lose his time sowing good seed on stony ground ; and then trifling, mocking, spirits take his place, because, troubling themselves very little about the truth, they do not look at things so closely, and are usually but little scrupulous as to the end or means.

We here sum up the principal kinds of mediumship, before presenting a kind of synoptical list, comprising those we have already described in the preceding chapters, indicating the numbers of those to which we shall add further details.

We have grouped the different varieties of mediums

by analogy with causes and effects, but do not propose there shall be anything absolute in this classification. Some are frequently met, others are rare and exceptional, which we have taken care to mention. These last indications have all been furnished by spirits, who, besides, have reviewed this descriptive list with an exceedingly particular care, and have completed it by numerous observations and new categories, so that it may be said to be their entire work. We have indicated by quotation marks their textual observations when we have thought it necessary to make them more prominent. They are mostly from *Erastus* and *Socrates.*

187. Mediums may be divided into two great classes.

MEDIUMS FOR PHYSICAL EFFECTS. Those who have the power to induce material effects or ostensible manifestations. (No. 160.)

MEDIUMS FOR INTELLECTUAL EFFECTS. Those who are more especially proper to receive and transmit intelligent communications. (No. 65, &c.)

All the other varieties more or less directly belong to one or the other of these classes ; some pertain to both. If the different phenomena produced under medianimic influence are analyzed, it will be seen that in all there is a physical effect, and that to the physical effects are most often joined an intelligent one. The boundary between the two is sometimes difficult to establish ; but that is of no consequence. We comprehend under the denomination *Mediums for Intellectual Effects* those who can more specially serve as intermediaries for regular and continuous communications. (No. 133.)

Varieties common to all Kinds of Mediumship.

188. *Sensitive Mediums.* Persons susceptible to the presence of spirits by a general or local, a vague or material impression. Most of them distinguish the spirits, good or bad, by the nature of the impression.

"Delicate and very sensitive mediums should abstain from communications with violent spirits, or those whose impression is painful, because of the fatigue resulting from it."

Natural or Unconscious Mediums. Those who produce the phenomena spontaneously, without any participation of their will, and often against it. (No. 161.)

Optional or Voluntary Mediums. Those who have the power of inducing the phenomena by an act of their will. (No. 160.)

"Whatever may be this will, they could do nothing should the spirits refuse, which proves the intervention of a foreign power."

Special Varieties for Physical Effects.

189. *Tipping Mediums.* Those by whose influence noises and rappings are produced. A very common variety, with or without the will.

Moving Mediums. Those who produce the movement of inert bodies. Very common. (No. 61.)

Mediums for Translations and Suspensions. Those who produce the aerial translations and the suspension in space, without support, of inert bodies. There are those who can raise themselves. More or less rare, according to the development of the phenomenon ; very rare in the latter case. (Nos. 75, &c., and No. 80.)

Musical Mediums. They induce the playing of instruments without contact. Very rare. (No. 74, question 24.)

Mediums for Apparitions. Those who can induce fluidic or tangible apparitions visible to those present. (No. 100, question 27, and No. 104.)

Mediums for Materialization. Those who can serve as auxiliaries to the spirits, to bring material objects. A variety of the moving mediums, and mediums for translations. Exceptional. (No. 96.)

Nocturnal Mediums. Those who obtain certain physical effects only in obscurity. I give the answer of a spirit to the question, if these mediums may be considered as forming a variety.

"A specialty may certainly be made of it; but this phenomenon pertains rather to surrounding conditions than to the nature of the medium or the spirits. I should add that some escape this influence of the surroundings, and that most of the nocturnal mediums could, by practice, succeed as well in the light as in the darkness. This variety is not very numerous; and it must be said, that under cover of this condition, which allows so much liberty in the employment of tricks, ventriloquism, and acoustic pipes, charlatans have too often played upon credulity, passing themselves off for mediums in order to make money. But what matter? Private as well as public jugglers will be cruelly unmasked, and the spirits will prove to them that it is not good to interfere with their affairs. Yes, I repeat it, certain charlatans will be rapped over the fingers in a rude enough fashion to disgust them with the part of false mediums. Besides, all that is but for a time.

"ERASTUS."

Pneumatographic Mediums. Those who obtain direct

writing. A very rare phenomenon, and one very easy to imitate by jugglery. (No. 177.)

Remark. The spirits have insisted, against our opinion, in classing direct writing among the physical phenomena, for the reason, they say, that "intelligent effects are those by which the spirits use the cerebral material of the medium, which is not the case in direct writing; the action of the medium is here wholly material, while with the writing medium, even when entirely mechanical, the brain always plays an active part."

Healing Mediums. Those who have the power of healing or soothing by laying on of hands, or by prayer.

"This faculty is not essentially medianimic; it belongs to all true believers, whether they are mediums or not; it is often only an exaltation of magnetic power, fortified, in case of need, by the concurrence of good spirits." (No. 175.)

Excitative Mediums. Persons who have the power of developing in others, by their influence, the faculty of writing.

"This is rather a magnetic effect, than mediumship proper, for nothing proves the intervention of a spirit. In all cases it belongs to the order of physical effects. (See chapter on the *Formation of Mediums*.)

Special Mediums for Intellectual Effects. — Various Aptitudes.

190. *Hearing Mediums.* Those who hear spirits. Quite common. (No. 165.)

"There are many who imagine they hear, when it is only imagination."

Speaking Mediums. Those who speak under the influence of spirits. Quite common. (No. 166.)

Seeing Mediums.   Those who see spirits in a waking state.

The accidental or unforeseen sight of a spirit under particular circumstances is quite frequent; but the habitual or optional sight of spirits without distinction is exceptional.. (No. 167.)

"It is an aptitude to which the actual state of the organs is opposed; this is why you must not always believe the word of those who say they see spirits."

Inspired Mediums.   Those to whom thoughts are suggested by spirits, most often against their will, be it for the ordinary acts of life, or for great intellectual labors.   (No. 182.)

Mediums for Presentiments.   Persons who, under certain circumstances, have a vague intuition of ordinary future events.   (No. 184.)

Prophetic Mediums.   A variety of the inspired or presentiment mediums ; they receive, by God's permission, and with more precision than presentiment mediums, the revelation of future events of a general interest, and which they are charged to make known to men for their instruction.

"If there are true prophets, still more are there of false ones, and of those who take the dreams of their imagination for revelations, when they are not impostors who pretend to be prophets, from ambition." (See *Book on Spirits*, No. 624, Characters of the true prophets.)

Somnambulistic Mediums.   Those who, in a state of somnambulism, are assisted by spirits.   (No. 172.)

Ecstatic Mediums.   Those who, in a state of ecstasy, receive revelations from spirits.

"Many ecstatics are the sport of their own imagination, and of deceiving spirits, who profit by their exaltation. Those who deserve perfect confidence are very rare."

Painting and Drawing Mediums. Those who paint or draw under the influence of spirits. We speak of those who obtain serious things, for this name cannot be given to certain mediums who are made to draw, by mocking spirits, things so grotesque that the merest scholar would disavow them. Frivolous spirits are imitators. At the time when the remarkable drawings of Jupiter appeared, there arose a great number of pretended drawing mediums, with whom the mocking spirits amused themselves by making them draw the most ridiculous things. One of them, among others, wishing to outdo the drawings of Jupiter, in dimensions, at least, if not in quality, made a medium draw a monument covering sheets enough to have reached two stories high. Many others drew so-called portraits which were veritable caricatures. (*Revue Spirite,* August, 1858.)

Medium Musicians. Those who execute, compose, or write music under the influence of spirits. There are mechanical, semi-mechanical, intuitive, and inspired medium musicians; the same as for literary communications. (See *Mediums for Musical Effects.*)

Varieties of Writing Mediums.

1. *According to the Methods of Execution.*

191. *Writing or Psychographic Mediums.* Those who have the faculty of writing under the influence of spirits.

Mechanical Writing Mediums. Those whose hand receives an involuntary impulse, and who have no con-sciousness of what they write. Very rare. (No. 179.)

Semi-mechanical Mediums. Those whose hand moves involuntarily, but who have instantaneous consciousness of the words or phrases as they write them. The most common.   (No. 181.)

Intuitive Mediums. Those to whom the spirit communicates by the thought, and whose hand is guided by the will. They differ from inspired mediums, insomuch as these last have no need to write, while the intuitive medium writes the thought suggested to him instantaneously on any given and induced subject. (No. 180.)

" They are very common, but also very subject to error, because often they cannot distinguish what emanates from the spirits, and what from their own ideas.'

Polygraphic Mediums. Those whose writing changes with the spirit who communicates, or who are apt to reproduce the writing the spirit had during his life. The first case is very common ; the second — that of the identity of the writing — is more rare.   (No. 219.)

Polyglot Mediums. Those who have the faculty of speaking or writing in languages unknown to them. Very rare.

Illiterate Mediums. Those who write as mediums, without knowing how to read or write in the ordinary state.

" More rare than the preceding ; there is a much greater material difficulty to overcome."

2. *According to the Development of the Faculty.*

192. *Novice Mediums.* Those in whom the faculty is not yet fully developed, and who lack the necessary experience.

Unproductive Mediums. Those who can succeed in

obtaining only insignificant things — monosyllables, signs, or letters, without connection. (See chapter on *Formation of Mediums.*)

Formed or Complete Mediums. Those in whom the medianimic faculties are completely developed, who transmit the communications they receive with facility and promptitude, without hesitation. It may be readily supposed that this result is not obtained without practice, while with *novice mediums* the communications are slow and difficult.

Laconic Mediums. Those whose communications, though easy, are brief and without development.

Explicit Mediums. The communications they obtain have all the fullness and extent that a perfect writer can attain.

"This aptitude is due to the expansion and the facility of habit, often acquired in a short time, while experience is the result of a serious study of al! the difficulties presented in the practice of Spiritism. Experience gives the medium the tact necessary to appreciate the nature of the spirits, who manifest themselves, to judge their qualities, good or bad, by the minutest signs, to discern the frauds of deceiving spirits, who shelter themselves under the appearance of truth."

The importance of this quality, in default of which all others are without real utility, may be easily comprehended ; the trouble is, many mediums confound experience, fruit of study, with aptitude, product of organization ; they believe themselves " passed masters " because they write easily ; they repudiate all advice, and become the prey of lying and hypocritical spirits, who take them captive by flattering their pride. (See after, chapter on *Obsession.*)

Flexible Mediums. Those in whom the faculty is most easily adapted to various kinds of communications, and by whom all spirits, or nearly all, can manifest themselves spontaneously, or by invocation.

" This variety of mediums approach very nearly to sensitive mediums."

Exclusive Mediums. Those by whom one spirit manifests himself by preference, and even to the exclusion of all others.

" This is always owing to a defect in flexibility; when the spirit is good, he may attach himself to the medium from sympathy, and with a praiseworthy object; when he is bad, it is always with a view to bringing the medium into subjection to him. It is a defect rather than a good quality, and almost obsession." (See chapter on *Obsession.*)

Mediums for Invocation. Flexible mediums are most fitted for this kind of communication, and to the questions in detail that may be addressed to spirits. There are, under this head, mediums who are entirely special.

" Their answers are almost always limited to a restricted outline, incompatible with the development of general subjects."

Mediums for Spontaneous Dictations. They receive, by preference, spontaneous communications from spirits who come without being called. When this faculty is special with a medium, it is difficult, sometimes even impossible, to make an invocation by him.

" Yet they are better furnished than those of the preceding shade. Understand that by furnishing here is understood cerebral material; for there needs often, I will even say always, a greater amount of intelligence for spontaneous dictations than for invocations.

Understand here, by spontaneous dictations, those which really deserve this name, and not a few incomplete phrases, or some ordinary thoughts to be found in every human head-piece.

3. *According to the Kind and Speciality of the Communications.*

193. *Versifying Mediums.* They obtain, more easily than others, communications in verse. Very common for bad verses, very rare for good ones.

Poetic Mediums. Without obtaining verse, the communications they receive are somewhat vaporous and sentimental; nothing expresses roughness: they are, more than others, suited to the expression of tender and affectionate expressions. All is vague, and it would be useless to ask anything exact of them. Very common.

Positive Mediums. Their communications have, in general, a character of clearness and precision which is easily accommodated to circumstantial details and exact teachings. Quite rare.

Literary Mediums. They have neither the vagueness of poetic mediums, nor the matter of fact of positive mediums; but they discuss with sagacity; their style is correct, elegant, and often remarkably eloquent.

Incorrect Mediums. They can obtain very good things, thoughts of irreproachable morality; but their style is diffuse, incorrect, full of repetitions and improper terms.

" Material incorrectness of style is, generally speaking, the fault of want of intellectual culture of the medium, who is not, in this respect, a good instrument for the spirit; the spirit attaches little importance to it; for him, the essential thing is the thought, and he leaves you free to give it a suitable form. It is not the same with the false and illogical ideas a communication may enclose ; they are always an indication of the inferiority of the spirit."

Historical Mediums. Those who have a special aptitude for historical developments. This faculty, like all the others, is independent of the knowledge of the mediums ; for unlearned persons, and even children, are often seen to treat of subjects far above their mental caliber. A rare variety of positive mediums.

Scientific Mediums. We do not say scientists, for they may be very ignorant, and, notwithstanding that, they may be more especially suited to communications relating to the sciences.

Medical Mediums. Their speciality is to serve more easily as interpreters to spirits for medical prescriptions. They must not be confounded with *healing mediums*, for these absolutely do nothing but transmit the thought of the spirit, and have, by themselves, no influence. Quite common.

Religious Mediums. They receive, more especially, communications of a religious character, or those that treat questions of religion without regard to their beliefs or their habits.

Moral Philosophic Mediums. Their communications have usually for their object questions of morals and higher philosophy. Very common for morals.

" All these shades are varieties of aptitudes of good mediums. As to those who have a special aptitude for certain communications, scientific, historical, medical, or others, beyond their actual caliber, be sure they have possessed these knowledges in another existence, and that they have remained with them in a latent state ; they make a part of the cerebral material necessary to the spirit who manifests himself; they are the elements which facilitate the way for him to communicate his own ideas ; for these mediums are but instruments for him, more intelligent and more easily managed than an animal would be.   ERASTUS."

Mediums for Trivial and Obscene Communications. These words indicate the kind of communications that certain mediums habitually receive, and the nature of the spirit who makes them.   Whoever has studied the spirit world in all the degrees of its scale, knows that there are those whose perversity equals that of the most depraved men, and who are pleased to express their thoughts in the grossest terms.   Others, less abject, are contented with trivial expressions.   These mediums should desire to be relieved from the preference these spirits accord them, and should envy those who, in the communications they receive, have never had an unwholesome word.   One must have a strange aberration of ideas, and an utter divorce from good sense, to believe such language could be that of good spirits.

4. *According to the Physical Qualities of the Mediums.*

194. *Calm Mediums.* They always write with a certain slowness, and without experiencing the least agitation.

Rapid Mediums write with a rapidity greater than they could voluntarily, in the ordinary state ; spirits communicate with them with the velocity of lightning ; it might be said, they have a superabundance of fluid, which permits their instantaneous identification with the spirit.   This quality has sometimes its inconvenience, the rapidity of the writing making it very difficult to read for any other but the medium.

"It is also very fatiguing, for it expends too much fluid uselessly."

Convulsive Mediums. They are in an almost feverish state of over-excitement ; their hand, and sometimes their whole person, is agitated with a trembling they cannot master. The primary cause is, without doubt, in the organization, but it depends also much on the nature of the spirits who communicate with them ; good and benevolent spirits always make a gentle and agreeable impression ; the bad, on the contrary, a painful one.

"Mediums should use but rarely their medianimic faculty, where the too frequent use of it may affect the nervous system." (Chapter on *Identity*, distinction between good and bad spirits.)

5. *According to the Moral Qualities of the Medium.*

195. We mention them summarily to memorize and complete the list ; but they will be developed by and by in the special chapters, — *On the Moral Influence of Mediums ; On Obsession ; On Identity of Spirits ;* and others to which we call particular attention ; the influence which the qualities and whims of the mediums can exercise on the certainty of communications, and who are those we can reasonably consider imperfect mediums, or good ones, will then be seen.

Imperfect Mediums.

196. *Obsessed Mediums.* Those who cannot rid themselves of importunate and deceiving spirits, but who are not deceived.

Fascinated Mediums. Those who are directed by deceiving spirits, and are deluded in the nature of the communications they receive.

Subjugated Mediums. Those who are subjected to a moral, and often material domination, on the part of bad spirits.

Trifling Mediums. Those who do not accept their faculty as serious, and use it only for amusement, or for futile things.

Indifferent Mediums. Those who draw no moral profit from the instructions, and in no way modify their conduct or their habits.

Presumptuous Mediums. Those who pretend that they alone are *en rapport* with superior spirits. They believe in their own infallibility, and regard as inferior and erroneous all that does not emanate from them.

Haughty Mediums. Those who are vain of the communications they receive; they think they have nothing more to learn of Spiritism, and do not take to themselves the lessons they often receive on the part of the spirits. They are not contented with the faculties they possess; they would have all.

Susceptible Mediums. A variety of the haughty mediums; they are wounded by the criticisms of which their communications may be the object; they are angry at the least contradiction, and if they show what they obtain, it is to have it admired, and not to ask advice. Generally, they take an aversion to the persons who do not applaud them without reserve, and desert the reunions they cannot impose upon and control.

" Let them go and strut elsewhere, and seek ears more complaisant, or withdraw into isolation; the reunions they deprive of their presence do not sustain a very great loss.   ERASTUS."

Mercenary Mediums. Those who sell their faculty.

Ambitious Mediums. Those who, without putting a

price on their faculty, yet hope to draw from it some advantages.

Insincere Mediums. Those who, having real faculties, simulate those they have not, for the sake of being important. The title of medium cannot be given to those who, having no medianimic faculty, produce effects only by jugglery.

Egotistic Mediums. Those who use their faculty only for personal use, and keep for themselves all the communications they receive.

Jealous Mediums. Those who see with envy other mediums better appreciated, and who are their superiors.

All these bad qualities have, necessarily, their counterparts in good.

Good Mediums.

197. *Serious Mediums.* Those who use their faculty only for good and for really useful purposes ; they would consider it profaned if used for the satisfaction of the curious and indifferent, or for trifles.

Modest Mediums. Those who take no merit to themselves for the communications they receive, however beautiful they may be ; they regard themselves, in connection with it, as strangers, and do not consider themselves proof against mystifications. Far from avoiding disinterested advice, they solicit it.

Devoted Mediums. Those who understand that the true medium has a mission to fulfill, and should, when it is necessary, sacrifice tastes, habits, pleasures, time, and even his material interests, to the good of others.

Certain Mediums. Those who, with facility of execution, deserve the most confidence, by their own character, the elevated nature of the spirits, whose assistants they are, and who are the least exposed to be deceived. We shall see, by and by, that this security depends not at all on the names, more or less respectable, that the spirits take.

"It is incontestable, you can readily see, that thus criticising the qualities and whims of mediums, will excite contrarieties, and even animosities, with some; but what matter? Mediumship is spreading day by day, and more and more, and the medium who would take these reflections amiss would prove one thing — that he is not a good medium, or is assisted by bad spirits. Then, too, as I have already said, it is but for a time; and bad mediums, or those who abuse or misuse their faculties, will suffer the sad consequences, as some have already done; they will learn to their cost what it is to turn to the profit of their worldly passions a gift which God has given them for their moral advancement. If you cannot lead them into the good path, pity them, for I can tell you they are cast away by God.   ERASTUS."

"This descriptive list is of great importance, not only for sincere mediums, who will truly seek, in reading it, to avoid the dangers to which they are exposed, but also for those who make use of mediums, because it will show them what they may rationally expect in it. It should be always kept in view by every one engaged in manifestations, the same as the *Spirit Scale*, which is its complement: these two descriptive lists sum up all the principles of the doctrine, and will contribute more than may be supposed to restore Spiritism to its true mission.   SOCRATES."

198. All these varieties of mediums present infinite degrees in their intensity: there are many which constitute but shades, properly speaking, but which are

not the less effects of special aptitudes. It may easily be supposed that the faculty of a medium being rigorously circumscribed to one single kind is quite rare ; the same medium can, doubtless, have several tendencies, but there is always a governing one, and to the cultivation of that one he should devote himself if it be useful.

It is a serious wrong to wish to press to the development a faculty one does not possess : all those whose germs are seen to be within us should be cultivated, but to pursue the others is, in the first place, to lose time, and, in the second place, to lose, perhaps, — weaken, certainly, — those with which we are endowed.

"When the principle, the germ of a faculty, exists, it is always shown by unequivocal signs. By adhering to his speciality the medium may excel, and obtain grand and beautiful things ; in trying to do all, he will do nothing well. Be it remarked, in passing, that the desire to extend indefinitely the circle of his faculties is a haughty presumption that the spirits never leave unpunished ; the good always abandon the presumptuous, who thus become the sport of lying spirits.

"Unhappily, it is not rare to see mediums discontented with the gifts they have received, and aspire, from self-love or ambition, to possess exceptional faculties, that they may be noticed ; this presumption destroys their most precious quality — that of *sure* mediums.

"SOCRATES."

199. The study of the speciality of mediums is necessary, not only for these, but for the invocator. According to the nature of the spirit whom it is desired to call, and the questions to be addressed to him, it is proper to choose the medium most suitable to the

purpose ; to take the first one at hand is to be exposed to the reception of incomplete or erroneous answers. Let us take a comparison from ordinary usage. An editorial, even a simple copy, would not be confided to the first comer, because he might know how to write. A musician wants a bit of singing executed, of his own composition ; he has at his disposal several singers, all skillful ; yet he does not take by chance : he will choose for his interpreter the one whose voice, expression, all whose qualities, in fact, best answer to the nature of the music. The spirits do the same with regard to the medium, and we should do as do the spirits.

It is, besides, to be remarked, that the shades that mediumship presents, and to which others might be added, are not always related to the character of the medium ; thus, for instance, a medium naturally gay and jovial, might habitually have grave, even severe communications, and *vice versa ;* here, again, is an evident proof that he acts under a foreign influence. We shall return to this subject in the chapter that treats of the *Moral Influence of the Medium*.

CHAPTER XVII.

FORMATION OF MEDIUMS.

Development of Mediumship. — Change of Writing. — Loss and Suspension of Mediumship.

Development of Mediumship.

200. WE shall speak here especially of writing mediums, because that is the most wide-spread mediumship, and because it is, at the same time, the simplest and most convenient, that which gives the most satisfactory and most complete results; it is also the one all persons desire. Unhappily, up to this time there is no diagnostic that can indicate, even approximately, the possession of this faculty; the physical signs in which some have believed they could discover such indications have in them no certainty. It is found in children and in the aged, among men and among women, whatever may be the temperament, the state of health, the degree of intellectual or moral development. There is but one single means to prove its existence; that is to make the trial.

Writing can be obtained, as we have seen, by means of baskets and planchettes, or directly with the hand; this last method being the easier, and, we may say, the only one at present employed, it is the one to which we shall give the preference. The process is of the simplest: it consists solely in taking pencil and paper,

246

and the position of writing, without other preparation ; but to succeed, several recommendations are indispensable.

201. As a material point, we recommend the avoidance of everything that can interfere with the free motion of the hand ; it is even preferable that it should not rest at all on the paper. The point of the pencil should rest enough to trace, but not enough to experience any resistance. All these precautions are useless when the person has come to write easily, for then no obstacle can arrest it : these are only the preliminaries of the scholar.

202. It is indifferent whether the pen or the pencil be used ; some mediums prefer the pen ; but it is only convenient to those who are formed and who write steadily ; there are some who write with such velocity that the use of the pen would be almost impossible, or, at least, very inconvenient ; it is the same when the writing is jerky and irregular, or when violent spirits are communicating, who strike with the point, and break it, tearing the paper.

203. The desire of all who aspire to be mediums is, naturally, to be able to converse with the spirits of persons who are dear to them ; but they must moderate their impatience, for communication with an especial spirit frequently offers material difficulties that render it impossible for the beginner. In order that a spirit may communicate, there must be between him and the medium fluidic relations, which are not always instantly established ; it is only as the faculty is developed that the medium acquires, little by little, the fitness to enter into relation with the first comer. It may be, then, that the one with whom communication is desired may not be in propitious condition to make it, *notwithstand-*

ing his presence, as it may also be that he has neither the possibility nor the permission to come at the call that is made. This is why it is best, in the beginning, not to persist in asking for one spirit to the exclusion of all others ; for it often happens that fluidic relations are not established with that one most easily, whatever may be the sympathy for him. So, before expecting to obtain communications from such or such a spirit, it is necessary to press the development of the faculty, and for that purpose make a general appeal, and, above all, address yourself to your guardian angel.

There is no particular form to be used ; whoever pretends to give one may boldly be taxed with jugglery, because, for spirits, form is nothing. The invocation should always be made in the name of God ; it may be made in the following terms, or in something equivalent : *I pray Almighty God to permit a good spirit to communicate with me, and make me write ; I pray, also, my guardian angel kindly to help me, and drive away bad spirits.* Then wait until a spirit manifests himself by writing something. It may be that it will be the one desired, or it may be the spirit of a stranger, or the guardian angel ; in any case he generally makes himself known by writing his name ; but then comes the question of *identity*, one that requires the most experience, for there are few beginners who are not liable to be deceived. We treat of this afterward in a special chapter.

When it is desired to call certain spirits, it is very essential, in the beginning, to address only those known to be good and sympathetic, and who might have a motive for coming, as relations or friends. In this case the invocation might be thus expressed : *In the name of Almighty God I pray the spirit of such a*

one, to communicate with me : or, *I pray Almighty God
to permit the spirit of so and so to communicate with
me :* or any other form answering to the same thought.
It is not the less necessary that the first questions
should be so contrived that the answer may be simply
yes or *no*, as, for instance, *Are you there ? Will you
answer me ? Can you make me write ?* &c. Later this
precaution will be useless : we are speaking only of the
beginning, when the relation is to be established : the
essential thing is, that the question be not useless ; that
it does not pertain to things of private interest ; and
above all, that it be the expression of a benevolent and
sympathetic sentiment for the spirit addressed. (See,
later, the special chapter on *Invocations.*)

204. One thing still more important to observe
than the mode of appeal, is calm and concentration of
thought joined to an ardent desire and a firm will to
succeed ; and, by will, we do not understand an ephemeral will, that acts by jerks, and is, at each minute,
interrupted by other preoccupations ; but a serious,
persevering, sustained will, *without impatience or feverish desire.* Concentration of thought is favored by
solitude, silence, and the removal of all that might dis-
tract the attention. But one thing more remains to be
done ; every day renew the effort for ten minutes or a
quarter of an hour, and that during fifteen days, a
month, two months, and more if necessary : we know
mediums who were not formed until after six months'
practice, while others write easily from the first.

205. To avoid useless attempts, a serious and advanced spirit can be interrogated through another
medium ; but we must here remark that when the
question of whether a person is or is not a medium is
addressed to the spirits, they almost always answer

affirmatively, which yet does not prevent the efforts from being unfruitful. This may be very naturally explained. A general question is put to the spirit; he answers in a general manner; for, as every one knows, nothing is more elastic than the medianimic faculty, as it can be displayed under the most varied forms, and in very different degrees. A person thus may be a medium without perceiving it, and in a different sense from the one thought of. To this vague question, Am I a medium? the spirit may answer, Yes: to the more exact one, Am I a writing medium? he may answer, No. The nature of the spirit questioned must also be taken into consideration; there are some so trifling and so ignorant that they answer at random, like veritable dunces: this is why we say, address enlightened spirits, who usually answer these questions willingly, and indicate the best method to pursue if there is a possibility of success.

206. One method, which often succeeds, consists in employing as temporary auxiliary a good, flexible writing medium already formed. If he rests his hand or his fingers on the hand that is wanted to write, it is seldom that it does not succeed immediately: this is easily comprehended: the hand that holds the pencil becomes, in a manner, an appendage to the hand of the medium, like a basket or a planchette; but that does not prevent this exercise from being very useful when it can be done, inasmuch as if, often and regularly repeated, it helps to overcome the material obstacle, and develop the faculty. Magnetizing strongly the arm and hand will sometimes suffice; often even the magnetizer may simply rest his hand on the shoulder, and we have seen persons write at once under this influence. The same effect may be pro-

duced without contact, by the sole effort of will. It may easily be seen that the confidence of the magnetizer to produce this result will make a great difference, and that a skeptical one would have little or no action.

The concurrence of an experienced guide is, besides, sometimes useful to make the beginner observe a number of little precautions, which he often neglects, to the detriment of the rapidity of his progress ; and especially to enlighten him on the nature of the first questions, and the manner of proposing them. His part is that of a professor, to be dispensed with when the person is sufficiently skillful.

207. Another means, that may also powerfully contribute to the development of the faculty, consists in gathering together a certain number of persons all animated by the same desire and by a community of intention ; then let all simultaneously, in absolute silence, and with a religious concentration, try to write, each appealing to his guardian angel or to some sympathetic spirit. One of them may, without special designation, and for all the members of the assembly, make a general appeal to good spirits, saying, for instance, *In the name of Almighty God, we pray good spirits to please communicate by the persons here present.* It is very seldom that among the number there will not be some who give prompt signs of mediumship, or even write easily in a very short time.

This can be readily explained. Persons united by a community of intention form a collective whole, whose power and susceptibility are increased by a kind of magnetic influence which aids in the development of the faculty. Among the spirits attracted by this concourse of wills, there are some who find the instrument suited to them ; if not one, it will be another, and they profit by it.

This method is suited to a circle of spiritists who are in want of mediums, or who have not a sufficient number.

208. Processes for the formation of mediums have been sought for as people seek diagnostics ; but as yet we know of none more efficacious than those we have indicated. In the persuasion that the obstacle to the development of the faculty is an entirely material resistance, some pretend to overcome it by a kind of gymnastics almost dislocating the arm and head. We do not describe this process, which comes to us from across the Atlantic, not only because we have no proof of its efficacy, but from the conviction we have that it may be dangerous to delicate constitutions by the disturbance of the nervous system. If the rudiments of the faculty do not exist, nothing can give them, not even electricity, which has been unsuccessfully employed for the same end.

209. Faith in the apprentice medium is not an absolute condition ; it seconds the efforts, certainly, but is not indispensable : purity of intention, desire, and good will are sufficient. Perfectly skeptical persons have been known to be surprised by writing in spite of themselves, while sincere believers could not ; which proves this faculty to be an organic predisposition. (Note 10.)

210. The first indication of a disposition to write, is a kind of trembling in the arm and hand ; little by little the hand is carried along by an impulse that it cannot master. It often traces, at first, but insignificant signs ; then the characters are drawn more and more clearly, and it ends by acquiring the rapidity of

ordinary writing. In all cases the hand must be abandoned to its natural movement, neither resisting nor propelling.

Some mediums write easily and rapidly from the beginning, sometimes even from the first sitting, which is quite rare; others for a long time make lines and genuine calligraphic exercises; the spirits say to limber the hand. If these exercises are too prolonged, or degenerate into ridiculous signs, there can be no doubt it is a spirit amusing himself, for good spirits never do anything useless: in such case it is necessary to appeal to them with redoubled fervor. If, in spite of that, there is no change, stop as soon as it is found nothing serious can be obtained. The attempt may be renewed daily, but it is best to cease at the first equivocal signs, so as not to give such satisfaction to mocking spirits.

To these observations a spirit adds, "There are mediums whose faculty cannot go beyond these signs; when, at the end of some months, they obtain nothing but insignificant things, *yes* or *no*, or letters without continuance, it is useless to persist in soiling paper in pure loss: they are mediums, but *unproductive mediums*. The first communications obtained should be considered only as exercises confided to secondary spirits; but slight importance should be atached to them, because of the spirits who are, so to say, employed as writing-masters to teach the beginner; for believe not that they are elevated spirits who take the medium through these preparatory exercises; only it happens that, if the medium have no serious end in view, these spirits remain, and attach themselves to him. Nearly all mediums have gone through this crucible to be developed; it is for them to do all they can to conciliate truly superior spirits.

211. The rock on which most debutants split, is having to do with inferior spirits; and they should think themselves happy when they are only trifling spirits. All their attention should be given to not allowing them to take footing; for once anchored it is not always easy to be relieved from them. This is such a special point, particularly in the beginning, that, without the necessary precautions, the fruit of the finest faculties may be lost.

The primary point consists in putting one's self, with a sincere faith, under the protection of God, and imploring the assistance of one's guardian angel, who is always good, while the familiar spirit, sympathizing with the good or bad qualities of the medium, may be trifling, or even bad.

The second point is to ascertain with scrupulous care, by every indication experience furnishes, the nature of the first spirits that communicate, and of whom it is always prudent to beware. If these indications are suspicious, a fervent appeal must be made to the guardian angel, and the bad spirit repulsed with the whole strength, proving to him that you are not his dupe, in order to discourage him. This is why a previous study of the theory is indispensable, if the dangers inseparable from inexperience would be avoided: fully developed instructions on this subject will be found in the chapters on *Obsession and Identity of Spirits.* We shall limit ourselves at this time to saying that, besides the language, all signs, figures, useless or trifling emblems, all absurd writing, jerky, designedly twisted, of exaggerated dimensions, or affecting ridiculous or unusual forms, are infallible proofs of the inferiority of the spirits ; the writing may be very bad, quite illegible even, which is more the fault of the medium than of the spirit, without being at all unusual. We have seen mediums so deceived that they measure the superiority of the spirits by the dimensions of the characters, and who attached great importance to letters modelled like print — a puerility evidently incompatible with real superiority.

212. If it is important not to fall unwillingly into the power of bad spirits, it is still more so not to put one's self into a state of dependence upon them voluntarily ; and an immoderate desire to write should not lead to the belief that it is indifferent to address the first comer, hoping to be rid of him later, if he should not suit, for assistance in anything is not asked of a bad spirit with impunity ; he can always make one pay dearly for his services.

Some persons, impatient for the development in themselves of the medianimic faculty, — too slow in its growth for them, — have had the idea of calling to their aid any spirit whatever, *even a bad one*, intending to dismiss him afterward. Many have been served to their wish, and have written at once ; but the spirit, not caring to be taken as a makeshift, has been less docile to go than to come. We know some who have been punished for their presumption in thinking themselves strong enough to drive them away as they pleased, by years of obsessions of every kind, by the most ridiculous mystifications, by a tenacious fascination, and even by *material* misfortunes and the most cruel deceptions. The spirit at first showed himself openly wicked, then hypocritical, in order to lead to a belief in his conversion, or in the pretended power of his victim, to drive him away at will.

213. The writing is sometimes very legible, words and letters perfectly detached ; but with some mediums it is difficult to decipher for any other than the one who writes it ; the habit must be acquired. It is quite often formed in large characters ; the spirits are little economical of paper. When a word or phrase is illegible, ask the spirit to please begin again, which he is usually willing to do. When the writing is habitually illegible, even for the medium, he can almost always succeed in obtaining clearer copy by frequent and continued practice, *bringing to it a strong will*, and earnestly requesting the spirit to be more correct. Some spirits often adopt conventional signs, which pass current in habitual circles. To mark when a question displeases them, or they do not wish to answer, they will, for instance, make a long bar, or something equivalent.

When the spirit has finished what he had to say, or will no longer answer, the hand remains immovable, and the medium, be his power and will what they may, can obtain no further word. On the contrary, until the spirit has finished, the pencil goes on without the hand being able to stop it. If he wish to say something spontaneously, the hand seizes the pencil convulsively, and begins to write without power to oppose it. The medium almost always feels within him something that indicates, if it is only a suspension, or if the spirit has ended. It is seldom he does not feel when he is gone.

Such are the most essential explanations we have to give concerning the development of psychography ; experience will show, in the practice, certain details useless to bring in here, and for which each one must be guided by general principles. Let every one try, and there will be found more mediums than are supposed.

214. All that we have said applies to mechanical writing; it is that all mediums seek to obtain, and with reason; but purely mechanical writing is very rare; it is more or less mixed with intuition. The medium, having the consciousness of what he writes, is, naturally, prone to doubt his faculty; he does not know if it comes from himself or the foreign spirit. He need not be disquieted, and should continue all the same; let him observe with care, and he will easily recognize in what he writes a crowd of things not in his thought, that even are contrary to it — evident proof that they do not come from him. Let him then continue, and doubt will be dissipated by experience.

215. If it is not given to a medium to be entirely mechanical, all attempts to obtain this result will be fruitless; yet he will do wrong to think himself disinherited: if he be endowed only with intuitive mediumship, he must be content with it, and it will not fail to be of great service to him, if he knows how to profit by it, and does not repulse it.

If, after useless attempts followed up for some time, no indication of involuntary movement is produced. or if these movements are too weak to give results, he should not hesitate to write the first thought suggested to him, without troubling himself as to whether it come from himself or a foreign source; experience will teach him to make the distinction. It very often happens that the mechanical movement will be ulteriorly developed.

We have said above that there are cases in which it is indifferent to know if the thought is from the medium or a foreign spirit ; when a purely intuitive or inspired medium writes a work of imagination, it is little matter if he should attribute to himself a thought suggested to him ; if good ideas come to him, let him thank his good genius, and he will have other good ones suggested to him. Such is the inspiration of poets, philosophers, and savants.

216. Let us now suppose the medianimic faculty completely developed ; that the medium writes with facility ; in a word, let him be what is called a formed medium ; it will be very wrong on his part to think he can dispense with all further instruction ; he has over-come only a material resistance ; but then begin for him the real difficulties, and he has, more than ever, need of the advice of prudence and experience, if he would not fall into the thousand traps that will be set for him. If he would fly with his own wings, it will not be long before he will be the dupe of lying spirits, who will try to make capital from his presumption.

217. When the faculty is developed with a medium, it is essential that he should not abuse it. The satis-faction it gives to some beginners excites in them an enthusiasm it is important to moderate ; they should remember that it is given to them to do good, and not to satisfy a vain curiosity ; this is why it is best to use it only at opportune moments, and not at every in-stant ; spirits not being constantly at their orders, they run the risk of being dupes of mystifiers. It is well to adopt certain days and hours for this purpose, for then greater concentration can be brought to it, and the spirits who desire to come are informed, and consequently prepared.

218. If, in spite of all efforts, mediumship is in no way revealed, it must be renounced, as a person gives

up singing who has no voice. One who does not know a language uses an interpreter ; he must do the same here, that is, have recourse to another medium. In default of a medium, he must not think himself deprived of the assistance of the spirits. Mediumship is for them a means of expressing themselves, but not an exclusive means of attraction ; those who love us are near us whether we be mediums or not : a father does not abandon his child because this child is deaf and blind, and can neither see him nor hear him ; he surrounds him with his solicitude as the good spirits do for us ; if they cannot transmit their thoughts to us materially, they come to aid us by inspiration.

Change of Writing.

219. A very ordinary phenomenon, with writing mediums, is the change of writing according to the spirits who communicate ; and what is more remarkable, the same writing is constantly reproduced with the same spirit, and sometimes it is identical with that he had while living ; we shall see, by and by, the results that may be drawn from this as to identity. The change of writing takes place only with those mediums who are mechanical or semi-mechanical, because with them the movement of the hand is involuntary, and directed by the spirit ; it is not the same with mediums purely intuitive, for in such case the spirit acts solely on the thought, and the hand is directed by the will, as in ordinary circumstances, but the uniformity of the writing, even with a mechanical medium, proves absolutely nothing against the faculty, change not being an absolute condition in the manifestations of the spirits ; it pertains to a special aptitude, with which the most mechanical mediums are not always

endowed.   We designate those who have this aptitude under the name of *polygraphic mediums*.

Loss and Suspension of Mediumship.

220. The medianimic faculty is subject to intermissions and temporary suspensions, whether for physical manifestations or for writing.   We give the answers of the spirits to some questions on this subject.

1. "Can mediums lose their faculty?"

"That very often happens, whatever kind it may be ; but often it is only a temporary interruption, which ceases with the cause that produced it."

2. "Is the cause of this loss the exhaustion of the fluid ? "

"With whatever faculty the medium may be endowed, he can do nothing without the sympathetic concurrence of the spirits ; when he obtains nothing, it is not always that the faculty is lacking, but that the spirits will, or can, no longer use him."

3. "For what cause would the spirits abandon him ? "

" The use he makes of his faculty is the most powerful with good spirits.   We may abandon him when he uses it for frivolities or for ambition ; when he refuses to impart our words or our facts to the incarnated who call to him, or who need to see in order to be convinced.   This gift of God is not granted to the medium for his good pleasure, and still less to serve his ambition, but for his own advancement, and to make known the truth to men.   If the spirit sees that the medium no longer answers his views, and does not profit by his instructions, and by the warnings he gives him, he retires to find a more worthy protégé.

4. "Might not the spirit who withdraws be replaced,

and thus the suspension of the faculty not be under-stood ? "

" Spirits are not wanting who ask nothing better than to communicate, and are ready enough to replace those who withdraw ; but when it is a good spirit who forsakes the medium, it may very well be that he leaves him only temporarily, and deprives him for a certain time of all communication in order to give him a lesson, and prove to him that his faculty *depends not on himself*, and that he should not be vain of it. This temporary impotence is also to give the medium a proof that he writes under a foreign influence ; other-wise there would be no intermittence in it.

" Yet the interruption of the faculty is not always in punishment ; it is sometimes a proof of the solicitude of the spirit for the medium, whom he loves ; he would by that means procure him a material rest, which he sees to be necessary, and in such case he does not permit other spirits to replace him."

5. " Yet we see mediums, very meritorious in a moral point of view, who experience no need of rest, and are annoyed by interruptions, whose motive they cannot understand."

" It is in order to put their patience to the proof, and to judge of their perseverance ; this is why the spirits assign no general end to this suspension ; they wish to see if the medium will become disheartened. It is often, also, to leave them time to meditate on the in-structions they have given them, and this meditation on our teachings we recommend to all truly serious spiritists ; we cannot give this name to those who, in reality, are only amateurs of communications."

6. " Is it necessary in this case for the medium to continue his attempts to write ? "

"If the spirit so advise him, yes: if he tells him to abstain, he should do so."

7. "Is there any way to abridge this trial?"

"Resignation and prayer. It is enough that he make the attempt for a few minutes every day, for it would be useless to lose time in fruitless efforts; the attempt has no other end but to see if the faculty is recovered."

8. "Does the suspension imply the absence of the spirits who were accustomed to communicate?"

"Not the least in the world; the medium is then like a person who has temporarily lost his sight, but is none the less surrounded by his friends, though he cannot see them. The medium can then, and should, continue to converse by thought with his familiar spirits, and feel convinced that he is heard by them. If the lack of mediumship can deprive him of material communications with spirits, it cannot deprive of moral communications."

9. "Then the interruption of the medianimic faculty does not always imply blame on the part of the spirits?"

"No, doubtless; for it may be a proof of good will."

10. "By what sign can blame be recognized in the interruption?"

"Let the medium question his conscience; let him ask himself what use he has made of his faculty; the good that has resulted from it to others; *the profit he has drawn* from the advice that has been given him, and he will have the answer."

11. "Cannot the medium who can no longer write have recourse to another medium?"

"That depends upon the cause of the interruption;

it may often have for a motive to leave you some time without communications, after having given you advice, in order that you may not become accustomed to do nothing without us ; in such case he will be no more satisfied in using another medium ; and in that is still a motive, to prove to you that the spirits are free, and that you cannot make them come and go at your will. It is also for this reason that those who are not mediums do not always have all the communications they desire."

Remark. It must be observed that he who has recourse to a third for communications, notwithstanding the quality of the medium, often obtains nothing satisfactory, while at other times the answers are very explicit. That depends so much on the will of the spirit, that you are no further advanced by changing the medium ; the spirits even seem in that respect to give each other the word, for if nothing is obtained from one, you get no more from another. We should be careful not to persist or become impatient, if we would not be the dupe of deceiving spirits, who will answer if we wish it with all our strength, and the good will allow them, to punish us for our persistence.

12. " For what reason has Providence endowed certain individuals with mediumship in a special manner ?"

" It is a mission with which they are charged, and which they are happy in filling ; they are interpreters between spirits and men."

13. " Yet there are mediums who employ their faculty only with repugnance."

" Those are imperfect mediums ; they do not know the value of the favor accorded to them."

14. " If it be a mission, how does it happen that it

is not the privilege of good men, and that this faculty should be given to people who merit no esteem, and who may abuse it ? "

" It is given to them because they need it for their own advancement, and in order that they may receive good instruction ; if they do not profit by it, they will suffer the consequences.   Did not Jesus prefer to give His word to fishermen, saying, He must give to him who has not ? "

15. " Should those who have a great desire to write, and who cannot succeed, conclude there is something against them in the kind feelings of the spirits on this account ? "

" No ; for God may have refused them this faculty, as He may have refused them the gift of poetry or music ; but if they have not this favor, they may have others."

16. " How can a man perfect himself by the instructions of spirits, when he has neither by himself, nor by other mediums, the means of directly receiving this teaching ? "

" Has he not books, as the Christian has the Gospel ? To practice the morality of Jesus, the Christian does not need to hear the words from His very mouth."

Chapter XVIII.

INCONVENIENCES AND DANGERS OF MEDIUMSHIP.

Influence of the Exercise of Mediumship on the Health; on the Brain; on Children.

221. 1. " Is the medianimic faculty an indication of a pathological state, or simply abnormal ? "

" Abnormal sometimes, but not pathological ; there are mediums of robust health ; those who are sick are so from other causes."

2. " Can the exercise of the medianimic faculty occasion fatigue ? "

" The too prolonged exercise of any faculty whatever leads to fatigue: mediumship is the same, principally those who apply themselves to physical effects ; it necessarily occasions an outlay of fluid which leads to fatigue, and is repaired by rest."

3. " Has the exercise of mediumship dangers of itself, in a hygienic point of view, even if not abused ? "

" There are cases where it is prudent, necessary even, to abstain from it, or, at least, to moderate its use ; that depends on the physical and moral state of the medium. Besides, the medium generally feels it, and when he experiences fatigue, he should abstain."

4. " Are there some persons for whom this exercise is more unsuitable than for others ? "

" I have said that it depends upon the physical and

moral state of the medium. There are persons to whom it is necessary to avoid every cause for excitement, and this is of the number." (Nos. 188–194.)

5. " Can mediumship produce insanity ? "

" No more than anything else, when there is no predisposition, owing to weakness of the brain. Mediumship will not produce insanity when the germ is not there ; but if the germ exists, which is very easy to know from the moral state, good sense says that careful management is necessary in every way, for the least shock might be injurious."

6. " Is there danger in developing mediumship in children ? "

" Certainly ; and I maintain that it is very dangerous ; for these tender and delicate organizations would be too much shaken, and their young imagination over-excited. Wise parents will remove all these ideas from them, or at least speak to them only of the moral consequences."

7. " Yet there are children who are naturally mediums for physical effects, for writing, and for visions : has that dangers ? "

" No ; when the faculty is spontaneous in a child, it is in its nature, and its constitution agrees with it ; it is not the same when induced and over-excited. Remark, that the child who has visions is generally very little impressed by them ; it seems to him a perfectly natural thing, to which he gives but little attention, and often forgets : later the fact returns to his mind, and if he knows anything of Spiritism, he can easily explain it."

8. " At what age, without danger, can a person practice mediumship ? "

" There is no precise age ; it depends upon development, physical, but still more upon moral.   There are children of twelve years who would be less affected by it than some grown persons.   I speak of mediumship in general, but that which applies to physical effects is more fatiguing, corporeally ; writing has one great danger for a child, on account of inexperience ; he might engage in it alone, and make it a matter of sport."

222. The practice of Spiritism, as we shall see, demands much tact to unmask the tricks of deceiving spirits ; if grown men are their dupes, childhood and youth are still more exposed, from their inexperience. It is well known that concentration of thought is a condition without which we can have no intercourse with serious spirits ; invocations made with carelessness, or in a joking way, are a real profanation, which gives easy access to mocking or mischievous spirits ; and as the necessary gravity for such an act cannot be expected of a child, it may readily be feared that, if left to himself, he would make a play of it.   Even under the most favorable conditions, it is to be desired that a child gifted with the medianimic faculty should exercise it only under the eye of experienced persons, who will teach him, by their example, the respect due to souls that have already lived.

It will be seen from this, that the question of age is subordinate to the circumstances as much of temperament as of character.   At all events, the clear results of the answers given above are not to press this faculty to development with children, when it is not spontaneous, and that, in all cases, it must be used with great circumspection ; that it must be neither excited nor encouraged in debilitated persons.   Those who have ever displayed the least symptoms of eccentricity, either in ideas or in weakness of mental faculties, should, by every possible means, be dissuaded from it ; for there is, with them, an evident predisposition to insanity, which any too exciting cause may develop. The spirit ideas have not a greater influence for this, but insanity, once aroused, would take the character of the predominant preoccupation, as it would take a religious character, if the person abandons himself to excess in devotional practices ; and every one would consider Spiritism responsible. The best thing to do with any one who shows a tendency toward a fixed idea, is to direct his mind to other things, that so the weakened organs may rest.

In this connection, we call the attention of our reader to paragraph XII. of the introduction to the *Book on Spirits.*

CHAPTER XIX.

ROLE OF THE MEDIUM IN SPIRIT COMMUNICATIONS.

Influence of the Personal Spirit of the Medium. — System of Inert Mediums. — Aptitude of some Mediums for Things they do not know: Languages, Music, Drawing, &c. — Dissertation of a Spirit on the Rôle of Mediums.

223. 1. "Is the medium, at the time of exercising his faculty, in a perfectly normal state?"

"He is sometimes in a state of crisis more or less pronounced; this is what fatigues him, and why he needs rest; but more often his state does not sensibly differ from the normal state, especially in writing mediums."

2. "Can written or verbal communications also proceed from the spirit incarnated in the medium?"

"The soul of the medium may communicate, like that of any other; if it enjoy a certain degree of liberty it recovers its qualities of spirit. You have the proof of this in the soul of living persons who come to visit you, and communicate to you by writing, often without your calling them.

"For you must know that among the spirits you invoke, there are some who are incarnated on the earth; *then they talk to you as spirits, and not as men.*

269

Why should you suppose it cannot be the same with that of the medium ? "

" This explanation seems to confirm the opinion of those who believe that all communications emanate from the spirit of the medium, and not from foreign spirits."

" They are wrong only because they are absolute ; for while it is certain that the spirit of the medium can act by himself, this is no reason that others cannot act through him."

3. " How may it be known if the spirit who answers is that of the medium, or a foreign spirit."

"By the nature of the communications. Study the circumstances and the language, and you will distinguish. It is more particularly in the state of somnambulism, or ecstasy, that the spirit of the medium manifests itself, because it is then more free ; but in the normal state, it is more difficult. Besides, there are answers it is impossible to ascribe to him : this is why I tell you to study and observe."

Remark. When a person speaks to us, we readily distinguish what comes from him, or what is only an echo ; it is the same with mediums.

4. " As the spirit of the medium may have acquired knowledge in his former existences, which he has forgotten under his corporeal envelope, but which he remembers as spirit, can he not draw from his own sources the ideas that seem to surpass the breadth of his instruction ? "

" That often happens in the somnambulic or ecstatic crisis ; but even then there are circumstances that admit no doubt ; study long and meditate."

5. " Are the communications coming from the me-

dium always inferior to those that might be made by foreign spirits ? "

" Not always ; for the foreign spirit may himself be of an order inferior to that of the medium, and then speak less sensibly. It is seen in somnambulism, for then it is most often the somnambulist's spirit who manifests himself, and who yet says some very good things."

6. " Does the spirit who communicates by a medium transmit his thought direct ; or has he the spirit incarnated in the medium as an intermediary ? "

" The spirit of the medium is the interpreter, because he is bound to the body that serves us to speak, and a chain is necessary between you and foreign spirits who communicate, as an electric wire is necessary to transmit news from afar, and at the end of the wire an intelligent person, who receives and transmits it."

7. " Does the spirit incarnated in the medium influence the communications he has to transmit from foreign spirits ? "

" Yes ; if he is not in sympathy with them, he may alter their answers, and assimilate them to his own ideas and inclinations ; *but he does not influence the spirits themselves ;* he is only a bad interpreter."

8. " Is this the cause of the preference of spirits for certain mediums ? "

" There is no other ; they seek the interpreter who best sympathizes with them, and who renders most exactly their thought. If there is not sympathy between them, the spirit of the medium is an antagonist, who brings a resistance, and becomes an ill-willed, and often unfaithful, interpreter. It is the same among you when the advice of a wise man is transmitted by a blunderer or an insincere person."

9. " It can easily be supposed that it may be thus with an intuitive medium, but not with those who are mechanical."

" You do not thoroughly take into consideration the part played by the medium; there is a law in it you have not yet grasped. Remember that to effect the movement of an inert body, the spirit needs a portion of animalized fluid, which he borrows from the medium, to animate, temporarily, the table, before it will obey his will. Well, understand, also, that for an intelligent communication he needs an intelligent intermediary, and that this intermediary is the spirit of the medium."

— " This does not appear applicable to what are called talking tables; for when inert objects, such as tables, planchettes, and baskets give intelligent answers, it seems as if the spirit of the medium has nothing to do with it."

" That is an error; the spirit can give to the inert body a momentary, factitious life, but not intelligence: never has an inert body been intelligent. It is, then, the spirit of the medium who receives the thought unwittingly, and gradually transmits it by the help of various intermediaries."

10. " It seems to result from these explanations that the spirit of the medium is never entirely passive."

" He is passive when he does not mingle his own ideas with those of the foreign spirit, but he is never absolutely null; his concurrence is always necessary as intermediary, even in what you call mechanical mediums."

11. " Is there not a greater guarantee of indepen-

dence in the mechanical medium than in the intuitive?"

"Without doubt; and for some communications a mechanical medium is preferable; but when the faculties of an intuitive medium are known, it is immaterial, according to circumstances; I mean, there are communications that require less precision."

12. "Among the different systems that have been set forth to explain the spirit phenomena, is one which consists in believing that the real mediumship is in a body completely inert — is in the basket or the card, for instance, which serves as the instrument; that the foreign spirit identifies himself with this object, and renders it not only living, but intelligent; from thence the name of *inert mediums* given to these objects. What do you think of it?"

"There is but one word to say to that : if the spirit had transmitted intelligence to the card, at the same time as life, the card would write alone, without the help of the medium; it would be strange if an intelligent man should become a machine, and an inert object should become intelligent. This is one of the many systems born of a preconceived idea, and which, like so many others, fall before experience and observation."

13. "A well-known phenomenon — that of tables, baskets, &c., which express, by their movements, anger or affection — might easily accredit the opinion that there is in animated inert bodies more than intelligence, even life."

"When a man shakes a stick in anger, it is not that the stick is angry, nor even the hand that holds the stick, but the thought that directs the hand; tables and baskets are no more intelligent than the stick;

they have not one intelligent sentiment, but obey an intelligence; in a word, it is not the spirit transformed into a basket, nor even that he lives in it."

14. "If it be not rational to attribute intelligence to these objects, may they be considered as a variety of mediums, designating them as inert mediums?"

"It is but a question of words, which is of little moment to us, provided you understand us. You are free to call a man a puppet."

15. "Spirits have but the language of thought; they have no articulate language; this is why there is, for them, but one single language; according to that, could a spirit express himself through a medium in a language he had never spoken during his lifetime, in such case, from whence would he draw the words he would use?"

"You have answered your own question by saying that spirits have but one language — that of thought; this language is understood by all, as well by men as by spirits. The wandering spirit, in addressing himself to the incarnated spirit of the medium, speaks to him neither French nor English, but the universal language, which is that of thought; to translate his ideas into an articulate, transmissible language, he draws his words from the medium's vocabulary."

16. "If this be so, the spirit would be able to express himself only in the language of the medium; whereas mediums are seen to write in languages unknown to them: is that not a contradiction?"

"Understand, in the first place, that all mediums are not fit for this kind of exercise; and secondly, that the spirits lend themselves to it only incidentally, when they consider it may be useful; but for ordinary communications, and those of some extent, they prefer to use a language familiar to the medium, because it presents less material difficulty to overcome."

17. "Does not the aptitude of some mediums for writing in a language foreign to them proceed from the fact of their having been familiar with this language in another existence, and that they may have preserved an intention of it?"

"That may be, certainly, but it is not a rule; the spirit can, with some effort, temporarily overcome the material resistance he encounters — exactly what happens when the medium writes in his own language words he does not understand."

18. "Could a person who does not know how to write serve as a writing medium?"

"Yes; but you can readily imagine that there would be a great mechanical difficulty to surmount, the hand being unaccustomed to the movement necessary to form the letters. It is the same with drawing mediums, who do not know how to draw."

19. "Could a medium of slight intelligence transmit communications of an elevated order?"

"Yes, by the same means that one can write in a language unknown to him. Mediumship, properly so called, is independent of intelligence as well as of the moral qualities, and in default of a better instrument, the spirit can use the one at hand; but it is natural that, for communications of a certain order, he should prefer the medium who offers the least material obstacles. And, then, another consideration: The idiot is often an idiot only from the imperfection of his organs, but his spirit may be more advanced than you suppose; you have a proof of it by certain invocations of idiots, dead or living."

Remark. This is a fact verified by experience; we

have several times invoked living idiots, who have
given proofs patent of their identity, and answered in
a very sensible and even superior manner.   This state
is a punishment for the spirit who suffers from the
constraint in which he is bound.   An idiot medium
may sometimes offer to the spirit who desires to manifest himself, greater resources than would be supposed.
(See *Revue Spirite*, July, 1860, article on Phrenology
and Physiognomy.)

20. "From whence comes the aptitude of some mediums to write in verse, notwithstanding their positive
ignorance of poetry?"

"Poetry is a language; they can write in verse as
they can write in a language they do not know; and
then, too, they may have been poets in another existence; and, as you have been told, knowledge acquired
is never lost to the spirit, who must attain perfection
in all things.   Thus, what they have known gives them,
doubtless, a facility they do not have in the ordinary
state."

21. "Is it the same for those who have a general aptitude for drawing and music?"

"Yes, drawing and music are also methods of expressing the thought; spirits use the instruments that
offer them the greatest facility."

22. "Does the expression of the thought by poetry,
drawing, or music, depend solely on the special aptitude of the medium, or on that of the spirit who communicates?"

"Sometimes on the medium, sometimes on the spirit.
The superior spirits have all aptitudes, the inferior
spirits have limited knowledge."

23. "Why does the man who has a transcendent
talent in one existence not have it in a following one?"

"It is not always so, for often he perfects in one existence what he began in a preceding one; but it may happen that a transcendent faculty sleeps during a certain time, to leave another more free to be developed; it is a latent germ, which will be found afterward, and of which there *always* remain some traces, or, at least, a vague intuition."

224. The foreign spirit doubtless understands all languages, as languages are the expression of thought, and as the spirit understands by thought; but to render this thought he needs an instrument; this instrument is the medium. The soul of the medium who receives the foreign communication can transmit it only by the organs of his body; and these organs cannot have the same flexibility for an unknown language which they have for the one familiar to them. A medium who knows only French might, incidentally, give an answer in English, for instance, should it please the spirit to do so; but spirits, who already find the human language too slow, considering the rapidity of thought, though they abridge as much as they can, are impatient òf the mechanical resistance they experience; this is why they do not always do it. This is also the reason a novice medium, who writes laboriously and slowly, even in his own language, usually obtains but very brief and undeveloped answers; so the spirits recommend that only simple questions be asked through him. For those of higher bearing it needs a formed medium, who offers no mechanical difficulty to the spirit. We would not take for our reader a scholar who spells. A good workman does not like to use poor implements.

Let us add another consideration of great gravity in what concerns foreign languages. Trials of this kind are always made from curiosity and for experiment, and nothing is more antipathetic to the spirits than the trials to which persons endeavor to subject them. The superior spirits never lend themselves to it, and leave as soon as this is begun. Inasmuch as they like useful and serious things, in so far they dislike to be engaged in frivolities and things without motive. Skeptics will say, "It is to convince us; and that is a useful motive, since it gains believers to their cause." To that the spirits answer, "Our cause has no need of those who have so much pride as to consider themselves indispensable: we call to us *those whom we wish*, and they are often the least and the most humble. Did Jesus perform the miracles demanded of him by the scribes, and what men did he use to revolutionize the world? If you desire to be convinced, you have other means than by tricks; begin first by submitting yourselves: it is not in order that the scholar should impose his will upon his teacher."

It thus results that, with some exceptions, the medium renders the thoughts of the spirits by the mechanical means at his disposal, and that the expression of this thought may, and most often must, partake of the imperfection of these means; thus, the uncultured man, the peasant, might say the most beautiful things, express the most elevated, most philosophical thoughts, speaking as a peasant, for it is well known that with the spirits the thought is all.

This answers the objections of some critics on the subject of the incorrectness of style and of orthography with which they may reproach the spirit, and which may come from the medium, as well as from the spirit. It is frivolous to care for such things. It is not less puerile to take great pains to reproduce such faults with minute exactness, as we sometimes see done. They may be corrected without scruple, at least, unless they be a characteristic type of the spirit who communicates, in which case it is useful to preserve them, as proof of identity. Thus, for instance, we have seen a spirit constantly write *Jule* (without the *s*) in speaking to his grandson, because, during his life, he wrote it in this way, and though his grandson, who served as medium, knew perfectly well how to write his name.

225. The following dissertation, given spontaneously by a superior spirit who revealed himself by communications of the highest order, recapitulates in the clearest and most complete manner, the question of the *rôle* of mediums : " Whatever may be the nature of writing mediums, whether mechanical, semi-mechanical, or simply intuitive, our processes of communication with them do not essentially vary. In fact, with the incarnated spirits themselves, as with the spirits proper, we communicate solely by the radiating of our thought.

" Our thoughts do not need the clothing of words to be understood by spirits, and all spirits perceive the thought you desire to communicate to them, simply by your directing the thought toward them, and this by reason of their intellectual faculties ; that is to say, a certain thought can be comprehended by certain ones according to their advancement, while to certain others the thought, awakening no remembrance, no knowledge in the depths of their heart or brain, is not perceptible to them. In such case the incarnated spirit who serves us as medium is more fit to render our thought for other incarnated beings, even should he not comprehend it, than a spirit decarnated and but little advanced could be to do so, were we forced to have recourse to his intervention ; for the terrestrial being puts his body at our disposal, which the wandering spirit could not do.

"Thus, when we find a medium whose brain is furnished with knowledge acquired during his actual life, and whose spirit is rich with latent anterior knowledge proper to facilitate our communications, we use him in preference, because with him the phenomenon of communication is much easier for us than with a medium whose intelligence is limited, and whose anterior knowledge may be insufficient. We will make ourselves understood by a few concise and exact explanations.

"With a medium whose actual or anterior intelligence is developed, our thought is communicated instantly, spirit to spirit, by a faculty proper to the spirit himself. In such case we find in the brain of the medium the elements suitable to give to our thought the word-clothing corresponding to the thought, and that whether the medium be intuitive, semi-mechanical, or mechanical pure. This is the reason that however great may be the number of spirits communicating through a medium, the dictations obtained by him, though proceeding from different spirits, bear the seal of form and color personal to the medium. Yes, even though the thought may be altogether strange to him, or the subject be one of the same kind he is accustomed to, or even if what we wish to say proceed in no way from him, he does not the less influence the form by the qualities, the properties belonging to his individuality. It is absolutely as when you look at different points with colored spectacles — green, white, or blue ; be the point of view or objects looked at entirely op-

posite, or totally independent of each other, they are
not the less always affected by the tint from the color
of the spectacles. Or, better, let us compare mediums
to those jars full of colored and transparent liquids
seen in the windows of druggists ; well, we are as lights
that illuminate certain points of view — moral, philosophic, and internal — through mediums of blue, green,
or red, in such a way that our luminous rays, obliged
to pass through glasses more or less cut, more or less
transparent, — that is to say, through mediums more
or less intelligent, — reach the object they wish to enlighten, only with the tint, or rather the form, peculiar
and special to these mediums. Finally, to end by a last
comparison, we spirits are like composers of music
who have composed, or would improvise, an air, and
we have at hand only a piano, or a violin, or a flute, or
a bassoon, or only a two-penny whistle. It is true that
with the piano, the flute, or the violin, we could execute our bit in a manner very comprehensible to our
auditors ; and though the sounds coming from a piano,
bassoon, or clarinet, may differ essentially, our composition will not be less identically the same, save for
the shades of sound. But if we have at our disposal
only a two-penny whistle — therein lies the difficulty
for us.

"When we are obliged to use mediums but little advanced, our work becomes longer, much more tedious,
because we are obliged to have recourse only to incomplete forms, which is a complication for us ; for then
we are forced to decompose our thought, word by word,
letter by letter, which is an annoyance and fatigue for
us, and a real hinderance to the promptitude and development of our manifestations.

"This is why we are glad to find mediums well appointed, well furnished, armed with materials ready to work, — in a word, good instruments, — because then our *périsprit*, acting on the *périsprit* of him whom we mediumize, has only to give impulsion to the hand which serves us as a pen-holder; while with insufficient mediums we are obliged to perform a labor analogous to that we do when we communicate by rappings, designating letter by letter, word by word, each of the phrases which form the translation of the thoughts we wish to communicate.

"It is for these reasons we address ourselves in preference to the enlightened and instructed classes for the divulgation of Spiritism, and the development of the scriptive medianimic faculties, though it may be among these classes we meet the most skeptical, the most rebellious, and the most immoral individuals. It is for the same reason we now leave to juggling spirits, and those but little advanced, the exercise of tangible communications, of rappings, of materialization, as, among you, men but little serious prefer phenomena that strike their eyes or their ears, to those which are purely spiritual, purely psychological.

"When we wish to work by spontaneous dictations, we act on the brain of the medium, and we mingle our materials with the elements he furnishes us, and that entirely without his will, just as if we should take the money in his purse, and arrange the different kinds in whatever order might seem to us most useful.

"But when the medium himself desires to question us in a special manner, it is well for him to reflect seriously, in order that he may question methodically, thus facilitating our labor in answering. For, as has been told you in a former instruction, your brain is often in inextricable confusion, and it is as painful as it is difficult for us to move in the labyrinth of your thoughts. Where questions involve each other, and should be made in proper succession, it is well, it is useful, that the series of questions should be communicated in advance to the medium, so that he may identify himself with the spirit of the invocator, and be impregnated with it, because we ourselves have then much greater facility to answer, by the affinity existing between our *périsprit* and that of the medium who serves us as interpreter.

"Certainly we could talk mathematics by means of a medium who seems to know nothing about it; but the spirit of this same medium may often possess this knowledge in a latent state, that is to say, personal to the fluidic being, and not to the incarnated, because his actual body is an instrument, rebellious or contrary to this knowledge. It is the same with astronomy, with poetry, with medicine, and the different languages, as well as all other knowledge pertaining to mankind. We still have the means of toilsome elaboration in use with mediums completely ignorant of the subject treated, putting together by words and letters, as in typography.

"As we have said, spirits do not need to clothe their thoughts; they perceive and communicate thought by the simple fact of its existence in them. Corporeal beings, on the contrary, perceive thought only when clothed. While the letter, the word, the substantive, the verb, the phrase, all are necessary to you in order to perceive even mentally, no visible or tangible form is necessary for us. ERASTUS and TIMOTHEUS."

Remark. This analysis of the *rôle* of mediums, and of the processes by help of which the spirits communicate, is as clear as it is logical. From it results this principle — that the spirit draws, *not his ideas*, but the materials necessary to express them, from the brain of the medium, and that the richer this brain is in materials, the easier is the communication. When the spirit expresses himself in the language familiar to the medium, he finds within him the words all formed with which to clothe the idea; if it is a language unknown to the medium, he does not find the words, but simply the letters ; the spirit then is obliged to dictate, as it were, letter by letter, exactly as you would do if you wished to make a person write German who is totally ignorant of that language. If the medium can neither read nor write, he does not possess even the letters ; it is then necessary to conduct the hand, as you would that of a scholar ; and there is a still greater material difficulty to overcome. These phenomena are possible ; we have numerous examples of them ; but it may readily be comprehended that this mode of procedure accords little with the extent and rapidity of communications, and that the spirits must prefer the most flexible instruments, or, as they express it, the mediums, from their point of view, best furnished with tools.

If those who ask these phenomena as a means of conviction had previously studied the theory, they would know under what exceptional conditions they are produced.

CHAPTER XX.

MORAL INFLUENCE OF THE MEDIUM.

*Various Questions. — Dissertations of a Spirit on
Moral Influence.*

226. 1. "Is the development of mediumship in proportion to the moral development of the medium ?"

"No ; the faculty proper pertains to the organism ;
it is independent of the moral ; it is not the same with
its use, which may be more or less good, according to
the qualities of the medium."

2. "It has always been said that mediumship is a
gift of God, a grace, a favor; why, then, is it not a
privilege of good men, and why do we see unworthy
people who are endowed in the highest degree, and
who misuse it ?"

"All faculties are favors for which we should give
thanks to God, for there are men who are deprived of
them. You might as well ask why God gives sight to
malefactors, adroitness to thieves, eloquence to those
who use it to say evil things. It is the same with
mediumship ; unworthy persons are endowed with it,
because they have greater need of it to be improved :
do you think God refuses the means of salvation to the
guilty ? He multiplies such means in their path ; *he
puts them in their hands ;* it is for them to profit by it.
Did not Judas, the traitor, as apostle, perform miracles,

and heal the sick ?   God permitted him to have this gift to render his treason more odious."

3. " Will mediums who make a bad use of their faculty, or who do not use it for doing good, or do not profit by it for their instruction, be obliged to bear the consequences ?"

" If they use it wrongly, they will be doubly punished, because they have a means of being enlightened, and do not profit by it.   He who sees clearly and stumbles is more blamable than the blind man who falls into the ditch."

4. " There are mediums to whom communications are, almost constantly, being made spontaneously, on the same subject, on certain moral questions, for instance, certain designated faults : has that any special motive ?"

" Yes ; and the motive is to enlighten them on a subject often repeated, or to correct them of certain faults ; for this reason they speak to one constantly of pride, to another of charity : only satiety can open their eyes.   There is not a medium misusing his faculty from ambition or interest, or compromising it by a capital fault, such as pride, egotism, levity, &c., who does not receive from time to time some warning from the spirits ; the evil is, that they rarely take the warning to themselves."

Remark.   Spirits often use management in giving their lessons ; they give them in an indirect manner, in order to leave more merit to him who knows how to apply and profit by them ; but with some people the blindness and pride are such that they cannot recognize themselves in the picture placed before their eyes ; much more if the spirit gives them to understand that they themselves are the ones in question, they become angry, and treat the spirit as a liar or jester. This plainly proves that the spirit was right.

5. " In the lessons that are dictated to the medium in a general manner, and without personal application, does he not act as a passive instrument for the instruction of others ? "

" Often the advice and counsel are not dictated for him personally, but for others to whom we can address ourselves only through his agency ; but he ought to take his share of it, if he is not blinded by self-love.

" Do not think the medianimic faculty has been given solely to correct one or two persons ; no, the end is greater ; it is a question of all mankind. A medium is an instrument of too little importance individually : this is why, when we give instructions for general profit, we use those who possess the necessary facilities ; but be assured there will come a time when good mediums will be so common that spirits will not need to use bad instruments."

6. " Since the moral qualities of the medium keep away imperfect spirits, how does it happen that a medium endowed with good qualities transmits false or gross answers ? "

" Do you know the inward recesses of the soul ? Besides, without being vicious, he may be light and frivolous, and then, also, sometimes he needs a lesson that he may be on his guard."

7. " Why do the superior spirits permit persons endowed with great power as mediums, and who might do much good, to be made the instruments of error ? "

" They try to influence them ; but when they allow themselves to be carried into an evil way, they let them go. This is the reason they use them with repugnance, *for truth cannot be interpreted by false-hood.*"

8. "Is it absolutely impossible to have good communications through an imperfect medium ?"

"An imperfect medium may sometimes obtain good things, because, if he have a fine faculty, good spirits may avail themselves of him in default of another, in one particular case ; but it is always only temporarily, for, as soon as they find one who suits them better, they give him the preference."

Remark. It is to be observed that when the good spirits perceive that a medium ceases to be well assisted, and becomes, by his imperfections, the prey of deceiving spirits, they almost always call forth circumstances that expose his irregularities, and withdraw from him serious and well-intentioned persons, whose sincerity might be abused. In such case, whatever may be their faculties, it is not to be regretted."

9. "What should a medium be, to be called perfect ?"

"Perfect! You well know that perfection is not on the earth, or you would not be here; say a good medium, and that is much, for they are rare. The perfect medium would be one on whom the bad spirits have never *dared* the attempt to deceive; the best is he who, sympathizing only with good spirits, has been least often deceived."

10. "If he sympathize only with good spirits, how can they allow him to be deceived ?"

"The good spirits sometimes allow it with the best mediums, in order to exercise their judgment, and teach them to discern the true from the false; and then, however good a medium may be, he is never so perfect that there may not be found some weak side in him hat can be approached ; it should serve him as a lesson. The false communications that he receives from time to time are warnings that he must not believe himself infallible, and pride himself upon it ; for the medium who obtains the most remarkable things has no more matter for glorification in it than the organ-grinder who produces the most beautiful airs by simply turning the crank of the instrument."

11. " What are the necessary conditions by which the words of the superior spirits may reach us pure from all adulteration ? "

" To will good ; to remove all pride and egotism : both are necessary."

12. " If the speech of the superior spirits reach us pure only under conditions difficult to attain, is it not an obstacle to the propagation of the truth ? "

" No ; for the light always comes to him who wishes to receive it. Whoever wishes to be enlightened must flee the darkness, and darkness is in impurity of heart.

"Spirits whom you consider the personification of good do not willingly answer the appeal of those whose hearts are soiled by pride, cupidity, and a lack of charity.

" Let those, then, who desire enlightenment, throw aside all human vanity, and humble themselves before the infinite power of the Creator : this will be the best proof of their sincerity ; and this condition every one can fulfill."

227. If the medium, as to execution, is only an instrument, yet, under the moral relation, he exercises a great influence. Since, in order to communicate, the foreign spirit identifies himself with the spirit of the medium, this identification can take place only so

far as there is sympathy, and, if one might say it, affinity between them. The soul exercises on the foreign spirit a kind of attraction or repulsion, according to the degree of their similarity or dissimilarity; thus, the good have an affinity for the good, and the bad for the bad; from whence it follows that the moral qualities of the medium have a powerful influence on the nature of the spirits who communicate through him. If he is vicious, the inferior spirits surround him, and are always ready to take the place of the good spirits who have been called. The qualities which best attract good spirits are, kindness, benevolence, simplicity of heart, love of the neighbor, detachment from material things; the faults that repel them are, pride, egotism, envy, jealousy, hatred, cupidity, sensuality, and all the passions by which man is attached to matter.

228. All moral imperfections are so many open doors which give access to evil spirits; but the one they can play upon most skillfully is pride, because it is the one people are least willing to confess, even to themselves: pride has ruined numberless mediums endowed with the finest faculties, and who, but for that, might have become remarkable and very useful subjects; but, become the prey of lying spirits, their faculties have been first perverted, then annihilated, and more than one have been humiliated by the most bitter deceptions.

Pride betrays itself in mediums by unequivocal signs, to which it is so much the more necessary to call attention, as it is one of the things which should soonest inspire a distrust of their communications. This is, first, a blind confidence in the superiority of these same communications, and in the infallibility of the spirit who gives them ; from thence a certain disdain for all that does not come to them, for they believe that they have the privilege of the truth. The prestige of great names, borrowed by the spirits whom they account as their protectors, dazzles them, and as their self-love would suffer in confessing themselves to be dupes, they repulse every kind of advice ; they even avoid it by withdrawing from their friends, and from whoever might be the means of opening their eyes : if they condescend to listen to them, they scorn their advice ; for to doubt the superiority of their spirit is almost a profanation. They are offended at the least contradiction, at a simple criticism, and even almost begin to hate the persons who have done them the service. Under cover of this isolation, brought about by spirits who want no contradictions, these have fine sport in keeping them in their illusions, and easily make them take the grossest absurdities for sublimities. Thus, absolute confidence in the superiority of what they obtain, contempt for what does not come from them, undue importance attached to great names, rejection of counsel, all criticism taken in ill part, withdrawal from those who might give disinterested advice, a belief in their skill in spite of their want of experience, — such are the characteristics of proud and vain mediums.

It is proper to say that pride is often excited in a medium by his surroundings. If he has greater faculties than ordinary, he is sought after and praised ; he considers himself indispensable, and soon affects airs of self-sufficiency and disdain when he lends his assistance. We have, more than once, had to regret the eulogiums we had given to certain mediums in order to encourage them.

229. By the side of this picture let us place that of the truly good medium — him in whom we may have confidence. Let us first suppose facility of execution so great as to permit the spirits to communicate freely, without being hampered by any difficulty of a material kind. This being given, what is most necessary to consider is, the nature of the spirits who habitually assist him ; and for that it is not the name that must be looked to, but the language. He should never lose sight of the fact that the sympathies he encourages among the good spirits will be in proportion to his withdrawal from the bad. Knowing that his faculty is a gift accorded to him for use in good, he seeks not self-laudation, he takes no merit for it to himself. He accepts the good communications made to him as a favor, of which he should endeavor to render himself worthy by kindness, benevolence, and modesty. The former prides himself on his relations with superior spirits ; the latter becomes more humble in consequence, always believing himself beneath such favor.

230. The following instruction has been given to us on this subject by a spirit, several of whose communications we have already given : —

" We have already said, mediums, as mediums, have but a secondary influence in the communications of spirits : their task is that of an electric machine, which transmits telegraphic despatches from one point of the earth to another far distant. So, when we wish to dictate a communication, we act on the medium as the telegraph operator on his instruments ; that is, as the *tac-tac* of the telegraph writes thousands of miles away, on a slip of paper, the reproduced letters of the dispatch, so we, from the immeasurable distance that separates the visible from the invisible world, the im-

material from the incarnated world, communicate what
we wish to teach you by means of the medianimic instrument. But, also, as the atmospheric influences act
upon, and often disturb, the transmissions of the electric
telegraph, the moral influence of the medium acts upon,
and sometimes affects, the transmission of our dis-
patches from beyond the tomb, because we are obliged
to make them pass through a medium whose nature is
contrary to them. At the same time, that influence is
most often annulled by our energy and our will, and
no disturbing element is manifest. Indeed, dictations
of a high, philosophic bearing, communications of
perfect morality, are sometimes transmitted through
mediums little suited to these superior teachings ;
while, on the other hand, communications anything
but edifying, sometimes come by mediums who are
very much ashamed of having been used as their
conductor.

"As a general rule it may be affirmed that spirits call
their like, and that spirits of an elevated plane rarely
communicate by bad conductors, where they have at
hand good medianimic instruments — good mediums.

"Light, trifling mediums call spirits of the same
nature ; and thus their communications are impressed
with vulgar expressions, frivolities, ideas disjointed
and often very heterodox, spiritually. To be sure they
can and do sometimes say good things, but it is in this
case, particularly, that it is necessary to subject them
to a rigid examination ; for, in the midst of these good
things, some hypocritical spirits skillfully, and with
calculating perfidy, insinuate inventions, lying asser-
tions, in order to deceive the sincerity of their auditors.
Then every equivocal word or phrase must be mercilessly stricken out, preserving only as much of the

dictation as is accepted by logic, or as is already
taught by the doctrine. Communications of this nature are to be dreaded only for isolated spiritists, for
circles newly formed, or not yet fully enlightened ; for
in reunions where the believers are more advanced,
and have gained experience, in vain the jackdaw borrows the peacock's feathers ; he is always mercilessly
expelled.

"I will not speak of mediums who are pleased to
solicit and listen to filthy communications ; let us leave
them to please themselves in the society of cynical
spirits. Besides, communications of this order seek,
of themselves, solitude and isolation ; in any case they
could only inspire disdain and disgust among the
members of philosophical and serious circles. But
where the moral influence of the medium makes itself
really felt, is when he substitutes his personal ideas
for those which the spirits endeavor to suggest to him ;
and again, when he draws from his own imagination
fantastic theories, which he himself sincerely believes
to be the result of an intuitive communication. Then
it is a thousand to one that this is the reflex of the
personal spirit of the medium ; then occurs this
strange fact — the hand of the medium is sometimes
moved almost mechanically, guided by a secondary
and mocking spirit. It is against this touchstone that
so many ardent imaginations are shattered ; for, carried away by the impetuosity of their own ideas, by
the tinsel of their literary learning, they despise the
modest dictation of a wise spirit, and abandon the substance for the shadow, substitute for it a high-flown
paraphrase. On this dreadful rock are personal ambi-
tions also stranded, when, in default of communications,
which the good spirits refuse to them, they present

their own work as the work of these same spirits. For this reason it is necessary that the chiefs of spiritist circles be possessed of exquisite tact and rare sagacity, in order to discern authentic communications, and not to wound those who delude themselves.

"' In doubt, abstain,' says one of your old proverbs ; admit nothing that has not certain evidence of truth. As soon as a new opinion is brought to light, if it seem ever so little doubtful, pass it through the crucible of reason and logic ; what reason and good sense refuse, reject boldly ; better reject ten truths than admit a single lie, a single false theory. For on this theory you might construct a whole system that would crumble at the first breath of truth, like a monument raised on the shifting sand ; while, should you reject some truths to-day, because they are not clearly and logically demonstrated, very soon a strong fact, an irrefutable demonstration, will come to show you its authenticity.

" Remember, nevertheless, O, spiritists, that there is nothing impossible for God, and for good spirits, except injustice and iniquity.

" Spiritism is now sufficiently diffused among men, and has so moralized the sincere believers of its holy doctrine, that spirits need no longer be reduced to employ bad instruments — imperfect mediums. If, now, a medium, whoever he may be, gives, by his conduct or his manners, by his pride, his want of love and charity, a legitimate cause for suspicion, — refuse, reject his communications, for there is a snake hidden in the grass. That is my conclusion on the moral influence of mediums. ERASTUS."

Chapter XXI.

INFLUENCE OF THE SURROUNDINGS.

231. 1. "Does the sphere of the medium exercise an influence on the manifestations?"

"All the spirits that surround the medium assist him, in good as in evil."

2. "Could not the superior spirits triumph over the bad will of the incarnated spirit, who serves them as interpreter, and over those who surround him?"

"Yes, when they consider it useful, and according to the intention of the person who addresses them. We have already said so ; the most elevated spirits can sometimes communicate by a special favor, notwithstanding the imperfection of the medium, and his sphere ; but then those surrounding spirits remain perfect strangers to it."

3. "Do the superior spirits seek to lead frivolous circles to more serious ideas?"

"The superior spirits do not go into circles where they know their presence to be useless. Where the surroundings are but slightly instructed, yet sincere, we go willingly, even should we find but feeble instruments ; but in instructed spheres, where irony governs, we do not go. Then it is necessary to speak to the eyes and ears ; that is the *rôle* of rapping or mocking spirits. It is right that persons who boast themselves of their science should be humiliated by spirits less learned and less advanced."

4. " Are the inferior spirits denied access to serious reunions ? "

" No ; they remain there, sometimes to profit by the instructions given to you ; but they are silent, *like the giddy in an assembly of the wise.*"

232. It would be an error to suppose that it is necessary to be a medium in order to attract to you beings from the invisible world. The whole of space is peopled with them ; we have them constantly around us, by our side ; they see us, observe us, mingle in our reunions, follow us or fly from us, as we attract or repulse them. The medianimic faculty is not needed for that ; it is only a means of communication. From what we have seen of the causes of sympathy or antipathy of spirits, it will easily be understood that we must be surrounded by those who have affinity for our own spirit, according as it is elevated or degraded. If we consider the moral state of our globe, we shall perceive what kind of spirits must predominate among the wandering spirits. If we take each people in particular, we can judge by the prevailing characteristics of the inhabitants, by their preoccupations, their sentiments, more or less moral and *humanitary*, of the order of spirits who would there rendezvous from preference.

Making this principle our starting-point, let us suppose a reunion of trifling, incongruous persons, occupied with their pleasures ; what kind of spirits would be found among them ? Not, assuredly, superior spirits, any more than our " savants " and philosophers would spend their time among them. So, whenever men gather together, they have with them an invisible assembly, which sympathizes with their qualities or their whims, and that *setting aside all thought of invo-*

cation. Let us admit, now, the possibility of holding intercourse with the beings of the invisible world by an interpreter, a medium ; who would answer to their call ? Evidently those who are there already, and only seeking an occasion to communicate. If, in a frivolous assembly, a superior spirit is called, he might come, and say some seasonable words, as a good pastor in the midst of his strayed sheep ; but the moment he finds himself neither understood nor listened to, he goes, as you would do in his place, and then the others have full liberty.

233. It is not always sufficient for an assembly to be serious to have communications of a high order ; there are people who never laugh, and whose hearts are none the more pure ; and it is the heart, above all, that attracts good spirits. No moral condition excludes spirit communications ; but if persons are in bad conditions, they talk with their like, who think it no harm to deceive us, and often embrace our prejudices.

By this may be seen the enormous influence of the sphere on the nature of intelligent manifestations ; but this influence is not exercised, as some have supposed, when the world of spirits was not as well known as it is now, and before convincing proofs had cleared away all our doubts. When communications agree with the opinion of the assistants, it is not because the opinion is reflected in the spirit of the medium, as in a mirror ; it is because you have with you spirits who are in sympathy with you, for good as for evil, and who have your conceits ; and what proves this is, that if you have the strength to attract to you other spirits than those who surround you, the same medium will hold an entirely different language, and tell you things far removed from your thoughts and your convictions. To recapitulate : the conditions of the sphere will be so much better as there may be more of homogeneity, for good, more pure and elevated sentiments, more sincere desire to be instructed, without afterthought.

Chapter XXII.

OF MEDIUMSHIP IN ANIMALS.

234. Can animals be mediums? This question has often been asked, and certain facts would seem to answer it affirmatively. The remarkable signs of intelligence displayed by some trained birds have given credit to this opinion; they have seemed to divine the thought, and draw from a pack of cards those that would give the exact answer to the question proposed. We have observed these experiments with very particular care, and have most admired the art displayed in their instruction. We cannot refuse them a certain degree of relative intelligence; but it must be conceded that, in this case, their perspicacity greatly surpassed that of man, for no one could flatter himself to be able to do as they do; for some experiments, it would even be necessary to suppose them to be endowed with a gift of second sight, superior to that of the most clear-seeing somnambulists. We know their lucidity is essentially variable, and that it is subject to frequent intermissions, while with these birds it would be permanent, and work up to a given point with a regularity and precision not seen in any somnambulist; in a word, they were never at fault. Most of the experiments that we have seen are of the nature of those of jugglers, and could leave us no doubt of the employment of some of their methods, notably that of forced cards. The art of legerdemain consists in concealing

300

these methods, without which the effect would have no charm. The phenomenon, even reduced to this proportion, is not the less very interesting, and the talent of the instructor is as admirable as the intelligence of the pupil ; for the difficulty is much greater than if the bird acted by virtue of his own faculties : now, in making the birds do things that pass the limit of the possible for human intelligence, is to prove by that alone the employment of a secret process.

There is, besides, one certain fact — that these birds reach this degree of skill only at the end of a certain time, and by means of particular and persevering cares, which would not be necessary if their intelligence was the only thing. It is no more extraordinary to train them to draw cards than to accustom them to repeat tunes or words. It has been the same when the legerdemain has attempted to imitate second sight ; they made the subject do too much to be of long duration. From the first time that we were at a *séance* of this kind, we saw only a very imperfect imitation of somnambulism, revealing ignorance of the most essential conditions of this faculty.

235. Whatever there may be in the above experiments, the principal question remains none the less entire in another point of view ; for even as the imitation of somnambulism prevents not the existence of the faculty, so the imitation of mediums, by means of birds, proves nothing against the possibility of an analogous faculty in them and in other animals. The thing is, to know if animals are fit, like men, to serve as intermediaries to spirits, for intelligent communications. It even seems logical enough to suppose that a living creature, endowed with a certain degree of intelligence, should be more suitable to this effect

than an inert body without vitality, like a table, for
instance; yet it is what does not happen.

236. The question of the medianimity of animals is
completely solved in the following dissertation given
by a spirit whose depth and sagacity may be appreciated by the quotations we have already had occasion
to make. To be entirely aware of the value of his
demonstration, it is only necessary to refer to the explanation he has given of the *rôle* of the medium in
communications, and which we have given above.
(No. 225.)

This communication was given at the end of a discussion that took place, on this subject, in the Paris
Society for Spirit Studies.

"I touch, to-day, upon the question of medianimity
in animals, raised and sustained by one of your most
fervent believers. He contends, by virtue of this
axiom, '*He who can do the most can do the least;*' that
we can medianimize birds, and use them in our communications with mankind. This is what you call, in
philosophy, or, rather, in logic, purely and simply a
sophism. 'You animate,' says he, 'inert matter;
that is, a table, a chair, a piano; *a fortiori*, you should
animate matter already animated, and notably birds.'
Well, in the normal state of Spiritism, this is not, and
it cannot be.

"First, let us look well at our facts. What is a
medium? It is the being, the individual, who serves
as point of union to the spirits, that they may easily
communicate with men — incarnated spirits. Consequently, without a medium, no communications,
tangible, mental, scriptive, physical, nor any sort
whatever.

"There is a principle which, I am sure, is admitted

by all spiritists : it is that likes act with their likes and as their likes. Now, what are the likes of spirits, if not the incarnated or non-incarnated spirits. Must it be repeated to you constantly? Well, I will repeat it again : your *périsprit* and ours are drawn from the same sphere, are of an identical nature, are like, in a word ; they possess a property of assimilation more or less developed, of magnetic action more or less vigorous, which allows us, spirits and incarnated, to put ourselves, very promptly and easily, *en rapport*. Finally, what specially pertains to mediums, what is even the essence of their individuality, is a special affinity, and at the same time a peculiar force of expansion, which annihilate in them all refractibility, and establish between them and us a sort of current, a kind of fusion, which facilitates our communications. It is this refractibility of matter which is opposed to the development of mediumship in most of those who are not mediums.

"Men are always prone to exaggerate. Some — I speak not here of materialists — refuse a soul to animals ; and some would give them one, so to speak, like our own. Why thus desire to confound the perfectible with the imperfectible? No, no; be convinced in this : the fire that animates the beasts, the breath that makes them act, move, and speak in their language, has no aptitude, as to the present, to be mingled, to be united, to be fused with the divine breath, the ethereal soul, the spirit which animates the being essentially perfectible — man ; this king of the creation. Now, is it not this very essential condition of perfectibility in which consists the superiority of the human species? Well, understand, then, that no individual of the other races living on the earth can be compared with man, alone perfectible in himself, and in his works.

"Is the dog, whose superior intelligence among animals has made him the friend and companion of man, perfectible of his own head, and from his personal initiative? No one would dare to sustain it, for the dog does not make his race progress; the best trained among them is always trained by his master. Since the world has been a world, the otter has always built his hut on the water, of the same proportions, and according to an invariable rule; the nightingales and the swallows have never constructed their nests otherwise than as did their fathers.

"A sparrow's nest before the deluge is a sparrow's nest of to-day, is always a sparrow's nest; built in the same conditions, and with the same system of interlacing blades of grass and rubbish, gathered in the spring, the season of love. The bees and ants, those little republican housekeepers, have never varied in their custom of laying up stores, in their mode of proceeding, in their manners, in their productions. The spider always weaves his web in the same way.

"On the other side, if you seek the thatched huts and the tents of the early ages of the earth, you will find in their place the palaces and castles of modern civilization; to the garments of skins have succeeded tissues of gold and silk; finally, at each step, you find the proofs of the incessant march of humanity towards progress.

"Of this constant, invincible, undeniable progress of the human species, and of this indefinite stationariness of the other animated species, conclude with me, that if there exist principles common to all that live and move on the earth, breath and matter, it is none the less true that you alone, incarnated spirits are subjected to that inevitable law of progress which presses you incessantly forward, and always forward. God has placed the animals by your side as auxiliaries, to nourish, to clothe, to help you. He has given them a certain degree of intelligence, because, in order to aid you, they must understand ; and He has proportioned their intelligence to the services they are called upon to render ; but, in His wisdom, He has not meant they should be subjected to the same law of progress ; such as they were created, such they have remained, and will remain until the extinction of their races.

"It has been said, The spirits medianimize inert matter, and make it move chairs, tables, pianos ; make it move, yes ; but medianimize it, no ! For, still again, without a medium not one of these phenomena could be produced. What is there extraordinary in the fact that by the help of one or several mediums we move inert or passive matter, which, by reason of its very passivity, its inertia, is proper to undergo the movement and impulsions we wish to impress upon it ? For that we need mediums — that is certain ; but it is not necessary that the medium be present, or *conscious*, for we can act with the elements he furnishes, unknown to him, and without his presence ; above all, in the facts of tangibility and materialization. Our fluidic envelope, more imponderable and more subtile than the most subtile and most imponderable of your gases, uniting, wedding, combining with the fluidic but *animalized* envelope of the medium, and whose property of expansion and penetrability cannot be grasped by your gross senses, and is almost inexplicable to you, allows us to move furniture, and even to break it, in inhabited places.

"Certainly spirits can make themselves visible and tangible to animals, and often some sudden fright they have, and which seems to you motiveless, is caused by the sight of one or several of these spirits ill-intentioned to the individuals present, or to those to whom the animals belong. Very often you see horses who will neither advance nor go back, or who rear up at an imaginary obstacle. Well, take it for certain that the imaginary obstacle is often a spirit, or group of spirits, who are pleased to hinder his advance.

"Recollect Balaam's ass, who, seeing an angel before her, and fearing his flaming sword, would not stir; before visibly manifesting himself to Balaam, the angel wished to be visible to the animal alone; but, I repeat, we medianimize directly neither animals nor inert matter; the concurrence, either *conscious* or *unconscious*, of a human medium is always necessary, and this we can find neither in animals nor in inert matter.

"M. T. has, he says, magnetized his dog. What happened? He killed him, for the miserable animal died after falling into a kind of atony, of languor, in consequence. Indeed, in filling him with a fluid taken from an essence superior to that special to his nature, he crushed him, — acted on him, though more slowly, in the manner of the thunderbolt. Then, as there is no assimilation possible between our *périsprit* and the fluidic envelope of animals, proper, we should crush them instantly by medianimizing them.

"This established, I perfectly recognize among animals the existence of various aptitudes; that certain passions, identical with human passions and sentiments, are developed in them; that they are feeling and grateful, vindictive and hating, according as they are well or ill treated. It is because God, who makes nothing incomplete, has given to animals, companions and servants of man, qualities of sociability that are utterly wanting in wild animals. But from thence to being able to serve as intermediaries for the transmission of spirit thought, there is a gulf — the difference of natures.

"You know we draw in the brain of the medium the elements necessary to give to our thought a perceptible form, one that you can grasp: it is by the aid of the material he possesses that the medium translates our thought into ordinary language: well, what element would you find in the brain of an animal? Are there words, numbers, letters, any signs whatever, similar to those existing with man, even the least intelligent? Yet, you will say, animals understand man's thought; they even divine. Yes, trained animals understand certain thoughts; but have you ever seen them reproduce them? No; conclude, then, that animals cannot serve us as interpreters.

"To recapitulate: medianimic facts cannot be manifested without the conscious or unconscious concurrence of mediums, and it is only among the incarnated, spirits like ourselves, that we can meet with those who can serve us as mediums. As to dogs, birds, or other animals, trained to certain exercises, that is your business, and not ours. ERASTUS."

Chapter XXIII.

ON OBSESSION.

Simple Obsession. — Fascination. — Subjugation. — Causes of Obsession. — Means of combating it.

237. OF the number of dangers which the practice of Spiritism presents, in the front rank must be placed *Obsession;* that is, the dominion some spirits know how to take over certain persons. It is never done except by inferior spirits, who seek to govern; with good spirits we experience no restraint; they advise, combat the influence of the bad, and if they are not listened to, withdraw. The bad, on the contrary, attach themselves to those whom they find exposed; if they gain dominion over any one, they identify themselves with his own spirit, and lead him like a veritable child.

Obsession presents various characteristics, which it is very necessary to distinguish, and which result from the degree of restraint, and the nature of the effects it produces. The word *obsession* is, in some sort, a generic term, by which we designate this kind of phenomenon, whose principal varieties are, *simple obsession, fascination,* and *subjugation.*

238. *Simple obsession* is when a malicious spirit imposes himself on a medium, intermeddles, in spite of him, in the communications he receives, prevents him

308

from communicating with other spirits, and substitutes himself for those invoked.

It is not obsession to be deceived by a lying spirit: the best medium is exposed to that, especially in the beginning, when he still lacks the necessary experience; the same as, with us, the most honest people may be duped by rascals. One can be deceived without being obsessed; obsession is in the tenacity of the spirit, of whom you cannot get rid.

In simple obsession the medium knows very well that it is a deceiving spirit, and the spirit does not conceal himself: he disguises none of his bad intentions and his desire to thwart. The medium easily recognizes the imposture, and as he is on his guard, is rarely deceived. This kind of obsession is simply disagreeable, and has no other inconvenience than to oppose an obstacle to the communications that might be desired with serious spirits, or with those whom we love.

Physical Obsession may be ranked in this class; those which consist in noisy and obstinate manifestations of certain spirits, who rap and make other noises spontaneously.

239. *Fascination* has much graver consequences. It is an illusion produced by direct action of the spirit on the medium's thought, and which in some measure paralyzes his judgment in regard to communications. The fascinated medium does not believe himself to be deceived; the spirit has the art to inspire him with a blind confidence, which prevents him from seeing the treachery, and from understanding the absurdity of what he writes, even when it is patent to everybody's eyes: the illusion may even go so far as to make him see sublimity in the most ridiculous language. It

would be an error to suppose that this kind of obsession could come to only simple, ignorant persons, and those without judgment ; men the most acute, the most learned, the most intelligent in other relations, are not exempt, which proves that this aberration is is the effect of a foreign cause, to whose influence they are subjected. We have said that the results of fascination are much more grave ; for, by means of the illusion, the spirit leads the one he masters as he would lead a blind man, can make him accept the most absurd doctrines, the falsest theories, as being the sole expression of truth ; still more, he can incite him to the most ridiculous, compromising, and even dangerous proceedings.

One can easily comprehend the great difference existing between simple obsession and fascination ; as also that the spirits who produce these two effects must differ in character. In the first, the spirit is a being troublesome only by his tenacity, and of whom one is impatient to be rid. In the second, it is quite another thing : to gain such ends needs an adroit, subtle, and profoundly hypocritical spirit, for he can create the delusion, and make himself accepted only by means of the mask he wears and of a semblance of virtue ; the grand words, charity, humility, and love of God, are as letters of credence ; but through all he shows signs of inferiority, which one must be fascinated not to perceive. He also dreads all people who see too clearly ; his tactics, therefore, are, almost always, to inspire his interpreter to withdraw from every one who could open his eyes : by this means, avoiding all contradiction, he is sure of being always right.

240. *Subjugation* is a bond that paralyzes the will of

him who is subjected to it, and makes him act in spite of himself. In a word, it is a real *yoke.*

Subjugation may be moral or corporeal. In the first case, the subjugated is instigated to do things often absurd and compromising, which he is deluded into believing sensible : it is a kind of fascination. In the second case, the spirit acts on the material organs, and provokes involuntary movements. It shows itself in the writing medium by an incessant desire to write, even at the most inopportune moments. We have seen those who, in default of pen or pencil, would write with the finger, wherever they might be, even in the streets, on the doors and walls.

Corporeal subjugation sometimes goes further ; it may urge to the most ridiculous acts. We knew a man, neither young nor handsome, under the dominion of an obsession of this nature, constrained by an irresistible force to kneel to a young girl whom he had never before seen, and ask her in marriage. At other times, he felt on his back and loins a violent pressure, which forced him, in spite of his opposing will, to kneel and kiss the ground in public and crowded places. This man passed for crazy among his friends, but we were convinced he was not at all so ; for he was perfectly conscious of the ridicule of which he was unwillingly the cause, and suffered horribly from it.

241. Formerly the name of *possession* was given to this dominion exercised by evil spirits, when their influence extended to the aberration of the faculties. Possession, for us, would be synonymous with subjugation. We have two reasons for not adopting this term ; the first, that it implies beings created for, and perpetually devoted to, evil, while really there are only beings, more or less imperfect, who can all be made

better ; the second, that it also implies the idea of
taking possession of the body by a foreign spirit — a
sort of cohabitation ; while really there is only constraint. The word *subjugation* perfectly renders the
thought. Thus, for us, there are no *possessed*, in the
ordinary sense of the word ; there are only *obsessed*,
subjugated, and *fascinated*.

242. Obsession, as we have said, is one of the greatest dangers of mediumship ; it is also one of the most
frequent : so we cannot take too much pains to combat it ; for, over and above the personal inconveniences
that may result, it is an absolute obstacle to the goodness and truth of communications. Obsession, to
whatever degree it may be carried, being always the
effect of a restraint, and this restraint never being
exercised by a good spirit, the result is, that every
communication given by an obsessed medium is of a
suspicious origin, and merits no confidence. If sometimes good is found in them, take the good, but reject
all that is even doubtful.

243. Obsession may be known by the following
characteristics : First. Persistence of a spirit in communicating, *bon gré*, *mal gré*, by writing, hearing, typtology, &c., and in opposing whatever other spirits
may do.

Second. Illusion, which, notwithstanding the intelligence of the medium, prevents him from seeing the
falsity and absurdity of the communications he receives.

Third. Belief in the infallibility and absolute identity of the spirits who communicate, and who, under
respected and venerated names, say false or absurd
things.

Fourth. Confidence of the medium in the eulogiams the spirits who communicate with him bestow upon him.

Fifth. A disposition to withdraw from persons who may give him useful advice.

Sixth. Taking in ill part all criticisms on the subject of the communications he receives.

Seventh. An incessant and inopportune desire to write.

Eighth. Any physical restraint whatever against the will, and being forced to act or speak in spite of one's self.

Ninth. Persistent noises and disturbances about one, and of which one is the cause, or object.

244. In the face of this danger of obsession it may be asked if it is not a pity to be a medium; is it not this faculty that induces it, and is it not a proof of the inexpediency of spirit communications? Our answer is easy, and we beg it may be carefully considered.

Neither mediums nor spiritists created the spirits, but the spirits have been the cause of there being spiritists and mediums: spirits being only the souls of men, there have been spirits as long as there have been men; and, consequently, they have, in all time, exercised their salutary or pernicious influence on humanity. The medianimic faculty is for them only a means of manifesting themselves; in default of this faculty, they do it in a thousand other ways, more or less occult. It would be an error to believe that spirits exercise their influence only by written or verbal communications; their influence is incessant, and those who do not concern themselves about spirits, or who do not even believe in them, are as exposed to it as others, and more than others, because they have no counterpoise. Mediumship is for the spirit a means of making himself known; if he is bad he always betrays himself, however hypocritical he may be; thus it may be said that mediumship allows one to see his enemy face to face, if it may be so expressed, and to fight him with his own weapons; without this faculty he acts in the dark, and, under cover of his invisibility, can do, and does, much harm. To how many actions have not people been urged, to their misfortune, and which they might have avoided had they possessed the means of being enlightened! The incredulous know not how truly they speak, when they say of a man who obstinately goes astray, "It is his evil genius urging him on to his destruction." Thus the knowledge of Spiritism, far from giving dominion to bad spirits, must, sooner or later, when it shall be widely spread, result in the destruction of that domination by giving to every one the means of being on his guard against their suggestions, and then he who yields will have no one to blame but himself.

General rule: whoever has bad spirit communications, written or verbal, is under an evil influence; this influence is exercised on him, whether he writes or whether he does not write; that is, whether he be a medium or not; whether he believe or disbelieve. Writing gives a person the means of knowing the nature of the spirits who act on him, and of fighting against them if they are evil, which can be done with much greater success when the motive which makes them act is known. If he is too much blinded to understand it, others can open his eyes.

To recapitulate: the danger is not so much in Spiritism itself, since it can, on the contrary, serve as a controlling influence, and save from him who incessantly pursues us against our will ; it is in the haughty propensity of some mediums to believe too easily that they are the exclusive instruments of superior spirits, and in the kind of fascination that prevents them from understanding the foolish things of which they are the interpreters. Those, even, who are not mediums, may be exposed to it. Let us make a comparison. A man has a secret enemy, who disseminates all kinds of calumnious reports that the blackest wickedness can invent ; he sees his fortune lost, his friends alienated, his internal happiness destroyed ; not being able to discover the hand that strikes him, he cannot defend himself, and yields ; but one day this secret enemy writes to him, and, in spite of his strategy, betrays himself. Now he faces the discovered foe, can put him to confusion, and recover himself. Such is the *rôle* of the evil spirits, whom Spiritism makes it possible to know and unmask.

245. The motives of the obsession vary according to the nature of the spirit ; sometimes it is a vengeance he exercises on an individual, against whom he has cause of complaint, either during his life or in another existence ; often, also, he has no other reason than the desire of doing evil ; as he suffers, he wishes to make others suffer ; he finds a kind of joy in tormenting and vexing them ; also the impatience they exhibit excites him, because such is his object, while, by being patient, we weary him ; in becoming irritated, and showing vexation, we do exactly what he wishes. These spirits sometimes act from hatred and jealousy of good ; this is why they cast their malicious eyes on the best people. One of them sticks like a leech to an honorable family of our acquaintance, whom he has not even the satisfaction of deceiving ; interrogated as

to his motive for attacking good people, instead of evil
men like himself, he answered, " *They give me no cause
for envy."* Others are guided by a sentiment of cowardice, which leads them to profit by the moral weakness of those who they know are incapable of resisting them. One of these, who subjugated a young
man of very limited intellect, interrogated as to the
motives of his choice, answered, " *I have a very great
need of tormenting some one: a sensible person would
repulse me. I attach myself to an idiot, who has no
means of opposing me."*

246. There are obsessing spirits without malice, who
even have some good, but who have the pride of false
knowledge ; they have their own ideas, their systems
of the sciences, social economy, morality, religion,
philosophy ; they want their opinion to prevail, and,
for that purpose, seek mediums credulous enough to
accept them with closed eyes, and whom they fascinate
to prevent them from discerning the true from the
false. They are the more dangerous because sophisms
cost them nothing, and they can gain credit for the
most ridiculous extravagances : as they know the prestige of great names, they do not scruple to borrow the
most respected, not even recoiling before the sacrilege
of calling themselves Jesus, or the Virgin Mary, or a
venerated saint. They seek to dazzle by pompous
language, more pretentious than profound, bristling
with technical terms, and adorned with the grand
words of charity and morality ; they are careful not to
give bad advice, because they know they will be rejected : so those whose confidence they abuse defend
them against every one, saying, " You can see they
say nothing wrong." But morality is to them but a
passport ; it is the least of their care ; what they want

is to govern, and to impose on others their ideas, however unreasonable they may be.

247. Spirits who have a system to advance are generally writers: this is why they look for mediums who write with facility, and of whom they try to make docile instruments, fascinating them that they may be enthusiasts. They are almost always verbose, very prolix, endeavoring to make up in quantity what they lack in quality. They please themselves by dictating to their interpreters voluminous writings, crude and often nearly unintelligible, which, happily, it is almost impossible for the masses to read. The really superior spirits are sober of speech; they say much in few words: so this prodigious fecundity should always be suspected.

One cannot be too circumspect when the question arises of publishing such writings: the Utopianisms and eccentricities in which they abound produce a lamentable impression on novices, by giving them a false idea of Spiritism, without counting the fact that they are arms furnished to its enemies to turn it into ridicule. Among these publications are those which, without being evil, and without evincing obsession, may yet be regarded as imprudent, *unseasonable*, or maladroit.

248. It frequently happens that a medium can communicate only with one single spirit, who attaches himself to him, and answers for those who are called by his mediation. This is not always an obsession, for it may pertain to a certain want of flexibility in the medium, and to a special affinity on his part for such or such a spirit. There is no obsession, properly called, except when a spirit imposes himself on a medium, and forces away others by his will; this is

never the case with a good spirit. Usually the spirit
who makes himself master of a medium with the view
of governing him, does not suffer the critical examination of his communications ; when he sees they are
not accepted, and that they are discussed, he does not
retire, but he inspires the medium with the thought of
isolating himself ; often he even commands him to do
so. Every medium who is wounded by the criticism
of the communications he obtains, is the echo of the
spirit who governs him, and this spirit cannot be
good if he inspires an illogical thought — that of refus-
ing examination. The isolation of the medium is
always a lamentable thing for him, because then he
has no critic for his communications. Not only should
he gain insight by the advice of others, but it is necessary for him to study all kinds of communications
in order to compare them ; in shutting himself up
in those he himself obtains, however good they may
appear to him, he is exposed to delusion as to their
value, without reckoning that he cannot know everything, and that they nearly always run in the same
groove. (No. 192, *Exclusive Mediums.*)

249. The means of combating obsession vary according to the character it takes. The danger does not
really exist for any thoroughly convinced medium to
be brought into relations with a lying spirit, as in
simple obsession ; it is only a disagreeable thing for
him. But precisely because it is disagreeable to him,
is a reason the more for the spirit to follow him persis-
tently to vex him. There are two essential things to
do in such case : to prove to the spirit that one is not his
dupe, and that it is *impossible* to deceive us ; secondly.
tire his patience by showing ourself more patient than
he ; if he is thoroughly convinced that he will lose his

time, he will end by retiring, as importunate persons do when we do not listen to them.

But that does not always suffice, and it may be long, for some of them are very tenacious, and months and years are but little to them. The medium should make a fervent appeal to his good angel, also to the good spirits who are sympathetic to him, and beg them to assist him. As for the obsessing spirit, however bad he may be, he should be treated with firmness, but with kindness, vanquishing him by good in praying for him. If he is really perverse, he will at first mock at it ; but in perseveringly moralizing with him, he will end by amending ; it is a conversion to undertake, a task often painful, ungrateful, even discouraging, but whose merit is in the difficulty, and which, if well accomplished, always gives the satisfaction of having fulfilled a duty of charity, and often that of having led a lost soul into the good road.

It is equally expedient to break off all written communication as soon as it is known to come from a bad spirit, who will not listen to reason, in order not to give him the pleasure of being listened to. In some cases, even, it might be necessary to cease writing for a time ; it must be regulated according to circumstances. But if the writing medium can avoid these discourses by abstaining from writing, it is not the same with the hearing medium, whom the obsessing spirit sometimes pursues every instant with his gross and obscene remarks, and who has not even the resource of closing his ears. There are persons who are amused by the frivolous language of these spirits, whom they encourage and urge by laughing at their follies, instead of imposing silence on them, and trying to teach them better. Our advice does not apply to those who will drown themselves.

250. There is, then, only disgust, and not danger, for any medium who will not allow himself to be abused, because he cannot be deceived ; it is .entirely otherwise with *fascination*, for then the dominion the spirit assumes over him whom he invades has no bounds. The only thing to do with him is to try to convince him he is deceived, and to lead his obsession to a case of simple obsession ; but it is not always easy, if it is not even sometimes impossible. The ascendency of the spirit may be such that he makes the one fascinated deaf to every kind of reasoning, and, when the spirit commits some gross scientific heresy, makes him go so far as to doubt if science itself is not wrong. As we have said, he generally takes advice in very ill part ; criticism annoys, irritates him, and makes him dislike those who do not partake his admiration. To suspect his spirit is almost a profanation in his eyes, and that is all the spirit asks, for what he wants is, that we should bend before his word. One of them exercised on a person of our acquaintance a most extraordinary fascination ; we invoked him, and after some romancing, seeing that he could not delude us as to his identity, he ended by confessing that he was not the one whose name he had taken. Having asked why he so deceived this person, he answered in these words, which very clearly expresses the character of spirits of this kind : " *I looked for a man I could lead ; I have found him, and here I stay.*" " But if we should make him see clearly, he will drive you away." " *We'll see about that !* " As there is none more blind than he who will not see, when we find the uselessness of every attempt to open the eyes of the fascinated, the best

thing to do is, to leave him to his delusions. A patient cannot be cured who persists in keeping his disease, and even delights in it.

251. Corporeal subjugation often takes from the obsessed the energy necessary to rule the bad spirit; for this reason the intervention of a third person is needed, acting either by magnetism or by his strength of will. In default of any assistance from the obsessed, this person should take the ascendency over the spirit; but as this ascendency can only be moral, it is given only to a being *morally superior* to the spirit to exercise it, and his power will be as much greater as his moral superiority is greater, for he commands the spirit who is forced to bend before him; this is why Jesus had such great power to drive out what were then called demons, that is, bad obsessing spirits.

We can give here only general advice, for there is no material process, no formula, nor any sacramental word that has the power to drive away obsessing spirits. Sometimes the obsessed lacks fluidic force; in such case the magnetic action of a good magnetizer might be a very useful help. Then it is always well to take, by a sure medium, the advice of a superior spirit, or of his guardian angel.

252. The moral imperfections of the obsessed are often an obstacle to his deliverance. Here is a remarkable example, which may serve as instruction to every one : —

Several sisters were, for a number of years, victims of very disagreeable depredations. Their clothing was constantly thrown about in every corner of the house, and even upon the roof, cut, torn, and riddled with holes, whatever care they might take to lock it up. These ladies, brought up in a small provincial

locality, had never heard of Spiritism. Their first
thought, naturally, was, that they were the butt of some
joker's tricks ; but the persistence and their precautions destroyed that idea   It was not until a long time
after, that, on some indications, they thought they
ought to address us to know the cause of the trouble,
and the means to remedy it, if possible. The cause
was not doubtful ; the remedy was more difficult.
The spirit who manifested himself by these acts was
evidently malicious.   He showed himself, in the invocation, of great perversity, and inaccessible to every
good sentiment.   Prayer seemed, nevertheless, to exercise a salutary influence ; but after a short respite, the
depredations recommenced.   The advice of a superior
spirit on this subject is here given.

" What these ladies had better do is, to pray their
spirit protectors not to abandon them ; and I have no
better advice to give them than to look into their con-
sciences, and confess to themselves, and examine if
they have always practiced the love of the neighbor
and charity ; I do not mean the charity that gives
and distributes, but the charity of the tongue ; for
unhappily they know not how to control theirs, and
do not justify, by their pious acts, their desire of being
delivered from him who torments them. They like
too well to slander their neighbor, and the spirit who
obsesses them is taking his revenge, for he was their
drudge during his life.   They have only to search
their memory, and they will soon see with whom they
have to do.

" At the same time, if they become better, their
guardian angels will return to them, and their presence will suffice to drive away the bad spirit, who
could not have troubled one of them, but that her

guardian angel had withdrawn to a distance from her on account of some reprehensible acts or bad thoughts. What they must do is, to pray fervently for those who suffer, and to practice the virtues enjoined by God to each one according to his condition."

On our observing that these words seemed to us a little severe, and that they ought to be somewhat softened before transmitting them, the spirit added, —

"I ought to say what I have said, and as I have said it, because the persons in question have the habit of believing they do no harm with the tongue, while they do a great deal. We must, therefore, strike their minds in such a way that it will be a serious warning."

From this may be drawn instruction of great signification — that moral imperfections give a footing to obsessing spirits, and that the surest means of ridding one's self of them is to attract the good by well doing. The good spirits have, without doubt, more power than the bad, and their will is sufficient to remove these last; but they assist only those who second them by the efforts they make to become better; otherwise they withdraw, and leave the field free to the bad spirits, who thus become, in some cases, instruments of punishment, for the good leave them to act for this purpose.

253. Yet we should beware of attributing to the direct action of the spirits all the annoyances that may arise: these annoyances are often the consequence of negligence or improvidence. A planter wrote to us, that for twelve years all sorts of misfortunes had befallen his animals. Sometimes his cows died, or would give no milk; sometimes the trouble was with the horses; again his sheep or his pigs. He hired new people, but without remedying the evil, no more than

the masses he had said, or the exorcisms he had made. Then, according to country prejudice, he was persuaded some one had cast an evil eye on his animals. Believing, no doubt, that we were endowed with greater power than the priest of his village, he sent to ask our advice. We obtained the following answer : —

" The mortality or the sickness of this man's beasts is, because his stables are infected, and that he does not have them repaired because *it costs*."

254. We close this chapter with the answers given by the spirits to some questions supporting what we have said.

1. " Why cannot certain mediums rid themselves of bad spirits who are with them, and how is it that the good spirits they call are not powerful enough to remove the bad spirits, and communicate directly ? "

" It is not power that is wanting to the good spirits, it is often the medium who is not strong enough to second them ; his nature adapts itself better to certain relations, or rather his fluid identifies itself sooner with one spirit than with another ; this is what gives such great sway to those who wish to take advantage of it."

2. " Nevertheless, it seems to us that there are very many meritorious persons, of irreproachable morality, who yet are prevented from communicating with good spirits."

" It is a trial ; and, besides, who can tell if the heart is not stained with an evil thought ? if pride does not a little govern the appearance of goodness ? These trials, by showing to the obsessed his weakness, should turn him to humility.

" Is there any one on the earth who can say he is perfect ? and he who has all the appearances of virtue may still have hidden defects, an old leaven of imperfection. Thus, for instance, you say of him who does no wrong, who is loyal in his social relations, This is a true and worthy man : but do you know if his good qualities are not tarnished by pride ; if there is not within him a fund of egotism ; if he is not avaricious, jealous, spiteful, slanderous, and a hundred other things you do not perceive, because your relations with him have not developed them ?   The most powerful means of striving against the influence of bad spirits is to make yourself as much as possible like the good."

3. " Is the obsession which prevents a medium's obtaining the communications he desires always a sign of unworthiness on his part ? "

" I did not say it was a sign of unworthiness, but that an obstacle might be there to oppose certain communications ; it is to remove the obstacle within him that all attention should be given ; without that all his prayers, his supplications, will be of no avail.   It is not enough for a sick person to say to his doctor, Give me health ; I want to be well : the doctor can do nothing if the patient does not do what is necessary."

4. " Would the privation, then, be a kind of punishment ? "

" In some cases, this may be a real punishment, as the possibility of communicating with them is a recompense you should endeavor to deserve."   (See *Loss and Suspension of Mediumship*, No. 220.)

5. " Cannot the influence of bad spirits be also overcome by giving them moral instruction ? "

" Yes ; this is what no one does, but it is what should not be neglected ; for it is often a task given to you, and one that you should accomplish charitably and religiously. By wise counsel they may be incited to repentance, and their advancement hastened."

"How can a man have more influence in this respect than the spirits themselves?"

"The perverse spirits are allied rather to men whom they seek to torment, than to spirits from whom they withdraw as far as possible. In this approach to man, when they find one who talks to them trying to improve their morals, they do not listen at first; they laugh at it; then, if you know how to take them, they will eventually allow themselves to be affected. The elevated spirits can speak to them only in the name of God, and that frightens them. Man, certainly, has not more power than the superior spirits, but his language is better identified with their nature, and in seeing the ascendency he can exercise over the inferior spirits, he comprehends better the solidarity existing between the heavens and the earth.

"Then, too, the ascendency that man can exercise over the spirits is by reason of his moral superiority. He cannot master the superior spirits, nor even those who, without being superior, are good and benevolent, but he can master the spirits who are morally inferior to him."

6. "Can corporeal subjugation carried to a certain length induce insanity?"

"Yes; a kind of insanity whose cause is unknown to the world, but which has no relation to ordinary insanity. Among those treated as insane, there are many who are only subjugated; a moral treatment is necessary for them, while they make them really insane by their corporeal treatments. When doctors understand Spiritism, they will know how to make a distinction, and will cure more patients than they are now curing with their shower-baths." (221.)

7. " What may be thought of those who, seeing danger in Spiritism, think to prevent it by interdicting spirit communications ? "

" If they can prevent some persons from communicating with spirits, they cannot prevent the spontaneous manifestations made to these same persons, for they cannot suppress the spirits, nor hinder their secret influence. It is like children shutting their eyes and thinking no one can see them. It would be folly to suppress a thing that offers great advantages because some imprudent persons might abuse it ; the way to prevent these abuses is, on the contrary, to search the thing to the bottom."

Chapter XXIV.

IDENTITY OF SPIRITS.

Possible Proofs of Identity.— Distinction of Good and Bad Spirits.— Questions on the Nature and Identity of Spirits.

Possible Proofs of Identity.

255. THE question of the identity of spirits is one that has given rise to the greatest controversy, even among the believers of Spiritism ; spirits do not bring us letters of introduction, and it is well known with what facility some of them take borrowed names ; so that, obsession aside, it is one of the greatest difficulties in the practice of Spiritism ; yet, in many cases, absolute identity is a secondary question, and without real importance.

The identity of the spirit of ancient personages is the most difficult to verify, often even impossible, and we are reduced to a purely moral valuation. Spirits, like men, are judged by their language ; if a spirit presents himself under the name of Fénélon, for instance, and gives us trivialities or puerilities, it very surely cannot be he ; if he says only things worthy the character of Fénélon, and which he would not disavow, there is, if not material proof, at least a moral probability, that it must be he. In such case, particularly, the real identity is an accessory question : if the spirit says only good things, it matters little under what name they are given.

It will, doubtless, be objected that the spirit who would take an assumed name, even to say only good, would not the less commit a fraud, and thus could not be a good spirit. Here there are delicate shades quite difficult to seize, but which we shall try to develop.

256. In proportion as spirits are purified and elevated in the hierarchy, the distinctive characters of their personality are, in some sort, obliterated in the uniformity of perfection, and yet they do not the less preserve their individuality : this is the case with the superior and with the pure spirits. In this condition, the name they had on the earth, in one of their thousand *ephemeral* corporeal existences, is quite an insignificant thing. Let us remark again that spirits are attracted to each other by the similarity of their qualities, and that they thus form sympathetic groups or families. Again, if we consider the immense number of spirits who, since the beginning of time, have reached the highest rank, and compare them with the very restricted number of men who have left a great name on the earth, it will be understood that, among the superior spirits who can communicate, the greater part must have no name for us ; but as names are necessary to us to fix our ideas, they can take that of any known personage whose nature is best identified with their own ; thus our guardian angels most often make themselves known under the name of one of the saints we venerate, and generally under his name for whom we have the most sympathy. It thus follows that if a person's guardian angel gives his name as St. Peter, for instance, there is no actual proof that it is the apostle of that name ; it may be he, or it may be

an entirely unknown spirit, belonging to the family of spirits of which St. Peter makes a part: it also follows that under whatever name the guardian angel is invoked, he comes to the call that is made, because he is attracted by the thought, and the name is indifferent to him.

It is always the same when a superior spirit communicates spontaneously under the name of a known personage; nothing proves that it is precisely the spirit of that personage; but if he says nothing that discredits the elevation of character of this latter, there is presumption that it is he, and, in all cases, it may be said that, if it is not he, it must be a spirit of the same degree, or, perhaps, one sent by him. In recapitulation, the question of name is secondary; we may consider the name as a simple indication of the rank the spirit occupies in the spirit scale.

The position is quite different when a spirit of an inferior order borrows a respectable name to give credence to his words, and this case is so frequent that we cannot too carefully guard against these substitutions; for it is under cover of these borrowed names, and with the help of fascination, that certain spirits, more vain than learned, seek to gain credence for the most ridiculous ideas.

The question of identity, then, is, as we have said, nearly a matter of indifference in regard to general instructions, for the best spirits can be substituted the one for the other without its being of any consequence. The superior spirits form, so to say, a collective whole, whose individualities are, with few exceptions, totally unknown to us. The matter of interest to us is, not their person, but their teachings: now, if this teaching be good, it matters little whether he who gives it calls

himself Peter or Paul ; we judge by his quality, and not
by his signature. If a wine is bad, the trade-mark will
not make it better. It is otherwise with private communications, because it is the individual, his very person, that interests us ; and it is right that, in this case,
we should be particular to assure ourselves that the
spirit who comes at our call is really he whom we
wish.

257. The identity of contemporaneous spirits is
much more easily proved, those whose character and
habits are known, for it is precisely these habits, which
they have not yet had time to throw aside, by which
they can be recognized ; and let us say here, that in
these very individual habits we find one of the most
certain signs of identity. Without doubt, the spirit
can give the proofs if asked, but he does not always do
so unless it is agreeable to him, and generally the asking wounds him ; for this reason it should be avoided.
In leaving his body, the spirit has not laid aside his
susceptibility ; he is wounded by any question tending
to put him to the proof. *It is such questions as one
would not dare to propose to him, were he living,* for
fear of overstepping the bounds of propriety ; why,
then, should there be less regard after his death?
Should a man enter a drawing-room and decline to
give his name, should we insist, at all hazards, that
he should prove his identity by exhibiting his titles,
under the pretext that there are impostors? Would
he not, assuredly, have the right to remind his interrogator of the rules of good breeding? This is what the
spirits do, either by not replying or by withdrawing.
Let us make a comparison. Suppose the astronomer,
Arago, during his life, had presented himself in a
house where no one knew him, and he had been thus

addressed : "You say you are Arago ; but as we do not
know you, please prove it by answering our questions :
solve this astronomical problem ; tell us your name,
your Christian name, those of your children, what you
did such and such a day, at such an hour, &c." What
would he have answered? Well, as a spirit, he will
do just what he would have done during his lifetime ;
and other spirits do the same.

258. While spirits refuse to answer puerile and im-
pertinent questions, which a person would have hesi-
tated to ask during their lives, they often spontaneously give irrefutable proofs of their identity by their
character, revealed in their language, by the use of
words that were familiar to them, by citing certain
facts, particularities of their life sometimes unknown
to the assistants, and whose truth has been verified.
Proofs of identity will spring up in many unforeseen
ways, which do not present themselves at first sight,
but in the course of conversations. It is better, then,
to wait for them without calling for them, observing
with care all that may flow from the nature of the communications. (See the fact given, No. 70.)

259. One means employed, sometimes with success,
to be assured of identity when the spirit who communicates is suspected, consists in making him affirm,
in the name of Almighty God, that he is the one he
pretends to be. It often happens that he who usurps
a name would recoil before a sacrilege, and after having begun to write, *I affirm, in the name of* —, he stops,
and traces some insignificant lines, or breaks the
pencil in anger : if he is more hypocritical, he eludes
the question by a mental reservation, writing, for instance, *I certify that I have told you the truth*; or, *I
attest, in the name of God, that it is I who speak to*

you, &c. But there are some not so scrupulous, and who swear whatever you want. One of them communicated to a medium, calling himself *God;* and the medium, highly honored by so high a favor, did not hesitate to believe him. Invoked by us, he did not dare sustain his imposture, and said, "I am not God, but I am His son." "You are, then, Jesus? That is not probable, for Jesus is too high to employ subterfuge. Dare then to affirm, in the name of God, that you are the Christ." "I do not say I am Jesus: I say I am the son of God, because I am one of His creatures."

We may conclude that the refusal on the part of a spirit to affirm his identity in the name of God, is always a manifest proof that the name is an imposture, but that the affirmation is only a presumption, and not a certain proof.

260. Among the proofs of identity may also be classed the similarity of the writing and the signature, but, as it is not always given to all mediums to obtain this result, it is not always a sufficient guarantee; there are forgers in the world of spirits as in this; so that this is but presumptive evidence, which acquires value only by accompanying circumstances. It is the same with all material signs that some give as talismans that cannot be imitated by lying spirits. For those who dare perjure themselves in God's name, or counterfeit a signature, no material sign whatever will offer an obstacle. The best of all the proofs of identity is in the language and in casual circumstances.

261. It will be said, doubtless, that if a spirit can imitate a signature, he can as well imitate the language. That is true: we have seen those who had the effron-

tery to take the name of the Christ, and in order to delude, simulated the evangelical style, constantly introducing at hap-hazard the well-known words, *Verily, verily, I say unto you;* but when the whole was studied without prejudice, the depth of the thoughts, the bearing of the expressions, scrutinized, — when, by the side of fine maxims of charity, ridiculous and puerile recommendations were seen, — he would needs be fascinated to mistake it. Yes, certain parts of the material form of the language can be imitated, but not the thought: never will ignorance imitate true knowledge, never will vice imitate true virtue; some part will always show, if but the tip of the ear; the medium, as also the invocator, need all their perspicacity, all their judgment, to unravel the truth from the falsehood. They must remember that the perverse spirits are capable of every stratagem, and the more elevated the name under which a spirit announces himself, the more it should inspire distrust. How many mediums have had apocryphal communications signed Jesus, Mary, or a venerated saint!

Distinction of Good and Bad Spirits.

262. If the absolute identity of the spirits is, in many cases, a secondary question, one of little importance, it is not the same with the distinction of good and bad; their individuality may be indifferent to us, their quality never. In all instructive communications, it is on this point the whole attention should be concentrated, because it alone can give us the degree of confidence we may accord to the spirit, whatever may be the name under which he manifests himself. Is the spirit good, or bad? To what degree of the spirit scale does he belong? That is the grand

question. (See *Spirit Scale* in the Book on Spirits, No. 100).

263. The spirits are judged, we have said, as men are judged, by their language. Suppose a man should receive twenty letters from as many unknown persons: from the style, from the thoughts, from many signs, he will decide who are educated or ignorant, polished or ill-bred, superficial, profound, frivolous, vain, serious, light, sentimental, &c. It is the same with spirits: they should be considered as unknown correspondents, and we should ask ourselves what we should think of the knowledge and character of a man who should write such things. It may be given as an invariable rule, and one without exception, that *the language of the spirits is always in accordance with the degree of their elevation.* Not only do the really superior spirits say only good things, but they say them in terms which exclude in the most absolute manner all triviality ; however good these things may be, if they are tarnished by a single expression that savors of lowness, it is an indubitable sign of inferiority ; still more if the whole of the communication outrages propriety by its grossness. The language always betrays its origin, whether by the thought it renders, or by its form ; and if a spirit should desire to delude us as to his pretended superiority, a little conversation suffices for us to estimate him at his proper value.

264. Goodness and benevolence are the essential attributes of purified spirits ; they have no hatred, neither for men nor for other spirits ; they pity weaknesses, they criticise errors, but always with moderation, without anger and without animosity. If it be admitted that truly good spirits can will only good, and say only good things, it must thence be concluded

that anything which, in the language of the spirits, betrays a want of goodness and benevolence, cannot emanate from a good spirit.

265. Intelligence is far from being a certain sign of superiority, for intelligence and morality do not always keep step. A spirit may be good and benevolent, and have very limited knowledge, while an intelligent and educated spirit may be very inferior in morality.

It is quite generally believed that in interrogating the spirit of a man who was learned in a speciality on the earth, the truth will be more certainly obtained : this is logical, yet not always true. Experience shows that savants, as well as other men, especially those who have but lately left the world, are still under the dominion of the prejudices of corporeal life ; they do not immediately rid themselves of the spirit of system. It may, then, be that, under the influence of the ideas they have cherished during their lives, and which have made for them a glorious title, they see less clearly than we think. We do not give this principle as a rule ; far from it ; we say only that it shows for itself, and that, consequently, their human science is not always a proof of their infallibility as spirits.

266. By subjecting all communications to a scrupulous examination, by scrutinizing and analyzing the thought and the expressions, as we should do were we judging a literary work, by *unhesitatingly* rejecting everything that sins against logic and good sense, everything that contradicts the character of the spirit reputed to be manifested ; the deceiving spirits are discouraged, and end by withdrawing, once thoroughly convinced that they cannot deceive us. We repeat it, this is the only means, but it is infallible, because no bad communication can resist a rigorous criticism.

The good spirits are never offended by it, for they themselves advise it, and because they have nothing to fear from the examination ; the bad alone take offence, and try to dissuade from it : this of itself proves what they are.

We give the advice of St. Louis on this subject : —

"However great may be the confidence with which the spirits who preside over your labors inspire you, it is a recommendation we cannot too often repeat, and which you should always bear in mind when you give yourself to your studies — to weigh and mature, that is, submit to the censorship of the severest reason, all the communications you receive ; as long as one point appears suspicious, doubtful, or obscure to you, not to neglect to ask the explanations necessary to satisfy you."

267. The means of recognizing the quality of the spirits may be recapitulated in the following principles : —

1. Good sense is the sole criterion by which to discern the value of the spirits. Every formula given for this purpose by the spirits themselves is absurd, and cannot emanate from superior spirits.

2. The spirits are judged by their language and by their actions. The actions of spirits are the sentiments they inspire and the advice they give.

3. It being admitted that good spirits can say and do only good, nothing bad can come from a good spirit.

4. The superior spirits have a language always worthy, noble, elevated, with not the least tincture of triviality ; they say everything with simplicity and modesty, never boast, never make a parade of their knowledge or their position among others. That of the inferior or ordinary spirit has always some reflex

of human passions ; every expression that savors of vulgarity, self-sufficiency, arrogance, boasting, acrimony, is a characteristic indication of inferiority, or of treachery if the spirit presents himself under a respected and venerated name.

5. We must not judge spirits by the material form and the correctness of their style, but probe its inmost sense, scrutinize their words, weigh them coolly, deliberately, and without prejudice. Any digression from logic, reason, and wisdom leaves no doubt of their origin, whatever may be the name under which the spirit is disguised. (224.)

6. The language of elevated spirits is always identical, if not in form, at least in the inmost. The thoughts are the same, whatever be the time and place ; they may be more or less developed, according to circumstances, to the needs and to the facilities of communicating, but they will not be contradictory. If two communications bearing the same name are in opposition, one of the two is, evidently, apocryphal, and the true one will be that where NOTHING contradicts the known character of the personage. For instance, between two communications signed by St. Vincent de Paul, of which one should preach union and charity, and the other should tend to sow discord, no sensible person could mistake.

7. Good spirits tell only what they know ; they are either silent or confess their ignorance of what they do not know. The bad speak of everything with boldness, without caring for the truth. Any notorious scientific heresy, any principle that shocks good sense, shows fraud, if the spirit pretends to be an enlightened spirit.

8. Again, we recognize trifling spirits by the facility

with which they predict the future and material facts not given us to know. The good spirits may presage future things when that knowledge is useful for us to know, but they never fix dates ; any announcement of an event at a fixed date is indicatory of mystification.

9. The superior spirits express themselves simply, without prolixity ; their style is concise, without excluding the poetry of ideas and expressions, clear, intelligible to all, and requires no effort for its comprehension ; they have the art of saying much in a few words, because each word has its signification. The inferior spirits, or false savants, hide under inflated language and emphasis the emptiness of their thoughts. Their language is often pretentious, ridiculous, or obscure, by way of wishing to seem profound.

10. Good spirits never command ; they do not force themselves on any one ; they advise, and if they are not listened to, they withdraw. The bad are imperious ; they give orders, wish to be obeyed, and remain, whether or no. Every spirit who forces himself on any one betrays his origin. They are exclusive and absolute in their opinions, and pretend that they alone have the privilege of truth. They exact a blind belief, and make no appeal to reason, because they know that reason will unmask them.

11. Good spirits do not flatter ; they approve when we do well, but always with reserve ; the bad give exaggerated eulogiums, stimulate pride and vanity, while preaching humility, and seek to *exalt the personal importance* of those with whom they would curry favor.

12. The superior spirits are above the puerilities of form *in everything*. Only ordinary spirits attach importance to petty details, incompatible with truly ele-

vated ideas. Any *over-particular prescription* is a certain sign of inferiority and treachery on the part of a spirit who takes an imposing name.

13. The odd and ridiculous names some spirits take, who wish to impose on credulity, should be distrusted; it would be exceedingly absurd to take these names seriously.

14. It is also necessary to distrust those who present themselves easily under extremely venerated names, and to accept their words with the utmost reserve; in this case a severe censorship is indispensable, for it is often but a mask they assume to gain credit for their pretended intimate relations with spirits beyond them. By this means they flatter the vanity of the medium, and make use of it often to draw him into doing ridiculous things, or things to be regretted.

15. The good spirits are very careful as to the steps they advise; they never have any but a *serious and eminently useful* aim. We should, then, regard with suspicion all motives that are not of this character, or that would be condemned by reason, and should deliberate seriously before undertaking them, for we might be exposed to disagreeable mystifications.

16. We recognize good spirits by their prudent reserve on all subjects that might prove compromising; they dislike to unvail evil; light or malevolent spirits are pleased with displaying it. While the good seek to smooth over injuries and preach indulgence, the bad exaggerate them, and stir up discord by perfidious insinuations.

17. Good spirits advise only good. Any maxim, any advice, which is not *strictly conformable to pure evangelical charity*, cannot be the work of a good spirit.

18. Good spirits advise only perfectly rational things.

Any recommendation which departs from *the right line of good sense, or from the immutable laws of nature*, shows a narrow spirit, and is, consequently, little worthy of confidence.

19. Again, bad or simply imperfect spirits betray themselves by material signs which cannot be mistaken. Their action on the medium is sometimes violent, and provocative of sudden and jerking movements, a feverish and convulsive agitation, totally opposed to the calm and gentleness of the good spirits.

20. Imperfect spirits often use the means of communication opened to them to give perfidious advice; they excite distrust and animosity against those who are antipathetic to them; those who could unmask their imposture are especially the objects of their animadversion.

Weak men are their best game; to induce them to evil. Employing by turns sophisms, sarcasms, insults, even material signs of their occult power the better to convince them, they strive to turn them from the path of truth.

21. The spirits of men who have had, in the world, a special preoccupation, whether material or moral, if they are not disengaged from the influence of matter, are still under the dominion of terrestrial ideas, and retain a part of their prejudices, of their predilections, and even of the fancies they had here below. This is easily discerned in their language.

22. The learning that some spirits display, often with a kind of ostentation, is not a sign of their superiority. Unalterable purity of moral sentiment is the true touchstone.

23. The simple interrogation of a spirit is not sufficient to know the truth. We should, before all things,

know whom we address ; for the inferior spirits, themselve ignorant, treat with frivolity the most serious questions.

Neither does it suffice that a spirit should have been a great man on the earth to have supreme science in the spirit world. Virtue alone, in purifying him, can bring him nearer to God and extend his knowledge.

24. On the part of superior spirits pleasantry is often fine and piquant, but never trivial. Among the joking spirits who are not gross, biting satire is often full of meaning.

25. In carefully studying the character of the spirits who present themselves, especially from a moral point of view, their nature and the degree of confidence to be accorded them is easily ascertained. Good sense cannot be deceived.

26. In order to judge spirits, as in order to judge men, one should know how to judge one's self. There are, unhappily, many men who take their personal opinion as exclusive measure for good and bad, for true and false ; all that contradicts their mode of seeing, their ideas, the system they have conceived or adopted, is bad in their eyes. Such persons evidently lack the first requisite for a healthy appreciation — rectitude of judgment ; but they do not suspect it ; in the very defect is their greatest delusion.

All these instructions flow from experience and the teachings of the spirits ; we complete them by answers given by them on the most important points.

268. *Questions on the Nature and Identity of Spirits.*

1. "By what signs can we discern the superiority or inferiority of spirits ?"

"By their language, as you distinguish a trifler from

a man of sense. We have already said, the superior spirits never contradict themselves, and say only good things; they will nothing but good: it is their whole thought.

"The inferior spirits are still under the dominion of material ideas; their discourses show their ignorance and imperfection. It is given only to the superior spirits to know all things, and to judge without passion."

2. "Is scientific knowledge always a certain sign of a spirit's elevation?"

"No, for if he is still under the influence of matter, he may have your vices and your prejudices. There are persons who, in this world, are excessively jealous and vain: do you believe that as soon as they leave here they lose these defects? There remains, after the departure from here, especially to those who have had very decided passions, a kind of atmosphere that envelops them, and leaves them all these bad things.

"These semi-imperfect spirits are more to be dreaded than bad spirits, because most of them combine astuteness and pride with intelligence. By their pretended knowledge they impose on simple people and on the ignorant, who accept without criticism their absurd and lying theories; though these theories cannot prevail against the truth, they none the less do temporary harm, for they hinder the progress of Spiritism, and mediums are willingly blind to the merit of what is communicated to them. This is what demands great study on the part of enlightened spiritists and mediums; all their attention should be given to distinguish the true from the false."

3. "Many spirit protectors designate themselves by

the names of saints or well-known personages ; what should we believe on this subject ? "

" All the names of saints and of well-known personages would not suffice to furnish a protector to each man ; among the spirits are few who have a name known on the earth ; this is why very often they give none ; but almost always you want a name ; then, to satisfy you, they take that of a man you know and respect."

4. " May not this borrowed name be considered a fraud ? "

" It would be a fraud on the part of a bad spirit who might want to deceive ; but when it is for good, God permits it to be so among spirits of the same order, because there is among them a solidarity and similarity of thought."

5. " So, when a spirit protector calls himself St. Paul, for instance, it is not certain to be the spirit or soul of that apostle ? "

" Not at all, for you find thousands of persons to whom it has been said that their guardian angel is St. Paul, or some other ; but what matters it, if the spirit who protects you is as elevated as St. Paul ? I have said, you want a name ; they take one to be called, and recognized by, as you take a baptismal name to distinguish you from the other members of your family. They can just as well take those of the archangel Raphael, St. Michael, &c., and it would be a matter of no consequence.

" Besides, the more elevated the spirit, the more multiple his radiation ; believe that a spirit protector of a superior order may have under his tutelage hundreds of incarnated beings. With you, on the earth, you have notaries who have charge of the affairs of one or two hundred families : why should you suppose that we, spiritually speaking, would be less capable of directing men morally than those of directing their material interests?"

6. "Why do the spirits who communicate so often take the names of saints?"

"They identify themselves with the habits of those to whom they speak, and take the names calculated to make the strongest impression on the man by reason of his belief."

7. "Do superior spirits, when invoked, always come in person? or, as some think, do they come only by mandataries charged to transmit their thought?"

"Why should they not come in person, if they can? but if the spirit cannot come, it will surely be a mandatary."

8. "Is the mandatary always sufficiently enlightened to answer as the spirit would who sends him?"

"The superior spirits know to whom they confide the care of replacing them. Besides, the more elevated the spirits, the more they are commingled in one common thought, in such manner that they are indifferent to personality; and it ought to be the same for you. Do you think that, in the world of superior spirits, there are only those you have known on the earth capable of instructing you? You are so prone to consider yourselves types of the universe, that you always believe out of your world there is nothing. Truly you are like those savages, who, never having left their own island, fancy the world does not go beyond it."

9. "We comprehend that this may be the case when it is a question of serious teaching; but how is it that the superior spirits permit spirits of a low class to avail

themselves of respectable names to lead into error by perverse maxims ? "

"It is not with their permission ; does it not happen the same among you ? Those who thus deceive will be punished, believe me, and their punishment will be in proportion to the gravity of the imposture. Besides, if you were not imperfect, you would have around you only good spirits, and if you are deceived, you should blame no one but yourselves. God permits it to be so to make trial of your perseverance and your judgment, and to teach you to distinguish truth from error ; if you do not, it is that you are not sufficiently elevated, and still need the lessons of experience."

10. " Are not spirits, slightly advanced but animated by good intentions and a desire to progress, sometimes delegated to replace a superior spirit, in order that they may exercise themselves in teaching ? "

" Never in great circles ; I mean serious circles for general instruction ; those who present themselves there do it from their own desire, and, as you say, to exercise themselves ; this is the reason their communications, though good, always bear traces of their inferiority. Where they are delegated, it is for communications of little importance, and those that may be called personal."

11. "Ridiculous spirit communications are sometimes intermingled with very good maxims: how reconcile this anomaly, which would seem to indicate the simultaneous presence of good and bad spirits ? "

" Bad or frivolous spirits mingle thus to make sentences, without much concern as to their bearing or signification. Are all those among you superior men ? No ; the good and bad spirits do not mingle ; it is the

constant uniformity of good communications by which
you may recognize the presence of good spirits."

12. "Do the spirits that lead persons into error
always do it purposely ? "

"No ; there are spirits, good, but ignorant, who
might deceive in all sincerity ; when they are conscious of their insufficiency, they say so, and tell only
what they know."

13. "When a spirit makes a false communication,
does he always do so with a malicious intention ? "

"No ; if it is a trifling spirit, he amuses himself by
mystifying, and has no other motive."

14. "As certain spirits can deceive by their language, can they also, to the eyes of a seeing medium,
take a false appearance ? "

"That may be done, but with great difficulty. In
all cases it never takes place, unless with an aim that
the bad spirits themselves do not know. They serve
as instruments to give a lesson. The seeing medium
can see frivolous and lying spirits, as others hear
them, or write under their influence. Frivolous spirits
may profit by this disposition in order to abuse him
by deceitful appearances ; that depends on the qualities of his own spirit."

15. "Is it sufficient that we are actuated by good
intentions, not to be deceived ; and are perfectly serious men, who mingle no sentiment of vain curiosity
with their studies, as liable to be deceived ? "

"Less than others, evidently ; but man has always
some hobby which attracts mocking spirits ; he thinks
himself strong, and often is not ; he should beware of
the weakness born of pride and prejudices. These
two causes, by which spirits profit, are not sufficiently

taken into consideration ; by flattering whims they are sure to succeed."

16. " Why does God permit bad spirits to communicate and say evil things ? "

" Even in what is worst there is instruction ; it is for you to know how to extract it. There must be communications of all kinds, for you to learn to distinguish good spirits from bad, and to serve as mirrors to yourselves."

17. " Can spirits, by means of written communications, inspire unjust suspicions against certain persons, and embroil friends ? "

" Perverse and jealous spirits can do in evil all that men can do ; it is, therefore, necessary to beware of them. The superior spirits are always prudent and reserved when they are obliged to blame ; they never speak evil ; they warn with caution. If they desire, for the interest of two persons, that they should never see each other, they will bring about incidents that shall separate them in a perfectly natural manner. Language calculated to sow trouble and discord is always from a bad spirit, whatever may be the name he assumes. Therefore receive with the greatest circumspection the evil that a spirit may say of one of you, especially when a good spirit has said good to you of the same ; and also mistrust yourselves and your own prejudices. In communications from spirits, take only what is good, great, rational, and what your conscience approves."

18. " By the facility with which bad spirits mingle in communications, it appears that one is never sure of the truth ? "

" Yes, if you have judgment to appraise them. In reading a letter, you know how to judge if it is a hodman or a refined person, a fool or a savant, who has written to you : why can you not do the same when spirits write to you? If you receive a letter from a far-off friend, what proves to you it is really from him? His writing, you will say : but are there not forgers who imitate all writing, rascals who might know your affairs? Yet there are signs in which you cannot be mistaken. It is the same with spirits. Imagine, then, that it is a friend writing to you, or that you are reading a literary work, and judge by the same means."

19. "Could superior spirits prevent bad spirits from taking false names?"

"Certainly they could do so; but the worse the spirits, the more headstrong they are, and they often resist injunctions. You must also know that there are persons in whom the superior spirits are more interested than they are in others ; and when they deem it necessary, they know how to preserve them from the injury of the lie : against these persons the deceiving spirits are powerless."

20. "What is the motive of this partiality?"

"It is not partiality ; it is justice : the good spirits are interested in those who profit by their advice, and labor seriously in their own improvement : these are their preferred ones, and they help them ; but they trouble themselves little about those with whom they lose their time in vain words."

21. "Why does God permit spirits to commit sacrilege, by falsely taking venerated names?"

"You should also ask why God permits men to lie and blaspheme. Spirits, as well as men, have their free will, in good as in bad ; but to neither will the justice of God be wanting."

22. "Is there any formula that will drive away deceiving spirits?"

"Formula is matter; good thought toward God is of more value."

23. "Some spirits have said they have inimitable graphic signs, a kind of emblems, by which they may be recognized and their identity established. Is that true?"

"The superior spirits have no other signs, by which they may be recognized, than the superiority of their ideas and of their language. Any spirit can imitate a material sign. As to the inferior spirits, they betray themselves in so many ways, that one must be blind to be deceived."

24. "Cannot deceiving spirits counterfeit thought, also?"

"They counterfeit thought, as theatrical decorators counterfeit nature."

25. "It appears, then, that it is always easy to detect fraud by an attentive study."

"Never doubt it; spirits deceive only those who allow themselves to be deceived. But it is necessary to have the eyes of diamond merchants to distinguish the true stone from the false; he who knows not how to distinguish one from the other goes to the lapidary."

26. "There are persons who allow themselves to be seduced by emphatic language, who think more of words than of ideas, who take false and common ideas for sublime: how can these persons, who are not even capable of judging the works of men, judge those of spirits?"

"When these persons have sufficient modesty to

know their own inefficiency, they will not trust to themselves ; when, through pride, they think themselves capable, when they are not, they must bear the penalty of their silly vanity. The deceiving spirits know whom they address : there are simple, uninstructed persons more difficult to deceive than others who have wit and learning. By flattering his passions they make a man do as they please."

27. "In writing, do not bad spirits often betray themselves by involuntary material signs ? "

"The skillful do not ; maladroits go astray. Any useless or puerile sign is a certain indication of inferiority ; elevated spirits do no useless thing."

28. " Many mediums recognize good and bad spirits by the agreeable or painful impression they experience at their approach. We ask if any disagreeable impression, convulsive agitation, any uneasiness, in short, are always indications of the evil nature of the spirits who manifest themselves ? "

"The medium experiences the sensations of the state in which the spirit is who comes to him. When the spirit is happy, he is tranquil, easy, sedate ; when he is unhappy, he is agitated, feverish, and this agitation naturally passes into the nervous system of the medium. It is the same with men on the earth ; he who is good is calm and tranquil, he who is wicked is constantly agitated."

Remark. There are mediums of greater or less nervous impressibility, so that the agitation cannot be regarded as a general rule ; as in all other things, we must, in this, take into account the circumstances. The painful and disagreeable character of the impression is an effect of contrast ; for if the spirit of the medium sympathizes with the bad spirit who manifests himself, he will be little or not at all affected by it. The rapidity of the writing, which pertains to the extreme flexibility of some mediums, must not be confounded with the convulsive agitation that the slowest mediums may experience from contact with imperfect spirits.

Chapter XXV.

ON INVOCATIONS.

General Considerations. — Spirits who may be invoked. — Language to hold with Spirits. — Utility of Special Invocations. — Questions on Invocations. — Invocations of Animals. — Invocations of Living Persons. — Human Telegraphy.

General Considerations.

269. SPIRITS can communicate spontaneously, or come at our call ; that is, on invocation. Some persons think we should abstain from invoking such or such a spirit, and that it is preferable to wait for the one who wishes to communicate. This opinion is founded on the fact that, in calling a designated spirit, we are not certain that it is he who presents himself, while he who comes spontaneously, and of his own impulse, better proves his identity, as he thus announces his desire to converse with us. In our opinion this is an error ; firstly, because there are always spirits around us, most often of a low class, who ask no better than to communicate ; in the second place, and for this last reason alone in not calling any one in particular, the door is open to all who wish to enter. In an assembly, not to give the word to any one is to leave it to every one ; and the result of that is well known. The direct appeal, made to a designated spirit, is a bond between him and us ; we call him by our desire,

and thus erect a kind of barrier against intruders.
Without a direct appeal, a spirit would often have no
motive for coming to us, unless it might be our familiar spirit. These two methods have each their advantages, and the difficulty would be only in the absolute
exclusion of one of the two.   There is no trouble in
regard to spontaneous communications where one is
master of the spirits, and is certain not to let the bad
gain any dominion ; then it is often useful to wait the
good pleasure of those who desire to communicate, because their thought is under no restraint ; and in this
way very admirable things may be obtained, while you
cannot be sure that the spirit you call will be disposed
to speak, or capable of doing so, in the sense that is
desired. The scrupulous examination we have advised
is a guarantee against evil communications.   In regular reunions, especially in those engaged on a continuous work, there are always the accustomed spirits,
who are at the rendezvous without being called, because, by reason of the regularity of the *séances*, they
are pre-engaged ; they often begin spontaneously to
treat a certain subject, develop a proposition, or pre-
scribe what should be done ; and then they are easily
recognized, whether by the form of their language, or
by their writing, or by certain habits familiar to them.

270. When it is wished to communicate with a *designated* spirit, he must of necessity be invoked. (No.
203.) If he can come, this answer is usually obtained :
Yes ; or, *I am here ;* or, *What do you want of me?*
Sometimes he enters directly into the matter, answering by anticipation the questions it is proposed to
address to him.

When a spirit is invoked for the first time, it is best
to designate him with some precision.   In the ques-

tions addressed to him, we should avoid dry, impera-
tive forms; they might be a reason for his withdrawal.
The forms should be affectionate or respectful according to the spirit, and in all cases testify the kindness
of the invocator.

271. We are often surprised at the promptitude
with which an invoked spirit presents himself, even
the first time; it might be said he has been forewarned; this is, indeed, what has been done when
we are thinking of making an invocation. This thinking is a kind of anticipated invocation, and as we
always have our familiar spirits, who are identified with
our thoughts, they prepare the way, so that nothing
opposes it; the spirit whom we wish to call is already
present. When this is not the case, the familiar spirit
of the medium, or of the interrogator, or one of the
habitués, goes to find him, which does not require
much time. If the invoked spirit cannot come instantly, the messenger (the heathens would have said
Mercury) asks for a delay, sometimes of five minutes,
a quarter of an hour, and even several days, and when
he arrives, says, *He is there;* and then we can begin
the questions we want to ask him.

The messenger is not always a necessary intermediary, for the appeal of the invocator may be heard
directly by the spirit, as is said, No. 282, Question 5,
on the mode of transmitting thought.

When we say, Make the invocation in the name of
God, we mean that our recommendation should be
taken seriously, and not lightly; those who see in it
only a formula, and of little consequence, would better
abstain from it.

272. Invocations often present more difficulties to
mediums than spontaneous dictation, especially when

exact answers are wanted to circumstantial questions.
For that end special mediums are required at once
flexible and *positive;* and we have seen (No. 193), that
these last are quite rare, for, as we have said, the fluidic
relations (*rapports*) are not always instantaneously established with the first spirit comer.   It is, therefore,
best that mediums should not attempt special invocations, until assured of the development of their faculty,
and of the nature of the spirits who assist them ; for
with those who are badly surrounded, the invocations
could have no character of authority.

273. Mediums are generally much more sought for
invocations of private interest than for communications of general interest ; this is explained by the very
natural desire we have to converse with those who
are dear to us.   We consider that we ought to make
several important recommendations on this subject to
mediums.   First, to accede to this desire only with the
utmost reserve with persons in whose sincerity they
cannot completely trust, and to be on their guard
against the snares that malicious persons might set for
them.   Secondly, not to lend themselves to it under
any pretext, if they discover motives of curiosity or
interest, and not a serious intention on the part of the
invocator ; to refuse themselves to all idle questions,
or those aside from the circle of questions that may
rationally be addressed to spirits.   The suggestions
should be put with clearness, perspicuity, and without evasion, if categorical answers are desired.

All those that have an insidious character should
be declined, for it is well known that spirits do not
like those intended to put them to the proof ; to insist
on questions of this nature is to wish to be deceived.
The invocator should go frankly and openly to the

desired end, without subterfuge or windings : if he fears to explain himself, he would better abstain. If invocations are made in the absence of the one who has requested them, it should be done with the greatest prudence ; it is even oftentimes preferable to abstain entirely, those persons alone being fit to criticise the answers, to judge of the identity, to challenge explanations if there is cause, and to put incidental questions brought up by circumstances. Besides, their presence is a bond which attracts the spirit, often little disposed to communicate with strangers for whom he has no sympathy. In a word, the medium should avoid all that could transform him into a consulting agent, which, in the eyes of many persons, is synonymous with a fortune-teller.

Spirits who may be invoked.

274. All spirits, to whatever degree of the scale they belong, may be invoked — the good, as well as the bad ; those who have left this life but lately, and those who have lived in the most remote times ; illustrious men and the most obscure ; our relatives, our friends, and those who are indifferent to us ; but it is not said that they will or can always come at our call : independently of their own will, or of the permission that may be refused them by a superior power, they might be prevented by motives which it is not always given us to penetrate. We would say, there is no absolute hindrance to communications except what we shall presently give ; the obstacles that might hinder the manifestation of a spirit are almost always individual, and pertain to circumstances.

275. Among the causes that might oppose the manifestation of a spirit, some are personal to him, some

foreign. We must place among the former his occupations, or the missions in which he is engaged, and from which he cannot turn aside to yield to our wishes; in such case, his visit is only postponed.

There is, again, his own situation. While the state of incarnation may not be an absolute obstacle, it may be a hindrance at certain given moments, especially when it takes place in inferior worlds, and when the spirit himself is but little dematerialized. In the superior worlds, in those where the ties of spirit and matter are very feeble, the manifestation is almost as easy as in the wandering state, and in all cases easier than in those where the corporeal matter is more compact.

The foreign causes pertain principally to the nature of the medium, to that of the invoker, to the sphere in which the invocation is made, and, lastly, to the end proposed. Some mediums receive more especially communications from their familiar spirits, who may be more or less elevated; others are capable of serving as intermediaries to all spirits; that depends on the sympathy or antipathy, the attraction or repulsion, which the personal spirit of the medium exercises over the foreign spirit, who may take him for interpreter with pleasure or with repugnance. That, again, setting aside the innate qualities of the medium, depends on the development of the medianimic faculty. Spirits come more willingly, are more explicit with a medium who offers them no material obstacle. All things, besides, being equal as to moral conditions, the greater facility a medium has in writing or expressing himself, the more his relations with the spirit world may be generalized.

276. The facility with which the habit of communi-

cating with such or such a spirit gives, must also be taken into consideration ; with time the foreign spirit identifies himself with the spirit of the medium, and with him who calls him. The question of sympathy aside, fluidic relations are established between them which render communications more prompt: this is why a first conversation is not always as satisfying as might be desired, and it is also why the spirits themselves often ask to be recalled. The spirit who is in the habit of coming is as if at home ; he is familiarized with his auditors, and with his interpreters ; he speaks and acts more freely.

277. To recapitulate : from what we have just said, it results that the power of invoking any spirit whatever does not imply that the spirit is at our orders ; he can come at one moment, and not at another, with such medium or such invocator as pleases him, and not with such other ; say what he pleases, without being constrained to say what he does not wish to say ; go when it is agreeable to him ; finally, from causes dependent or not upon his will, after having shown himself assiduously during some time, he may suddenly cease to come. It is from all these motives that when we desire to call a new spirit, it is necessary to ask our guide protector, if the invocation is possible ; in cases where it may not be, he quite generally gives the motives, and then it is useless to insist.

278. An important question presents itself here — that of knowing whether or not there would be disagreeable consequences from invoking a bad spirit. That depends on the end proposed, and the ascendency that can be had over them. There is no difficulty when we call them with a serious and instructive aim, or with a view of improving them ; it is very great, on

the contrary, if it is from pure curiosity or pleasantry, or if one puts himself in their power by asking of them any service whatever.

The good spirits, in such case, can very well give them the power to do what is asked of them, safe to punish severely afterward the rash man who dared to invoke their help and believe them more powerful than God. It is vain that he may have promised himself tp make a good use of it in the end, and to dismiss the servitor once the service is rendered ; the very service solicited, however minute it may be, is a veritable pact concluded with the bad spirit, and he never lets himself be used easily. (See No. 212.)

279. Ascendency is exercised over the inferior spirits only by *moral superiority*.

The perverse spirits feel their masters in good men ; with those who oppose to them only strength of will, a kind of brute force, they struggle, and are often the stronger. A person tried in this way to tame a rebellious spirit by his will ; the spirit answered him, " *Let me alone, with your bullying airs, you who are no better than I ; they might say, a thief preaching to a thief.*"

One is astonished that the name of God invoked against them should often be powerless. St. Louis has given the reason in the following answer : —

"The name of God has influence over imperfect spirits only in the mouth of him who can use it with authority by his virtues ; in the mouth of a man who has no moral superiority over the spirit, it is a word the same as another. It is the same with the holy things opposed to them. The most terrible arms are inoffensive in hands unskilled in their use, or incapable of bearing them."

Language to hold with Spirits.

280. The degree of superiority or inferiority of the spirits naturally indicates the tone it is proper to take with them. It is evident that the more elevated they are, the more right they have to our respect, to our regard, and to our submission. We should show them as much deference as we should have done during their lives, but from different motives; on the earth we should have considered their rank and their social position; in the world of spirits our respect is addressed only to moral superiority. Their very elevation raises them above the puerilities of our adulatory forms. It is not by words that we can secure their kind feeling, but by the sincerity of our sentiments. It would be ridiculous, then, to give them the titles which our usages consecrate to the distinction of ranks, and which, during their lives, might have flattered their vanity; if they are really superior, not only will they not care for them, but to do so will displease them. A good thought is more agreeable to them than the most flattering epithets; if it were otherwise, they would not be above humanity. The spirit of a venerable ecclesiastic, who, in this world, was a prince of the church, a good man, practicing the law of Jesus, answered once to a person who invoked him under the title of "my Lord," "You should at least say, ex-my Lord, for here there is no other Lord but God; know that I see who on earth knelt before me, and those before whom I myself bowed."

As to the inferior spirits, their character shows us the language proper to use with them. Among the number there are some who, though inoffensive, and even kind, are trifling, ignorant, stupid: to treat them the same as serious spirits, as some persons do, is about the same as to bow before a scholar or an ass muffled up in a professor's cap. A tone of familiarity would not be out of place with them, and they do not take offense at it; on the contrary, they willingly receive it.

Among the inferior spirits there are some who are unhappy. Whatever may be the faults they are expiating, their sufferings entitle them to our consideration, so much the more as no one can flatter himself that he does not deserve these words of the Christ: " Let him who is without sin among you cast the first stone." The kindness we show them is a comfort to them : in default of sympathy, they should find the indulgence we should wish them to show to us.

The spirits who reveal their inferiority by the cynicism of their language, their lies, the baseness of their sentiments, the perfidy of their counsels, are assuredly less worthy of our interest than those whose words show their repentance ; we owe them, at least, the pity we accord the greatest criminals, and the way to reduce them to silence is to show ourselves superior to them : they indulge in their perversity only among persons with whom they think there is nothing to fear ; for the perverse spirits feel their masters in good men as in superior spirits.

To recapitulate : as much as it would be irreverential to treat the superior spirits as equals, just so much would it be ridiculous to extend the same deference to all without exception. Have veneration for those who deserve it, gratitude for those who protect and assist us, for all the others that kindness we may some day need for ourselves. In penetrating into the incorporeal world we learn to know it, and this knowledge should regulate us in our relations with those who inhabit it. The ancients, in their ignorance, elevated altars to them ; for us, they are only creatures more or less perfect, and we raise our altars only to God.

Utility of Special Invocations.

281. The communications obtained from very superior spirits, or from those who have animated the great personages of antiquity, are precious from their exalted teachings. These spirits have acquired a degree of perfection which permits them to embrace a more extended sphere of ideas, to penetrate mysteries beyond the ordinary limits of humanity, and, consequently, to initiate us better than others into certain things. It does not follow that communications from less elevated spirits should be without utility ; the observer may draw more than one instruction. To know the manners of a people, it must be studied in every degree of the scale. He who has seen it under one aspect only, would illy know it. The history of a people is not that of its kings and upper social circles ; to judge it, one should see it in its private life and customs.

Now, the superior spirits are the upper circles of the spirit world : their very elevation places them so much above us that we are frightened at the distance that separates us. Spirits more *bourgeois* (may they excuse the expression) make the circumstances of their new existence more palpable to us. With them, the tie between corporeal life and spirit life is more intimate ; we comprehend it better, because it touches us more nearly. In learning from themselves what has become of the men of all conditions and of all characters, what they think, what they experience, good, as well as vicious, the great and the small, the happy and the unhappy of the age, in a word, the men who have lived among us, whom we have seen and known, with whose real life we are acquainted, whose virtues and whims we know, — we comprehend their joys and their sufferings, we are associated with them, and draw therefrom a moral instruction as much more profitable as the relations between them and us are more intimate. We put ourselves more easily in the place of him who has been our equal than of him whom we see only through the mirage of a celestial glory.

Ordinary spirits show us the practical application of the great and sublime truths of which the superior spirits teach us the theory. Besides, in the study of a science nothing is useless; Newton found his law of the forces of the universe in the simplest phenomena.

The invocation of ordinary spirits has, besides, the advantage of putting us *en rapport* with suffering spirits who can be comforted, and whose advancement may be facilitated by useful advice, so that we can be useful while, at the same time, instructing ourselves; there is egotism in seeking only one's own satisfaction in intercourse with the spirits, and he who disdains to extend a helping hand to the unhappy gives proof of pride. Of what use to obtain grand teachings from spirits of the highest order, if it does not make us inwardly better, more charitable, more benevolent for our brothers, both in this world and in the other? What would become of the diseased if the doctors refused to touch their sores?

282. *Questions on Invocations.*

1. "Can we invoke spirits without being mediums?"

"Every one can invoke spirits, and if those you call

cannot manifest themselves materially, they are never-theless near you, and listen to you."

2. " Does the spirit invoked always come at the call made to him ? "

" That depends on the conditions in which he is, for there are circumstances in which he cannot do so."

3. " What causes might prevent a spirit from coming at our call ? "

" Firstly, his will ; then his corporeal state, if he is re-incarnated ; the missions with which he may be charged ; and still further, permission may be refused him. There are spirits who can never communicate — those who, by their nature, belong still to worlds in-ferior to the earth. Neither can those who are in the spheres of punishment, at least without a superior per-mission, which is granted only for the general good. That a spirit may be able to communicate, he must have attained the same degree of advancement as that of the world to which he is called ; otherwise he is strange to the ideas of that world, and has no point of comparison. It is not the same with those who are sent on missions, or in expiation, to inferior worlds ; they have the necessary ideas to reply."

4. " For what motives may the permission to com-municate be refused to a spirit ? "

" It may be a trial or a punishment for him, or for the one who calls him."

5. " How can spirits, dispersed in space or in differ-ent worlds, hear from all points of the universe the in-vocations that are made ? "

" They are often forewarned by the familiar spirits that surround you, who go to seek them ; but here is a phenomenon difficult to explain to you, because you cannot yet understand the transmission of thought among spirits. All I can tell you is, that the spirit you invoke, however distant he may be, receives, as it were, the rebound of the thought as a kind of electrical commotion, which calls his attention to the side from whence comes the thought addressed to him. It might be said he hears the thought, as on earth you hear the voice."

" Is the universal fluid the vehicle of thought, as the air is that of sound ? "

" Yes, with this difference, that sound can be heard only within a very limited radius, while thought attains the infinite. The spirit, in space, is like the traveler in the midst of a vast plain, who, hearing his name suddenly pronounced, directs his attention to the side on which he is called."

6. " We know that distances are but trifles to spirits ; yet one is astonished to see them sometimes respond as promptly to the call as if they had been all ready."

" And so, indeed, they are sometimes. If the invocation is premeditated, the spirit is forewarned, and often finds himself there before he is called."

7. " Is the thought of the invocator more or less easily heard according to circumstances ? "

" Without doubt ; the spirit called by a sympathetic and kind sentiment is more quickly touched : it is to him the voice of a friend which he recognizes ; without that it often happens that the invocation *miscarries*. The thought that springs from the invocation strikes the spirit ; if it is not well directed, it strikes in the void. It is with spirits as with men ; if he who calls them is indifferent or antipathetic, they may hear, but do not often listen."

8. " Does the spirit invoked come voluntarily, or is he constrained to come ? "

" He obeys the will of God, that is, the general law that rules the universe ; and yet constraint is not the word ; for he judges if it be useful to come , and there still is his free will. A superior spirit always comes when he is called for a useful end ; he refuses to anwer only in circles of persons either not serious, or treating the thing as a joke."

9. " Can the invoked spirit refuse to come at the call made on him ? "

" Perfectly ; or where would be his free will ? Do you think all the beings in the universe are at your orders ? And do you consider yourselves obliged to answer all who pronounce your name ? When I say he can refuse, I mean on the demand of the invocator, for an inferior spirit may be constrained to come by a superior spirit."

10. " Is there any means by which the invocator may oblige a spirit to come against his will ? "

" None, if the spirit is your equal or your superior in morality ; I say in *morality*, not in intelligence, because you have no authority over him : if it is your inferior, you can, if it is for his good, for then other spirits will second you." (No. 279.)

11. " Is there any difficulty in invoking inferior spirits ? and is there any danger, in calling them, of putting ourselves in their power ? "

" They rule only those who allow themselves to be ruled. He who is assisted by good spirits has nothing to fear : he controls the inferior spirits ; they do not control him. In isolation, mediums, especially those who are beginning, should abstain from such invocations " (No. 278.)

12. " Is it necessary to be in any particular frame of mind for invocations ? "

"The most essential of all dispositions is concentration of thought, when we desire aught of serious spirits. With faith and the desire of good, one is more powerful to invoke superior spirits. In elevating the soul by concentration of thought, at the moment of invocation, we are identified with good spirits, and attract them to us.

13. "Is faith necessary in invocations?"

"Faith in God, yes; faith will come for the rest if you desire good, and wish for instruction."

14. "Have men more power to invoke spirits when united by community of thought and intention?"

"When all are united by charity and for good, they obtain grand things. Nothing is more injurious to the result of invocations than divergence of thought."

15. "Is making a chain by joining hands for some minutes, at the beginning of reunions, of any use?"

"The chain is a material means, which does not promote union among you if it exist not in the thought: what is more useful is to be united in one common thought, each one calling to his side good spirits. You do not know all you might obtain in a serious reunion, from whence is banished every sentiment of pride and personality, and where reigns a perfect sentiment of mutual cordiality."

16. "Are invocations for fixed days and hours preferable?"

"Yes, and, if it be possible, in the same place; the spirits come to it more willingly: it is the constant desire you have that aids the spirits to come and put themselves into communication with you. Spirits have their occupations, which they cannot leave at a moment's warning for your personal satisfaction. I say, in the same place; but do not suppose this to be an absolute obligation, for spirits come everywhere: I mean, a place consecrated to that is preferable, because there concentration of thought is more perfect."

17. "Have certain objects, such as medallions and talismans, the property of attracting or repelling spirits, as some pretend?"

"This is a useless question, for you know very well that matter has no action on spirits. Be very sure that no good spirit ever advises such absurdities; the virtue of talismans, of whatever nature they be, has never existed save in the imaginations of credulous people."

18. "What must we think of spirits who give rendezvous in dismal places, and at undue hours?"

"These spirits amuse themselves at the expense of those who listen to them. It is always useless, and often dangerous, to yield to such suggestions: useless, because one gains absolutely nothing but to be mystified; dangerous, not for the evil the spirits might do, but on account of its influence on weak brains."

19. "Are there days and hours more propitious than others for invocations?"

"For spirits that is perfectly indifferent, as is everything material, and it is a superstition to believe in the influence of days and hours. The most propitious moments are those in which the invocator can be the least disturbed by his accustomed occupations; when his body and mind are most calm."

20. "Is invocation an agreeable or a painful thing for spirits? Do they come voluntarily when they are called?"

"That depends on their character and the motives from which they are called. When the object is praiseworthy, and when the surrounding is sympathetic to them, it is agreeable to them, and even attractive ; the spirits are always happy in the affection testified for them. There are those to whom it is a great happiness to communicate with men, and who suffer from the indifference in which they are left. But, as I have said, it depends upon their character ; among spirits there are also misanthropes, who do not like to be disturbed, and whose answers show their ill humor, especially when they are called by indifferent people, in whom they are not at all interested. A spirit has often no motive for coming at the call of an unknown person, who is indifferent to him, and almost always moved by curiosity ; if he comes, he usually makes but short visits, unless there may be a serious and instructive end in view in the invocation."

Remark. We see people who invoke their relations only to ask them the most ordinary things of material life ; for instance, one to know if he shall rent or sell his house, another to know what profit he shall have from his merchandise, the place where money is deposited, whether or no a certain business will be advantageous. Our relations from beyond the tomb are interested in us only by reason of the affection we have for them. If all our thought is limited to thinking them sorcerers, if we think of them only to ask favors of them, they cannot have any very great sympathy for us, and we should not be astonished at the little benevolence they sometimes evince.

21. "Is there a difference between good and bad spirits, in regard to their readiness to come at our call."

"There is a very great difference ; bad spirits come voluntarily only inasmuch as they hope to govern and make dupes ; but they experience a strong contrariety when they are forced to confess their faults, and only ask to go away again, like a pupil called up for correction. They can be constrained to come, by the superior spirits, as a punishment, and for the instruction of the incarnated. Invocation is painful for good spirits when they are called uselessly, for frivolities ; then they do not come at all, or soon withdraw."

"You may take it as a principle, that spirits, whatever they be, like no more than yourselves to serve as amusement for the curious. Often you have no other end, in invoking a spirit, than to see what he will tell you, or to question him on the particulars of his life, which he does not care to tell you, because he has no motive for giving you his confidence ; and think you he is going to put himself at the bar for your good pleasure ? Undeceive yourselves : what he would not have done during his lifetime, he will not do as a spirit."

Remark. Experience proves, in fact, that invocation is always agreeable to spirits, when made with a serious and useful motive ; the good come with pleasure to instruct us ; those who suffer find comfort in the sympathy shown them ; those whom we have known are satisfied with our remembrance. Frivolous spirits like to be invoked by frivolous persons, because that gives them an opportunity to amuse themselves at their expense ; they are ill at ease with grave persons.

22. "In order to manifest themselves, do spirits always need to be invoked ? "

"No ; they very often present themselves without being called, and that proves that they come willingly."

23. "When a spirit comes of himself, can we be sure of his identity ? "

" Not at all ; for deceiving spirits often employ this means, the better to delude."

24. "When we invoke the spirit of a person by thought, does he come to us even when there are no manifestations by writing or otherwise ? "

"Writing is a material means by which the spirit may attest his presence ; but it is the thought that attracts him, and we show it by writing."

25. When an inferior spirit manifests himself, can we oblige him to withdraw ? "

" Yes ; by not listening to him. But how do you expect him to withdraw when you amuse yourselves with his vileness ? The inferior spirits attach themselves to those who listen to them with complacence, like the fools among you."

26. " Is invocation, made in the name of God, a guarantee against the intermeddling of bad spirits ? "

"The name of God is not a check for all perverse spirits, but it restrains many ; by this means you always remove some, and you would remove many more, if it were made from the bottom of the heart, and not as a common formula."

27. " Could several spirits be invoked by name at the same time ? "

" There is no difficulty in that ; and if you had three or four hands to write, three or four spirits could answer you at the same time : this is what does happen when there are several mediums."

28. "When several spirits are simultaneously invoked, and there is but one medium, which one answers ? "

"One answers for all, and he expresses the collective thought."

29. " In a *séance*, could the same spirit communicate with two mediums at the same time ? "

" As easily as you have men who can dictate several letters at the same time."

Remark. We have seen a spirit answer at the same time by two mediums, — to one in English, to another in French, — and the answers were identical in sense ; some were the literal translation of the others. Two spirits, invoked simultaneously by two mediums, might establish a conversation with each other ; this mode of communication not being necessary for them, as they can read each other's thought, they sometimes do it for our instruction. If they are inferior spirits, as they are still imbued with terrestrial passions and corporeal ideas, it might happen that they would dispute and apostrophize each other with big words, upbraid each other with their wrongs, and even throw pencils, baskets, planchettes, &c., at each other.

30. " Can a spirit, invoked at the same time in different places, answer simultaneously to the questions addressed to him ? "

" Yes, if it is an elevated spirit."

—" In this case does the spirit divide himself? or has he the gift of ubiquity ? "

" The sun is one, yet he radiates all around, throwing his rays afar without subdividing himself : it is the same with spirits. The thought of the spirit is like a star that projects its light to a distance, and may be seen from all points of the horizon. The purer the spirit, the more his thought radiates and extends, like the light. The inferior spirits are too material ; they can answer only to a single person at once, and cannot come if they are called elsewhere. A superior spirit, called at the same time to two different points, will answer both invocations, if they are equally serious and fervent ; if not, he will give his preference to the more serious."

Remark. The same with a man who can, without changing his place, transmit his thought by signals seen from different points.

In a *séance* of the Parisian Society for Spirit Studies, when the question of ubiquity had been discussed, a spirit dictated spontaneously the following communication : " You asked, this evening, what is the hierarchy of spirits as to ubiquity ? Compare us to an aeronaut, who rises little by little in the air. When he leaves the ground, a very small circle can perceive him ; as he rises, the circle enlarges for him ; and when he has reached a certain height, he appears to an infinite number of persons. So with us : a bad spirit, who is still attached to the earth, remains in a very restricted circle, in the midst of persons who see him. If he grows in grace, if he becomes better, he can talk with several persons ; and when he has become a superior spirit, he can radiate like the light of the sun, show himself to many persons, and in many places, at the same time.   CHANNING."

31. " Can the pure spirits be invoked — those who have ended their series of incarnations ? "

" Yes, but very rarely : they communicate only with pure and sincere hearts, and not with the *haughty* and *egotistical:* you must be careful to distrust inferior spirits, who take this quality to give themselves more importance in your eyes."

32. " How is it that the spirit of the most illustrious men comes as readily and familiarly at the call of the most obscure ? "

" Men judge spirits by themselves, and that is an

error: after the death of the body, terrestrial rank no longer exists; there is but the distinction of goodness among them; and those who are good go wherever there is good to be done."

33. "At what length of time after death can a spirit be invoked?"

"It can be done at the very instant of death; but as, at this moment, the spirit is still in trouble, he answers but imperfectly."

Remark. The duration of the trouble being very variable, there can be no fixed time to make the invocation; yet it is rare if, at the end of eight days. the spirit has not sufficiently recovered to be able to answer: he can sometimes very well do so two or three days after death; it can, in any case, be tried with care.

34. "Is the invocation at the moment of death more painful for the spirit than if made later?"

"Sometimes; it is as if you were torn from sleep before you are fully awakened. There are some, however, who are not at all disturbed by it, and even whom it helps out of their trouble."

35. "How can the spirit of a child, who has died very young, answer with knowledge, when, during his life, he had as yet no consciousness of himself?"

"The soul of a child is a spirit *still enveloped in the swaddling-clothes of matter;* but, disengaged from matter, he enjoys his spirit faculties, for spirits have no age; which proves that the spirit of the child has already lived. Yet, until he shall have become completely disengaged, he may preserve in his language some traces of the character of childhood."

Remark. The corporeal influence which makes itself felt on the spirit of the child, for a longer or shorter time, is sometimes remarked, in the same way, on the spirit of a person dying in a state of insanity. The spirit himself is not crazy, but we know that some spirits, for a time, believe themselves still in this world : it is, then, not astonishing that the spirit of an insane person should still feel the fetters which, during life, opposed his free manifestation, until he become completely disengaged. This effect varies according to the causes of the insanity, for there are some maniacs who recover the lucidity of their ideas immediately after their death.

283. *Invocation of Animals.*

36. " Can the spirit of an animal be invoked ?"

" After the death of the animal, the intelligent principle that was in him is in a latent state ; he is immediately utilized, by spirits charged with such cares, to animate new beings, in whom he continues the work of his elaboration. Thus, in the spirit world there are no spirits of wandering animals, but only human spirits. This answers your question."

" How is it, then, that some persons have invoked animals and received answers ? "

" Invoke a stone and it will answer you. There is always a crowd of spirits ready to speak for anything."

Remark. Just the same if you invoke a myth, or an allegorical personage, it will answer ; that is, it will be answered for, and the spirit who would present himself would take its character and appearance. One day, a person took a fancy to invoke *Tartufe*, and *Tartufe* came immediately ; still more, he talked of *Orgon*, of *Elmire*, of *Damis*, and of *Valire*, of whom he gave news ; as to himself, he counterfeited the hyp-

ocrite with as much art as if *Tartufe* had been a real
personage. Afterward, he said he was the spirit of
an actor who had played that character.

Trifling spirits always profit by the inexperience of
interrogators, but they take good care never to address
those who they know are enlightened enough to discover their impostures, and who would give no credit
to their stories.

It is the same among men.

A gentleman had in his garden a nest of gold-
finches, in which he was much interested ; one day the
nest disappeared ; being certain that no one about the
house had been guilty of its destruction, he thought
of invoking the mother of the little ones ; she came,
and said, in very good French, " Do not accuse any
one, and be easy about my little ones ; the cat over-
threw the nest by jumping ; you will find, under the
grass, all the little ones that have not been eaten."
He looked, and found it so. Must he conclude that
the bird had answered him ? No, assuredly ; but
simply that a spirit knew the history of it. This
proves how much appearances should be distrusted,
and how just the above reply: Invoke a stone, and
it will answer you. (See, further the chapter on
Mediumship among Animals, No. 234.)

284. *Invocation of Living Persons.*

37. " Is the incarnation of the spirit an absolute
obstacle to his invocation ? "

" No ; but the state of the body must be such, at
the time, as to permit the spirit to disengage himself.
The incarnated spirit comes as much more easily as
the world in which he finds himself is of a more

elevated order, because the bodies there are less material."

38. "Can the spirit of a living person be invoked?"

"Of course, as you can invoke an incarnated spirit. The spirit of a living person can also, in his moments of liberty, come *without being invoked;* that depends on his sympathy for the person with whom he communicates." (See No. 116 — *History of the Man and the Snuff-box.*)

39. "In what state is the body of the person when the spirit is invoked?"

"He sleeps, or is dozing; it is then the spirit is free."

"Could the body awaken while the spirit is absent?"

"No; the spirit is obliged to *reënter* it; if, at the moment, he may be talking to you, he leaves you, and often tells you the reason for so doing."

40. "How is the spirit, when absent from the body, warned of the necessity of its return?"

"The spirit of a living body is never completely separated; to whatever distance it may transport itself, it is held to the body by a fluidic bond, which serves to recall it when necessary; this tie is broken only by death."

Remark. This fluidic tie has often been noticed by seeing mediums. It is a kind of phosphorescent train, which is lost in space in the direction of the body. Some spirits say it is by that they recognize those who are still boumd to the corporeal world.

41. "What would happen, if, during sleep, and in the absence of the spirit, the body should be mortally wounded?"

"The spirit would be warned, and would reënter before death."

— "So it could not happen that the body could die in the absence of the spirit, and that on his return he could not reënter it?"

" No ; it would be contrary to the law regulating the union of the soul and body."

—"But if the blow was struck suddenly, and without premeditation?"

" The spirit would be warned before the mortal blow could be given."

Remark. The spirit of a living person interrogated on this point, answered, —

"If the body could die in the absence of the spirit, it would be too convenient a method of committing hypocritical suicides."

42. " Is the spirit of a person invoked during sleep as free to communicate as that of a dead person?"

" No ; matter always influences it more or less."

Remark. A person in this state, to whom this question was addressed, answered, —

" *I am always chained to the ball I drag after me.*"

—"In this state. could the spirit be hindered from coming because of its being elsewhere?"

" Yes ; the spirit might be in a place where it pleased him to remain ; then he would not come at the invocation, especially if it were made by some one in whom he felt no interest."

43. " Is it absolutely impossible to invoke the spirit of a person who is awake?"

" Though difficult, it is not absolutely impossible ; for if the invocation *carries*, it may produce sleep in the person ; but the spirit can communicate, as spirit, only in those moments when its presence is not necessary to the intelligent activity of the body."

Remark. Experience proves that invocation made

during a waking state may produce sleep, or, at least, an absorption bordering on sleep; but this can take place only through a very energetic will, and when the ties of sympathy exist between the two persons; otherwise the invocation *does not carry*. Even in a case where the invocation causes sleep, if the moment is inopportune, the person not wishing to sleep will resist, and, if he yield, his spirit will be troubled, and answer with difficulty. It thus results that the most favorable moment for the invocation of a living person is during his natural sleep, because his spirit, being free, can as well come toward the one who calls him as to go elsewhere.

When the invocation is made with the consent of the person, and he seeks to sleep for the purpose, this very desire may retard the sleep and trouble the spirit; an unforced sleep is preferable.

44. "Has a living person, on waking, a conscious·ness of having been invoked?"

"No; you are yourselves invoked more often than you think. The spirit alone knows it, and may some-times leave with him a vague impression, like a dream."

—"Who can invoke us if we are but obscure beings?"

"In other existences you may have been known either in this world or in others, and have had your relations and friends the same in this world or in others. Suppose your spirit may have animated the body of the father of another person: well, then, he invokes his father; it is your spirit who is invoked, and who answers."

45. "Would the invoked spirit of a living person answer as spirit, or with the ideas pertaining to a waking state?"

"That depends on his elevation; but his judgment

is more healthy, and he has fewer prejudices, exactly like somnambulists ; it is a nearly similar state."

46. " If the spirit of a somnambulist in a state of magnetic sleep were invoked, would he be more lucid than that of other persons ? "

" He would, doubtless, answer more lucidly, because more disinthralled ; all depends on the degree of the spirit's independence of the body."

— "Could the spirit of a somnambulist answer a person at a distance, who might invoke him, at the same time that he is verbally answering another person ? "

" The faculty of communicating simultaneously at two different points pertains only to spirits completely disengaged from matter."

47. " Can the ideas of a person in a waking state be modified by acting upon his spirit during sleep ? "

" Yes, sometimes ; the ties that bind the spirit to matter are not then so close ; he is more accessible to moral impressions, and these impressions may influence his mode of seeing in the ordinary state."

48. " Is the spirit of a living person free to say or not to say what he will ? "

" He has his facul.ies of spirit, and consequently his free will ; and as he has more perspicacity, he is even more circumspect than when in a waking state."

49. " In invoking a person, can he be constrained to speak when he wishes to be silent ? "

" I have said that the spirit has his free will ; but it can very well be that, as spirit, he attaches less importance to certain things than in the ordinary state ; his conscience may speak more freely. Besides, if he does not wish to speak, he can easily escape importunities by leaving, for a spirit cannot be retained as you can retain his body."

50. "Can the spirit of a living person be forced by another spirit to come and speak, as can be done among wandering spirits?"

"Among spirits, whether of the dead or the living, there is no supremacy, save from moral superiority; and you may well believe that a superior spirit will never lend his support to a cowardly indiscretion."

Remark. This abuse of confidence would, in fact, be a bad action, which, however, would have no result, since you cannot tear from a spirit a secret he desires to keep, at least unless, influenced by a sentiment of justice, he avows what, under other circumstances, he would withhold. A person, by this means, desired to know of one of his relatives if his will was in her favor. The spirit answered, "Yes, my dear niece, and you shall soon have the proof of it."

The thing was true; but a few days afterward the relative destroyed his will, and was mischievous enough to let her know of it, though he did not know he had been invoked. An instinctive feeling, doubtless, urged him to execute the resolution his spirit had taken at the time of his having been questioned. It is cowardly to ask of a spirit, either of the dead or living, what you would not have dared to ask him in person, and this cowardice is not even compensated by the expected result.

51. "Can one invoke a spirit whose body is still in the mother's womb?"

"No; you know that, at such time, the spirit is in utter trouble."

Remark. The incarnation takes place actually only at the moment of the child's first breath; but from the conception the spirit designated to animate it is seized with a trouble, which increases as the birth approaches, and takes from him his self-consciousness, and consequently the faculty of answering. (See *Book on Spirits* — Return to the Corporeal Life, Union of the Soul and Body, No. 344.)

52. "Could a deceiving spirit take the place of a living invoked person?"

"That is not doubtful, and it very often happens, particularly when the intention of the invocator is not pure. But the invocation of living persons is interesting only as a psychological study : it is necessary to abstain always when it can have no instructive result."

Remark. If the invocation of wandering spirits does not always *carry*, — to use their own expression, — it must be much more frequent for those who are incarnated ; then, especially, do deceiving spirits take their place.

53. "Are there dangers in the invocation of a living person?"

"It is not always without danger ; that depends on the person's position, for if he is sick, it might add to his sufferings."

54. "In what case could the invocation of a living person have most dangers?"

"You should abstain from invoking children of a very tender age, persons seriously ill, infirm old men ; indeed, there are dangers in all cases when the body is very much enfeebled."

Remark. The sudden suspension of the intellectual faculties during a waking state might also be dangerous, if the person at the moment should find himself in need of his presence of mind.

55. "During the invocation of a living person, does the body experience fatigue by reason of the work his absent spirit performs?"

"A person in this state, who said his body was fatigued, answered this question : 'My spirit is like a balloon tied to a post ; my body is the post, which is shaken by the strugglings of the balloon.'"

56. "As the invocation of living persons may be dangerous when made without precaution, does not the danger exist when we invoke a spirit we do not know to be incarnated, and who might not find himself in favorable conditions ? "

"No ; the circumstances are not the same : he will come only if in a position to do so ; and besides, have I not told you to ask, before making an invocation, if it be possible ? "

57. "When, at the most inopportune moments, we experience an irresistible desire to sleep, does it warn us that we are invoked by some one ? "

"It may occur, but most often it is a purely physical effect ; either the body or the spirit has need of its liberty."

Remark. A lady of our acquaintance, a medium, one day invoked the spirit of her grandson, who was sleeping in the same room. His identity was confirmed by the language, by the familiar expressions of the child, and by the exact recital of several things that had happened at his boarding-school ; but one especial circumstance confirmed it. Suddenly the hand of the medium paused in the middle of a sentence, and it was impossible to obtain anything further: at this moment, the child, half awake, moved in his bed. Some moments after, he again slept ; the hand went on anew, continuing the interrupted talk.

The invocation of living persons, made under good conditions, proves, in the least contestable manner, the distinct action of the spirit and the body, and consequently, the existence of an intelligent principle independent of matter. (See *Revue Spirite* of 1860, pages 11 and 18, several remarkable examples of invocation of living persons.)

285. *Human Telegraphy.*

58. "Could two persons, by invoking each other, transmit their thoughts, and thus correspond?"

"*Yes ; and this human telegraphy will some day be a universal means of correspondence.*"

"Why should it not be practiced at present?"

"So it is, with some persons, but not with every one : men must *purify themselves*, in order that their spirit may be disengaged from matter ; and this is still another reason for making the invocation in the name of God. Until then it is confined to *chosen and dematerialized souls*, who are rarely met in the actual state of the world's inhabitants."

Chapter XXVI.

QUESTIONS THAT MAY BE ADDRESSED TO SPIRITS.

Preliminary Observations. — Questions sympathetic or antipathetic to the Spirits. — Questions on the Future. — On Past and Future Existences. — On Moral and Material Interests. — On the Fate of Spirits. — On the Health. — On Inventions and Discoveries. — On Hidden Treasures. — On the other World.

Preliminary Observations.

286. Too much importance cannot be attached to the manner of putting questions, and still more to their nature. Two things are to be considered in those addressed to spirits — the form and the subject. As to the form, they should be compiled with clearness and precision, avoiding complexity. But there is another point not less important — the order that should preside in their arrangement. When a subject requires a series of questions, it is essential that they be put together with method, so as to flow naturally into each other ; the spirits then answer much more readily and clearly than when they are put by chance, passing abruptly from one object to another. For this reason it is always best to prepare them in advance, intercalating those which, during a *séance*, are brought out by circumstances. The compiling is better done with the

head quiet; and this preparatory work is, as we have already said, a kind of anticipated invocation at which the spirit may have assisted, and be prepared to answer. It will be remarked that, very often, the spirit answers by anticipation to certain questions, which proves him to have already known them.

The subject-matter of the question requires a still more serious attention, for it is often the nature of the request that draws forth a true or false reply; there are those to which the spirits cannot or ought not to reply, from motives unknown to us: it is, therefore, useless to insist; but what we should especially avoid are questions calculated to put their perspicacity to the proof. When a thing is, it is said they ought to know it; but it is precisely because the thing is known to you, or that you have the means of verifying it for yourselves, that they do not give themselves the trouble of answering; this suspicion annoys them, and nothing satisfactory is obtained.

Have you not daily examples of this with yourselves? Would superior men, who are conscious of their value, answer all the foolish questions calculated to subject them to examination like scholars? The desire of making a believer of such or such a person is not, for spirits, a motive for satisfying a vain curiosity; they know that conviction will come sooner or later, and the means they employ to lead to it are not always those you think. Suppose a grave man, occupied with useful and serious matters, incessantly harassed by the puerile questions of a child, and you will have an idea of what the superior spirits think of all the nonsense with which they are credited. It does not follow that very useful teachings and excellent advice may not be obtained from spirits; but they answer according to the knowledge they themselves possess, according to the interest you deserve on their part and the affection they have for you, and according to the end proposed and the usefulness they see in the thing ; but if all our thoughts are limited to thinking them better fitted to teach us of the things of this world, they cannot have a very profound sympathy for us ; then they make visits very short or very often, according to the degree of their imperfection, evincing their annoyance for having been uselessly troubled.

287. Some persons think it preferable to abstain from asking questions, and that it is best to wait the teaching of the spirits without calling it forth ; that is an error. Spirits, certainly, give spontaneous instructions of a very high bearing, which it would be wrong to neglect ; but there are explanations we should often await a long time were they not solicited. Without the questions we have asked, the *Book on Spirits* and the *Book on Mediums* would be still to make, or, at least, would have been much less complete, and a crowd of problems of great importance would be still to solve. Questions, far from having the least danger attending them, are of great utility as to instruction, when we know how to keep them within the prescribed limits. They have another advantage ; they help to unmask deceiving spirits, who, being more vain than learned, rarely undergo to their advantage the trial of questions of close logic, by which they are driven to their last intrenchments. As spirits truly superior have nothing to dread from such a censorship, they are the first to offer explanations on obscure points ; the others, on the contrary, fearing to meet a stronger party, take great care to avoid them ; thus, in general, they recommend to the mediums they wish to govern,

and to make accept their theories, to abstain from all controversy at the place of their teachings.

If what we have already said in this work has been thoroughly understood, some idea can be formed of the circle in which it is best to confine the questions to be addressed to spirits ; yet, for greater certainty, we give below the answers that have been made on the principal subjects on which persons of slight experience are usually disposed to interrogate them.

288. *Questions sympathetic or antipathetic to Spirits.*

1. " Do spirits answer willingly to questions that are addressed to them ? "

" That is according to the questions. Serious spirits always answer with pleasure to those which have for their end good, and the means to advance you. They do not listen to futile questions."

2. " Is it sufficient that a question be serious to obtain a serious answer ? "

" No ; that depends on the spirit who answers."

— " But does not a serious question drive away trifling spirits ? "

" It is not the question that drives away trifling spirits ; *it is the character of him who asks it.*"

3. " What are the questions especially antipathetic to good spirits ? "

" All those that are useless, or are asked from a motive of curiosity or test ; then they do not answer, but withdraw."

— " Are there any questions antipathetic to imperfect spirits ? "

" Only those that might unmask their ignorance or their fraud when they try to deceive ; otherwise they answer all, without troubling themselves about the truth."

4. "What is to be thought of persons who see in spirit communications only a distraction or a pastime, or a means of obtaining revelations on what interests them?"

"These persons are very pleasing to inferior spirits, who, like them, wish to be amused, and are content when they have mystified them."

5. "Where spirits do not answer certain questions, is it the effect of their own will, or, rather, that a superior power is opposed to certain revelations?"

"Both; there are things that cannot be revealed, and others that the spirit does not know."

—"By strongly insisting, would the spirit end by answering?"

"No; the spirit who does not wish to answer can always leave. It is, therefore, necessary to wait when you are told to do so; and do not be obstinate in wishing to make us answer. To insist upon having an answer when we do not wish to give one, is a certain means of being deceived."

6. "Can all spirits understand the questions put to them?"

"Very far from it; the inferior spirits are incapable of comprehending some questions, which does not, however, prevent them from answering well or ill, just as it happens among yourselves."

Remark. In some cases, and when the thing is useful, it frequently happens that a more enlightened spirit comes to the assistance of the ignorant spirit, and breathes to him what he ought to say.

The contrast between the answers is easily recognized; and, besides, the spirit often acknowledges it himself. This happens only for spirits really ignorant, never for those who make a parade of false knowledge.

289. *Questions on the Future.*

7. " Can spirits tell us of the future ? "

" If man should know the future, he would neglect the present. And there is where you always insist upon having a precise answer ; it is a great wrong, for the manifestation of spirits is not a means of divination. If you will, absolutely, have an answer, it will be given to you by a foolish spirit ; we tell you so always." (See *Book on Spirits* — Knowledge of the Future, No. 868.)

8. " Are there not future events sometimes spontaneously and truly announced by spirits ? "

" It may happen that the spirit may foresee things he thinks it useful to make known, or that he has a mission to make known ; but there is greater cause for suspecting it to be deceiving spirits, who are amusing themselves by making predictions. Only by taking all the circumstances together can we ascertain the degree of confidence they merit."

9. " What kind of predictions should we most mistrust ? "

" All that have no motive of *general utility*. Personal predictions may almost always be considered apocryphal."

10. " What is the motive of spirits who announce spontaneously events that do not come to pass ? "

" Most often it is to be amused by the credulity, the terror, or the joy they cause ; then they laugh at the disappointment. Yet these lying predictions have sometimes a more serious aim — that of putting to the test him to whom they are made, to see how he takes them, the nature of the sentiments, good or bad, they may awaken in him."

Remark. Such, for instance, as the announcement of what might excite cupidity or ambition, the death of a person, or a prospective inheritance, &c.

11. "Why do serious spirits, when they predict an event, ordinarily fix no date; is it because they cannot, or will not?"

"Both; they may, in some cases, *predict* an event; then it is a warning they give you. As to giving a precise date, often they ought not; often, also, they cannot, because they do not know themselves. The spirit may foresee that a thing will take place, but the precise moment may depend on events not yet accomplished, and which God alone knows. Trifling spirits, who make no scruple of deceiving you, indicate the days and the hours, without troubling themselves with the issue. For this reason, all *circumstantial* predictions should be distrusted.

"Once again, our mission is to make you progress; we aid you as much as we can. He who asks wisdom of the superior spirits will never be deceived; but do not believe that we lose our time listening to your nonsense, and telling your fortunes; we leave that to frivolous spirits, whom it amuses, like mischievous children.

"Providence has imposed limits to the revelations that may be made to man. Serious spirits keep silence on everything forbidden to be made known. By insisting on an answer, you are exposed to the impostures of inferior spirits, always ready to seize every occasion to lay snares for your credulity."

Remark. Spirits see, or foresee, by induction, future events; they see them fulfilled in a space of time which they do not measure as we do ; in order to give the exact date, they must identify themselves with our method of computing duration, which they do not always judge necessary ; this is often a cause of apparent error."

12. "Are there not men endowed with a special faculty, which makes them foresee the future?"

" Yes ; those whose souls are disengaged from matter ; then it is the spirit who sees ; and when it is useful, God permits them to reveal some things for good ; but there are more impostors and charlatans. This faculty will be more common in the future."

13. "What must be thought of spirits who predict a person's death at a certain day or hour?"

"These are malicious jesters, — very malicious, — who have no other motive than to enjoy the fears they cause. Never believe them."

14. "How is it that some persons are warned by presentiment of the time of their death?"

" Most often it is their own spirit, who knows it in his moments of liberty, and preserves an intuition of it on awakening. These persons, being prepared, are not frightened nor moved. They see in this separation of the body and soul only a change of situation, or, if you like better, and to be more common, the change from a thick coat to a silk one. The fear of death will diminish as spirit belief is extended."

290. *Questions on Past and Future Existences.*

15. "Can the spirits acquaint us with our past existences?"

"God sometimes permits them to be revealed according to the end ; if for your edification and instruction, they will be true, and in such case the revelation is almost always made spontaneously, and in a totally unforeseen manner ; but He never permits it to satisfy a vain curiosity."

—"Why do some spirits never refuse to give such revelations ?"

"They are bantering spirits, who amuse themselves at your expense. In general, you should regard as false, or, at least, suspicious, all revelations of this nature that have not one eminently serious and useful aim. Mocking spirits please themselves in flattering self-love, by pretended origins. There are mediums and believers, who accept for current coin all that is said on this subject, and who do not see that the actual state of their spirit justifies in nothing the rank they pretend to have occupied ; a small vanity, with which the bantering spirits are as much amused as men. It would be more logical and more in conformity with the progression of beings, that they should ascend, not have descended ; it would be more honorable to them. In order that these revelations should be worthy of confidence, they should have been made spontaneously by various mediums, strangers to each other, to whom they should have been anteriorly revealed : then there would be evident reason for believing them."

—"If we may not know our anterior individuality, is it the same as to the kind of existence we have had, the social position we have occupied, the qualities and defects that have predominated in us ?"

"No ; that may be revealed, because you may profit by it, for your advancement ; but in studying your present, you can yourselves deduce your past." (See *Book on Spirits*— Forgetfulness of the Past, No. 392.)

16. " Can anything be revealed to us of our future existence ? "

" No ; all that some spirits tell you on this subject is simply a jest, — easily understood to be so ; your future existence is not decreed in advance, for it will be what you yourself have made it, by your conduct in the world, and by the resolutions you will have made when you shall have become spirits. The less you have to expiate, the happier you will be ; but to know where and how this existence will be, is impossible, except in the special and rare cases of spirits who are on the earth only to accomplish an important mission, because then their way is in some sort traced in advance.

291. *Questions on Moral and Material Interests.*

17. " Can one ask advice of spirits ? "

" Yes, certainly ; good spirits never refuse to aid those who invoke them with confidence, principally on what concerns the soul ; but they repulse hypocrites, *those who seem to ask for light, and yet delight in darkness.*"

18. " Can the spirits give advice on things of private interest ? "

" Sometimes, according to the motive. It depends, also, upon those to whom you address yourself. Advice concerning your private life is given with more certainty by the familiar spirit, because he attaches himself to a person, and interests himself in what concerns him. This is the friend, the confidant of your most secret thoughts ; but often you tire him with questions so little to the purpose that he leaves you. It would be as absurd to ask about your private affairs of spirits who are strangers to you, as to address yourself, for that purpose, to the first person you might meet on your road. You should never forget that puerility of questions is incompatible with the superiority of the spirits. You must also take into account the qualities of the familiar spirit, who may be good or bad, according to his sympathies for the person to whom he attaches himself. The familiar spirit of a wicked man is a wicked spirit, whose advice may be pernicious, but who removes and yields his place to a better spirit if the man himself becomes better. Like to like."

19. "Can the familiar spirits favor material interests by revelations?"

"They can and do sometimes, according to circumstances; but be assured that good spirits never lend themselves to serve cupidity. The bad will display to your eyes a thousand attractions, to incite it, and mystify you, at last, by deception. Be very sure, also, that if your lot is to undergo a certain vicissitude, your protecting spirits may aid you to support it with more resignation, may sometimes soften it ; but in the interest of your future, it is not permitted them to deliver you from it; as a good father does not give to his child all he may desire."

Remark. Our spirit protectors can, in many cases, indicate to us the better way, without, at the same time, leading us in a leash ; otherwise we should lose all initiative, and would not dare to take a step without having recourse to them, and this to the prejudice of our perfecting. To progress, man often has to gain experience at his own expense; for this reason wise spirits, even while advising us, leave us to our own energy, as a skillful teacher does for his pupils. In the ordinary circumstances of life, they counsel us by inspiration, and thus leave us all the merit of the good, as they leave us all the responsibility of the bad choice. It would be an abuse of the condescension of the familiar spirits, and a mistake as to their mission, to question them every instant about the most ordinary things, as do some mediums. There are those who, for a yes or no, take the pencil, and ask advice for the most simple action. This habit denotes poverty of ideas; at the same time, it is a presumption to suppose we have always a spirit at our command, having nothing else to do but to be occupied with us and our small interests. It will also serve to destroy one's own judgment, and reduce one's self to a passive part, profitless for the present life, and most surely prejudicial to future advancement. If it is childish to interrogate the spirits for trifling things, it is not less so on the part of the spirits who occupy themselves spontaneously with what one might call the details of the household : they may be good, but assuredly they are very terrestrial.

20. " If a person, in dying, leaves his affairs embarrassed, can one ask his spirit to aid in disentangling them, and can one also question him upon the real estate he has left, in a case where the estate may not be known, if such questioning be in the interests of justice ? "

" You forget that death is a deliverance from the cares of the world ; do you think that the spirit who is happy in his liberty willingly returns to take up his chains, and occupy himself with things he no longer cares for, to satisfy the cupidity of those who, perhaps, are rejoiced at his death, in the hope that it will be profitable to them ? You speak of justice, but the justice is in cheating their covetousness ; it is the beginning of the punishment which God reserves for their greediness for the goods of the world. Besides, the confusion which the death of a person sometimes leaves, makes a part of the trials of life, and it is not in the power of any spirit to deliver you from them, because they are in the decrees of God."

Remark. The above answer will, doubtless, disappoint those who imagine that spirits have nothing better to do than to serve us as auxiliary clairvoyants, to guide us, not toward heaven, but on the earth. Another consideration comes to the support of this answer. If a man, during his life, has left his affairs in disorder from negligence, it is not likely that, after his death, he will take more care, for he would be happy to be freed from the trouble they caused him, and however little he may be elevated, he will attach less importance to them as spirit than as man. As to the unknown goods he may have left, he has no reason to interest himself for greedy heirs, who would probably think no more of him if they did not hope to gain something ; and if he is still imbued with human passions, he may take a malign pleasure in their disappointment. If, in the interest of justice and of persons he loves, a spirit deems it useful to make revelations of this kind, he makes them spontaneously, and for that there is no need of being a medium, or of having recourse to one ; he leads to the knowledge of the things by apparently accidental circumstances, but never on a question put to him about it ; inasmuch as this question cannot change the trials to be suffered, it would rather tend to increase them, because it is almost always an indication of cupidity, and proves to the spirits that they think of him only from interested motives. (See No. 295.)

292. *Questions on the Fate of Spirits.*

21. "May we ask of spirits information of their situation in the world of spirits?"

"Yes; and they give it willingly, when the question is dictated by sympathy or the desire of being useful, and not by curiosity."

22. "Can spirits describe the nature of their sufferings, or their happiness?"

"Perfectly; and these revelations are of great instruction for you, for they initiate you into the true nature of future pains and recompenses, destroying the false ideas you have had on this subject; they tend to reanimate faith and your confidence in the goodness of God. The good spirits are glad to describe to you the happiness of the chosen; the bad can be constrained to describe their sufferings to incite them to repentance; they sometimes find a comfort in it; the unhappy pour out their complaint in the hope of compassion.

"Do not forget that the essential, exclusive end of Spiritism is your advancement, and it is to attain it that the spirits are permitted to initiate you into the future life, offering you examples by which you may profit. The more you identify yourself with the world that awaits you, the less you will regret the one in which you now are. This is, in short, the actual end of the revelation."

23. "In invoking a person whose fate is unknown, may we know from himself if he is still living?"

"Yes, if the uncertainty concerning his death is not a *necessity*, or a trial for those who are interested in knowing it."

"If he is dead, can he give us the circumstances of his death, so that they can be verified?"

"If he attaches any importance to it, he will do it; otherwise he cares little about it."

Remark. Experience proves that, in such case, the spirit is not impressed by the motives of interest there may be to know the circumstances of his death; if he chooses tô reveal them, he does it of himself, either through a medium or by visions or apparitions, and can then give more exact indications; if he does not desire it, a deceiving spirit may perfectly counterfeit him, and be amused by the vain search he causes.

It frequently happens that the disappearance of a person, whose death cannot be officially confirmed, creates confusion in family affairs. It is only in very rare and exceptional cases that we have known the spirits show the way of getting at the truth, after being asked to do so; if they wish to do it, doubtless they can, but often it is not permitted if the embarrassments are trials for those who might be interested in disentangling them.

It is, therefore, but a chimerical hope we follow, when we take such means of recovering an inheritance; the most certain thing about it will be the money spent in the effort.

There are not wanting spirits well disposed to flatter such hopes, who make no scruples of inciting to proceedings of which one is often very happy to be relieved at the expense of a little ridicule.

293. *Questions on the Health.*

24. "Can spirits give us advice for our health?"

"Health is a condition necessary for the work one should accomplish in the world; for this reason they willingly attend to it ; but as there are ignorant and learned among them, it is not proper for that, any more than for anything else, to address yourself to the first comer."

25. " In addressing one's self to the spirit of a medical celebrity, is one more certain of obtaining good advice ? "

" Terrestrial celebrities are not infallible, and have, often, systematic ideas which are not always true, and from which death does not immediately deliver them. Terrestrial science is a very small thing compared with celestial science ; the superior spirits alone have this last science ; without having names known among you, they may know much more than your learned men about everything. Science alone does not make spirits superior, and you would be very much astonished at the rank certain learned men occupy among us. The spirit of a learned man may not know more than when he was in the world, if he has not progressed as a spirit."

26. " Cannot the learned, after becoming a spirit, recognize his scientific errors ? "

" If he have reached a sufficiently high degree to be rid of his vanity, and to understand that his development is not complete, he recognizes and avows them without shame ; but if he is not sufficiently dematerialized, he may preserve some of the prejudices with which he was imbued in the world."

27. " Could a doctor, by invoking those of his patients who are dead, obtain from them some enlightenment on the cause of their death, the faults he may have committed in the treatment, and thus acquire an addition to his knowledge ? "

" He can ; and that would be very useful should he

have the assistance of enlightened spirits, who could supply the defects in the knowledge of some of the patients. But for that he must make this study in a serious and assiduous manner, with a humanitary design, and not as a means of easily acquiring knowledge and fortune."

294. *Questions on Inventions and Discoveries.*

28. "Can spirits guide in scientific researches and discoveries ? "

" Science is the work of genius ; it must be acquired only by labor ; for by labor alone is man advanced on his road. What merit would there be if he had only to question the spirits in order to know everything? Any simpleton could become learned at that price. Industry alone can give us inventions and discoveries. Then there is another consideration ; everything must come in its time, when ideas are ripe to receive it : if man had this power he would overturn the order of things, pushing forward fruit before its season.

" God has said to man, Thou shalt draw thy nourishment from the earth by the sweat of thy face : admirable figure! which pictures his condition here below. He must progress in everything by the effort of labor ; if we give him things already made, of what use would be his intelligence? He would be like the scholar whose duty another person performs."

29. " Are the 'savant' and the inventor never assisted by spirits in their researches ? "

" O, that is very different. When the time has come for a discovery, the spirits charged with its direction seek the man capable of conducting it to a good end, and inspire him with the necessary ideas, in such a way as to leave him all the merit of it ; for these ideas he must elaborate and work out. It is thus with all the grand achievements of human intelligence. The spirits leave each man in his sphere ; of him who is fit only to cultivate the earth, they will not make a confidant of God's secrets ; but they know how to draw from obscurity the man capable of seconding His designs. Do not allow yourselves to be carried away, by curiosity or ambition, into a path which is not the end of Spiritism, and which will lead only to the most ridiculous manifestations."

Remark. A more enlightened knowledge of Spiritism has calmed the fever for discoveries which, in its incipiency, were expected to be reached by this means. It was supposed persons had only to ask of the spirits recipes to color the hair or to make it grow, to cure corns on the feet, &c. We have seen many persons who thought their fortunes made, and who received only more or less ridiculous processes for it. It is the same when persons desire, by the aid of spirits, to pry into the mysteries of the origin of things ; some spirits having, on such subjects, systems often worth no more than those of men, and which it is prudent to receive with the utmost reserve.

295. *Questions on Hidden Treasures.*

30. "Can spirits discover to us hidden treasures?"

"The superior spirits are not engaged in such matters ; but mocking spirits often indicate treasures that do not exist, or can make you fancy one in a spot in a directly contrary direction from where it is ; and that has its usefulness in order to show that true fortune is in labor. If Providence destines hidden riches for some one, he will find them naturally ; otherwise not."

31. "What are we to think of the belief of spirit guardians for hidden treasures ?"

"Spirits who are not dematerialized are attached to things. Misers who have hidden their treasures might still watch over and guard them after their death, and the trouble of seeing them carried away is one of their punishments, until they understand how useless they are to them. There are also spirits of the earth, charged to direct its interior transformations, who have been allegorically made the guardians of natural riches."

Remark. The question of hidden treasures is in the same category as that of unknown inheritances ; very silly would he be who should reckon upon the pretended revelations that might be made to him by the jokers of the invisible world. We have said that when spirits will or can make such revelations, they do it spontaneously, and have no need of mediums for that. We give an example. A lady lost her husband, after thirty years of married life, and found herself on the brink of being expelled from her home, without any resource, by her step-son, to whom she had been as a mother. Her despair was at its height, when, one evening, her husband appeared to her, told her to follow him into his study ; there he showed her his writing desk, which was still under seal, and by a kind of second sight he made her see its interior ; he pointed out a secret drawer that she had not known, explained to her its mechanism, and added, " I foresaw what would happen, and wished to make sure of your comfort : in this drawer is my last will ; I have given you the use of this house, and a yearly income :" then he disappeared. When the day came to remove the seals, no one could open the drawer ; then the lady related what had happened to her. She opened it as her husband had told her, and there found the will, in terms exactly as he had mentioned.

296. *Questions on other Worlds.*

32. " What degree of confidence may we place in the descriptions spirits give us of the different worlds ? "

" That depends on the degree of *real* advancement the spirits who give these descriptions may have reached ; for you understand that ordinary spirits are as incapable of teaching you, in that respect, as an ignoramus in the world is to describe all the countries of the earth. You often ask scientific questions about these worlds that these spirits cannot solve: if they are sincere, they speak according to their personal ideas ; if they are trifling spirits, they amuse themselves by giving you absurd and fantastic descriptions ; inasmuch as these spirits, who are not deprived of imagination in the wandering state, any more than on earth, draw on this faculty for the recital of many things that have no reality. Yet, there is no absolute impossibility of having some enlightenment on these worlds ; good spirits are even pleased in describing to you those who inhabit them, in order to serve as instruction and for your advancement, and to induce you to follow the road that will lead you thither ; it is a means of fixing your ideas of the future, so as not to leave you with a vague impression."

" What certainty can we have of the exactness of these descriptions ? "

" The best is the agreement between them ; but remember, they have your moral advancement for their object, and that, consequently, it is on the moral state of the inhabitants you may receive the best teachings, and not on their physical or geological state. With your actual knowledge you could not even comprehend it ; its study would not serve your progress here below, and you will have every means of making it when you are there."

Remark. Questions on the physical constitution and astronomical elements of the worlds enter into the order of scientific researches, of which the spirits ought not to spare you the trouble ; otherwise an astronomer would find it very convenient to have them make his calculations, which, doubtless, he would not hesitate to do. If spirits could, by revelation, spare the labor of a discovery, it is probable that they would do so in favor of a " savant " modest enough to avow openly the source, rather than to allow those to profit by it who deny them, and for whose self-love, on the contrary, they often contrive deceptions.

CHAPTER XXVII.

CONTRADICTIONS AND MYSTIFICATIONS.

Of Contradictions.

297. THE adversaries of Spiritism do not fail to object that its believers do not agree among themselves; that all do not partake the same beliefs; in fact, that they contradict each other. If, they say, the teachings are given to you by the spirits, how is it that they are not identical? Nothing but a serious and profound study of the science can reduce this argument to its just value.

Let us hasten to say, first, that these contradictions, of which some persons make great account, are in general more apparent than real; that they more often pertain to the superficies than to the depth of the thing, and, consequently, are unimportant. The contradictions proceed from two sources, men and spirits.

298. The contradictions of human origin have been sufficiently explained in the chapter on *Systems*, No. 36, to which we refer our readers. Every one will understand that, in the beginning, when the observations were still incomplete, divergent opinions arose on the causes and the consequences of the spirit phenomena, three quarters of which opinions have fallen before a more serious and searching study. With very few exceptions, and aside from those persons who do not easily give up ideas they have embraced, or to which

they have given birth, it may be said that, at present, there is unity among the immense majority of spiritists, at least as to general principles, if not in insignificant details.

299. In order to comprehend the cause and the value of the contradictions of spirit origin, one must become identified with the nature of the invisible world, and have studied it under every aspect. At first sight, it may seem astonishing that the spirits do not all think the same; but that cannot surprise any one who will consider the infinite number of degrees that must be passed through before attaining the height of the scale. To suppose them to have an equal appreciation of things would be to suppose them all at the same level; to think they should all see correctly would be to admit that they have all reached perfection, which is not and cannot be, if it be remembered that they are but human beings stripped of the corporeal envelope. Spirits of every rank being able to manifest themselves, the result is, that their communications bear the seal of their ignorance or their knowledge, of their moral inferiority or superiority. The instructions we have given are to enable the true to be distinguished from the false, the good from the bad.

It must not be forgotten that among spirits, as among men, there are false and half-learned scientists, haughty and presumptuous spirits, and systematists. As it is given only to the perfected spirits to know everything, there are for others, as well as for us, mysteries which they explain in their own way, according to their ideas, and on which they may have opinions more or less correct, which from self-love they desire to have prevail, and which they like to put forth in their communications. The wrong is, that some of their interpreters have too lightly embraced opinions contrary to good sense, and of which the authors should be made responsible. Thus, the contradictions of spirit origin have no cause but the diversity of intelligence, knowledge, judgment, and morality of spirits who are, as yet, unfitted to know everything, or to comprehend everything. (See *Book on Spirits. Introduction,* § XIII.; *Conclusion,* § IX.)

300. Some persons will say, Of what use are the teachings of the spirits if they offer to us no greater certainty than human teachings? The answer is easy : We do not accept the teachings of all men with equal confidence, and between two doctrines we give the preference to that whose author seems to us most enlightened, most capable, most judicious, least accessible to passion ; we must act the same with the spirits.

If in the number there are some who are not above humanity, there are many who are far beyond it ; and these could give us instructions, we should seek in vain among the most learned men. We must distinguish them from the rabble of inferior spirits, and a profound knowledge of Spiritism will certainly lead us to this distinction.

But even these instructions are limited, and if it is not given to spirits to know everything, for still greater reason should it be the same with men. Thus, there are things on which they are questioned in vain, either that it is forbidden to reveal them, or because they are themselves ignorant of them, and could give us only their personal opinion ; but these very personal opinions are what vain spirits give as absolute truths. It is especially on what should remain hidden, as the future, and the principle of things, that they insist the most, in order to appear to be in the secrets of God ; so it is on these points there are the most contradictions. (See the preceding chapter.)

301. The following answers were given by spirits to questions relative to contradictions : —

1. "Can the same spirit, communicating to two different circles, transmit to them contradictory answers on the same subject ?"

"If the two circles differ in opinions and thoughts, the answer might reach them travestied, because they are under the influence of different columns of spirits : it is not the answer that is contradictory ; it is the manner in which it is rendered."

2. "We understand that an answer might be altered ; but when the qualities of the medium exclude all idea of bad influence, how does it happen that superior spirits hold a different and contradictory language on the same subject with persons perfectly serious ?"

"The really superior spirits never contradict themselves, and their language is always the same *with the same persons*. It may be different according to the persons and places ; but it is necessary to pay attention to this — the contradiction is often only apparent ; more in the words than in the thought ; for on reflection it will be found that the fundamental idea is the same. Then the same spirit may answer differently on the same question, according to the degree of perfection of those who invoke him, for it is not always good that all should have the same answer, while they are not as advanced. It is exactly as if a child and a 'savant' should ask you the same question ; surely you would answer to each in such a way as to be comprehended, and to satisfy them ; the answer, though different, would always have the same groundwork."

3. "From what motive do serious spirits seem to agree with ideas and prejudices of some persons, while in others they assail the same?"

"It is necessary that we make ourselves understood. If a person has a very confirmed conviction on a doctrine even false, we must turn him from this conviction, but little by little; for this reason we often use *his terms*, and appear to partake of his ideas, in order that he may not be suddenly disconcerted, and cease to allow us to instruct him. Besides, it is not good to shock prejudices too abruptly; it might be the means of not being listened to: for this reason the spirits often speak in the sense of the opinion of those who hear them, in order to lead them little by little to the truth. They appropriate the language of the persons, as you would do yourself, were you a somewhat skillful orator; thus they would not speak to a Chinese or to a Mohammedan, as they would to a Frenchman or to a Christian, for they would be sure to be repulsed.

"You must not take as a contradiction what is often but a skillful elaboration of the truth. All spirits have their tasks marked out by God; they accomplish them in the conditions He judges right for the good of those who receive their communications."

4. "Even apparent contradictions might engender doubts in the spirit of some persons; by what means can we know the truth?"

"To discern errors from truth, the answers must be examined thoroughly, and meditated long and seriously; it is an entire study. Time is necessary for this, as for all other studies.

"Study, compare, examine thoroughly; we tell you this constantly; knowledge of the truth is at this price. How do you expect to reach the truth when you interpret everything after your own narrow ideas, which you take for great ones? But the day is not far distant when the teachings of the spirits will be everywhere uniform in the details, as in the fundamentals. Their mission is to destroy error, but that can come only by degrees."

5. "There are persons who have neither time nor capacity for a serious and thorough study, and who accept what is taught them without examination. Is there no danger that they may thus give credence to error?"

"Let them practice good and do no evil; that is the essential thing; for that there are not two doctrines. Good is always good, whether it be done in the name of Allah or Jehovah, for there is only one God for the universe."

6. "How can spirits, who appear to be developed in intelligence, have ideas evidently false on certain things?"

"They have their doctrine. Those who are not sufficiently advanced, but who think they are, take their own ideas of the truth. It is the same among you."

7. "What are we to think of that doctrine which says that only one spirit can communicate, and that one is God or Jesus?"

"The spirit who teaches that is one who desires to govern; for that reason he wants to have it believed that he is alone; but the wretch who dare take the name of God will bitterly expiate his pride. As to these doctrines, they refute themselves, because they are in contradiction to the most proved facts; they do not deserve serious examination, for they have no root.

"Reason tells you that good proceeds from a good source, and bad from an evil one: why should you desire a good tree to bring forth evil fruit? Did you ever gather grapes from an apple tree? The diversity of the communications is the most patent proof of the diversity of their origin.

"Besides, the spirits who pretend that they alone communicate forget to say why the others cannot. Their pretension is the negation of the most beautiful and consoling facts of Spiritism — the relations of the visible and invisible worlds, of mankind with the beings dear to them, and who would otherwise be lost to them without return. These relations identify man with his future, and detach him from the material world; suppress them, he is again plunged into the doubt that makes his torment — given food for his egotism.

"In examining with care the doctrines of these spirits, we see, at every step, unjustifiable contradictions, the traces of their ignorance of the most evident thing, and, consequently, the certain signs of their inferiority. SPIRIT OF TRUTH."

8. "Of all the contradictions we observe in the communications of spirits, one of the most striking is that relating to re-incarnation. If re-incarnation is a necessity of spirit life, how is it that all the spirits do not teach it?"

"Do you not know that there are spirits whose ideas are limited to the present, as among many men of the earth? They believe that what is for them must last forever; they do not see beyond the circle of their perceptions, and trouble themselves neither about whence they come, nor whither they go; and yet they must undergo the law of necessity. Re-incarnation is, for them, a law of necessity, of which they will not think until it comes; they know that the spirit progresses, but how is for them a problem. Then, if you ask it of them, they will talk to you of the seven heavens, one above the other, like stagings : there are some, even, who will talk of the sphere of fire, the sphere of stars, then the city of flowers, and the city of the chosen."

9. "We can easily imagine that spirits but little advanced would not comprehend this question ; but then, how is it that spirits of a notoriously moral and intellectual inferiority speak spontaneously of their different existences, and of their desire to be re-incarnated, to make amends for their past ? "

"There are many things occurring in the world of spirits difficult for you to comprehend. Have you not among you persons very ignorant on some things, and enlightened on others ; persons who have more judgment than instruction, and others who have more instruction than judgment ? Do you not know, also, that some spirits are pleased to keep men in ignorance, while pretending to instruct them, profiting by the ease with which their words gain credit ? They may seduce those who do not go to the bottom of things, but when they are pressed to extremity by reasonings, they cannot long sustain their *rôle.*

"Notice, especially, the prudence with which the spirits in general promulgate the truth ; a too vivid and too sudden light dazzles without illuminating. They might, in certain cases, consider it useful to spread it only gradually, according to the times, the places, and the persons. Moses did not teach all that the Christ taught, and the Christ himself said many things the understanding of which was reserved for future generations. You speak of re-incarnation, and are astonished that this principle has not been taught in certain countries ; but remember, that in a country where the prejudice of color reigns supreme, where slavery is rooted in the manners, they would have rejected Spiritism, if only for that it proclaimed re-incarnation, for the idea that he who is master may become a slave, and the reverse, would have appeared monstrous. Was it not better that the general principle should be first accepted, safe, later, to bring its consequences ? O, mankind ! how short-sighted to judge the designs of God ! Know that nothing can be done without His permission, and without a motive which, very often, you cannot penetrate.

"I have told you that unity would come in the spirit belief ; take it as a certainty that it will come, and that the disagreements, already deeply-seated, will be effaced, little by little, as men are enlightened, and will disappear completely ; for such is the will of God, against which error cannot prevail.

"SPIRIT OF TRUTH."

10. "Will not the erroneous doctrines that some spirits teach have the effect of retarding the progress of true science ?"

"You would have everything without trouble : understand that there is no field where weeds will not grow for the laborer to root out. These erroneous doctrines are a consequence of the inferiority of your world ; if men were perfect, they would accept only the true ; errors are like false stones, which an experienced eye alone can distinguish ; you need an apprenticeship to distinguish the true from the false : well, these false doctrines are useful in exercising you to distinguish truth from error."

—"Are not those who adopt the error retarded in their progress ?"

"If they adopt error, it is because they are not sufficiently advanced to comprehend truth."

302. "While awaiting the coming of unity, each person believes he himself has the truth, and maintains that he alone is in the true ; an illusion that does not fail to call to him deceiving spirits : on what can an impartial and disinterested man base his judgment ? "

"The purest light is obscured by no cloud ; the diamond without flaw is most valuable : judge, then, the spirits by the purity of their teachings. Unity will come from that side where good has never been mingled with bad ; to that side man will rally by the law of events, for they will judge that there is the truth. Remark, besides, that the fundamental principles are everywhere the same, and should unite you in a common thought — the love of God and the practice of good. Whatever may be the mode of progression supposed for souls, the final end is the same, and the means of attaining it is also the same — do good ; and there are not two methods of doing it.

"Should there arise capital differences as to the principle, even, of doctrine, you have a certain rule for valuing them — the following : The best doctrine is that which best satisfies the heart and the reason, and which contains the most elements to lead men to good ; it is, I assure you, the one that will prevail.

"Spirit of Truth."

Remark. The contradictions that present themselves in spirit communications may arise from the following causes : the ignorance of some spirits ; the deceptions of the inferior spirits, who, either from malice or mischief, say the very contrary from what the spirit whose name they have usurped has already said elsewhere : the will of the spirit, who talks according to the times, the places, and persons, and considers it useful not to say everything to everybody ; the insufficiency of human language to express the things of the incorporeal world ; the insufficiency of the means of communication which do not always permit the spirit to render his whole thought ; finally, to the interpretation each one may give of a word or an explanation, according to his ideas, his prejudices, or the point of view from which he sees the thing. Study, observation, experience, and the abnegation of all sentiment of self-love, alone can teach us to distinguish these different shades.

Of Mystifications.

303. If it be disagreeable to be deceived, it is still more so to be mystified ; and it is one of the dangers from which it is easiest to be preserved. The means of unmasking the tricks of deceiving spirits are shown by all the preceding instructions ; for that reason we say but little. We give the answers of spirits on the subject : —

1. " Mystifications are among the greatest disagreeables in the practice of Spiritism: is there any way to be preserved from them ? "

" It seems to me you can find the answer in all you have been taught. Yes, certainly, there is a very simple means ; it is, not to ask of Spiritism more than it can or ought to give you ; its end is the moral amelioration of humanity ; so long as you depart not from that, you will never be deceived, because there are not two methods of comprehending true morality, which every man of good sense will admit.

" The spirits come to instruct and guide you into the

way of good, and not into that of honors and fortune,
or to serve your mean passions.   If nothing trifling is
ever asked of them, or nothing beyond their attributes,
no foothold is given to deceiving spirits ; from whence
you may conclude, that he who is mystified has only
what he deserves.

" The *rôle* of the spirits is not to teach you about
the things of this world, but to guide you surely in
what may be useful to you in the other.   When they
talk to you of things here below, it is because they
judge it to be necessary, but not on your asking.   If
you look upon spirits only as supplying the place of
diviners or sorcerers, you will surely be deceived.

" If men had but to ask the spirits in order to know
everything, they would no longer have their free-will,
and would turn aside from the path marked out by
God for humanity.   Man should act for himself ; God
does not send the spirits to smooth the road of material
life, but to prepare that of the future."

" But there are persons who ask nothing, and who
are unworthily deceived by spirits who come spontaneously, without being called."

" If they ask nothing, they allow themselves to tell
what happens to them all the same.   If they meet
with reserve and distrust all that is not the essential
object of Spiritism, trifling spirits will not so easily
take them for dupes."

2. " Why does God permit sincere persons, those
who accept Spiritism sincerely, to be mystified ?   May
not that shake their belief ? "

" If it shake their belief, it must be because their
faith is not very solid : those who renounce Spiritism
from a simple disappointment would prove that they
do not understand it, and do not belong to the serious

party. God permits mystifications to test the perseverance of true believers, and to puniuh those who make it an object of amusement.

" SPIRIT OF TRUTH."

Remark. The turnings and doublings of the mystifying spirits sometimes surpass anything that can be imagined ; the art with which they draw up their batteries and arrange their means of persuading would be a curiosity, were it always only for innocent pleasantries ; but these mystifications may have disagreeable consequences for those who are not on their guard : we are happy that we have been able, *in time*, to open the eyes of some persons who have asked our advice, and to have spared them from ridiculous and compromising actions. Among the means these spirits employ, we must place in the front rank, as being most frequent, those which have for their aim to tempt cupidity, such as the revelation of pretended hidden treasures, the announcement of inheritances, or other sources of fortune.

At first sight we ought especially to suspect all predictions for a fixed time, as well as all precise indications touching material interests ; to beware of every step prescribed or advised by spirits when the motive is not eminently rational ; never to allow ourselves to be dazzled by the names they take to give an appearance of truth to their words ; to mistrust bold scientific theories and systems ; anything, in short, foreign to the true moral end of the manifestations. We could fill a volume with the history of all the strange mystifications that have come to our knowledge.

CHAPTER XXVIII.

CHARLATANISM AND JUGGLERY.

Self-interested Mediums. — Spirit Frauds.

Self-interested Mediums.

304. As everything can become a subject for making capital, it is not astonishing that persons should wish to make capital out of the spirits; it remains to be seen how they will take the thing, if such a speculation should be introduced. We will say, first, that nothing lends greater aid to charlatanism and jugglery than such doings. If we see false somnambulists, still oftener do we see false mediums; and this reason alone should induce distrust. Disinterestedness, on the contrary, is the most peremptory answer to those who see nothing in the facts but a skillful maneuver. There is no disinterested charlatanism. What motive could persons have for using deception without profit? still more, when their proved honor places them above suspicion?

If the gain a medium may draw from his faculty may be an object of suspicion, this would not be a proof that the suspicion is well founded; he might have a real aptitude, and act in perfect sincerity, while making it pay: let us see if, in this case, we can reasonably expect a satisfactory result.

305. If all that we have said of the conditions necessary to serve as interpreter to good spirits; of the num-

berless causes that may repel them; of the circumstances, independent of their will, which are often an
obstacle to their coming : of all the *moral* conditions
that may exercise an influence over the communications, — if all this has been thoroughly comprehended,
how can it be supposed that a spirit, however little
elevated, can be, at all hours of the day, at the orders
of a director of *séances*, and subject to his require-
ments to satisfy the curiosity of the first comer ?

We know the aversion of the spirits for everything
that savors of cupidity and egotism, the few cases in
which they help in material things ; and yet they are
expected to assist in making money by their presence !
The very thought is repugnant, and one must know
very little of the spirit world to believe that this may
be. But, as trifling spirits are less scrupulous, and
only seek occasion to amuse themselves at our expense, it results that if persons are not mystified by a
false medium, there is every chance of their being so
by such spirits. These reflections alone will show the
measure of the degree of confidence that should be
given to communications of this kind. For the rest,
why employ paid mediums, when now, if a person has
not the faculty himself, he can surely find it in his
family or among his friends and acquaintances ?

306. Interested mediums are not the only ones who
may exact a fixed payment ; self-interest is not always
seen in the hope of a material gain, but also in ambitious views of every kind on which personal hopes
may be founded ; that again is a trait on which mocking spirits know very well how to seize, and how to
profit by, with an address and skill truly remarkable, —
rocking to sleep by deceitful illusions those who place
themselves under their control. To recapitulate : me-

diumship is a faculty given for good, and good spirits withdraw from every one who would make it a stepping-stone for aught that does not answer to the views of Providence. Egotism is the sore spot in the social system; the good spirits combat it, and it cannot be supposed that they come to serve it. This is so rational that it would be useless to insist further on this point.

307. Mediums for physical effects are not in the same category; these effects are usually produced by less scrupulous, inferior spirits. We do not say that these spirits may necessarily be bad: one can be a porter and a very honest man; a medium of this category, who would make money of his faculty, might have one who would help him without repugnance; but here again is another danger. The medium for physical effects has received his faculty no more for his pleasure than has the medium for intelligent communications: it has been given to him on condition that he make a good use of it; and if he abuse it, it will be withdrawn or turned to his detriment, for, peremptorily, the inferior are under the control of the superior spirits.

The inferior spirits like well to mystify, but they do not like to be mystified; if they lend themselves willingly to jesting, to things for curiosity, because they like amusement, they no more than others like to be used for money-making or selfish views; and they prove at every instant that they have their will; that they act when and how seems good to them, so that the medium for physical effects is still less sure of the regularity of the manifestations than the writing medium. To pretend to produce them at fixed days and hours would be a proof of the most profound ignorance. What, then, will be done to earn his money? Simulate the phenomena : this is what happens not only with those who make it a regular business, but even with persons apparently simple, who find this easier and more agreeable than to work. If the spirit does not give, they supply it : imagination is so fertile when money is in question! Self-interest being a legitimate motive of suspicion, it gives the right for rigorous examination, and none can be offended by it without justifying suspicions. But as far as suspicion is legitimate in such case, just so far is it offensive toward honorable and disinterested persons.

308. The medianimic faculty, even restricted to the limit of physical manifestations, has not been given to make a parade on the platform, and whoever pretends to have at his orders spirits, to exhibit in public, may justly be suspected of charlatanism or jugglery more or less skillful. Let this be held for truth, every time an announcement of pretended *séances* of *Spiritism* or *Spiritualism* is made, wherever the place ; and let every one remember the right he purchases with his entrance.

From all that precedes we conclude that the most absolute disinterestedness is the best guarantee against charlatanism ; if it does not always insure the goodness of intelligent communications, it takes from bad spirits a powerful means of action, and silences detractors.

309. There remains what may be called amateur jugglery ; that is, innocent frauds of mischievous jesters. They may doubtless practice it, by way of pastime, in trifling and frivolous circles, but not in serious assemblies, where only serious persons are admitted. A person may please himself by a momentary mysti-

fication, but he must be endowed with singular patience to play this part for months and years, and
each time for several consecutive hours. Interest of
some kind can alone give this perseverance ; and this
interest, we repeat, makes everything suspicious.

310. It will, perhaps, be said, that a medium who
gives his time to the public, in the interest of the
thing, cannot give it for nothing ; for he must live.
But is it in the interest of the thing, or in *his own*,
that he gives it ? and is it not rather because he sees
in it a lucrative business ? You can always find devoted people at that price. Has he no other industry
at his disposal ? Let us not forget that spirits, whatever may be their superiority or inferiority, are the
souls of the dead ; and when morality and religion
make it a duty to respect their remains, the obligation
is still greater to respect their spirits.

What would be said of one who should take a corpse
from the tomb to exhibit it for money, because there
might be something about it to arouse curiosity?

Is it less disrespectful to exhibit the spirit than the
body, under the pretext that it is curious to see a
spirit act ? It is also to be remarked that the price of
seats is according to the wonders they can perform,
and the attraction of the spectacle. Surely, during
his life, had he been a comedian, he could hardly
have supposed that, after his death, he would find a
manager who would make him play comedy gratis for
said manager's own profit.

It must not be forgotten that physical as well as intelligent manifestations are permitted by God only for
our instruction.

311. These moral considerations aside, we will not
aver that there cannot be interested mediums, honora-

ble and conscientious, because there are honest men in all trades ; we speak only of the abuse : but it will be readily agreed that there is more reason for the abuse in paid mediums, than with those who, regarding their faculty as a favor, employ it only to render a service.

The degree of confidence or mistrust that may be given to a paid medium depends entirely upon the esteem his character and morality may command, independent of circumstances. The medium who, with an eminently serious and profitable aim, would be prevented from utilizing his time in any other way, and for that reason *exonerated*, must not be confounded with the *speculating* medium, him who, from premeditated design, would make a trade of his mediumship. According to *the motive and the end*, the spirits could condemn, absolve, or even favor ; they judge the intention rather than the material fact.

312. Somnambulists who utilize their faculty in a lucrative manner are not in the same case. Though this may be subject to abuse, and disinterestedness be a greater guarantee of sincerity, the position is different, as it is their own spirit that acts ; it is, consequently, always at their disposal, and, in reality, they simply make money of themselves, because they are free to dispose of their person as they understand it, while speculating mediums use the souls of the dead. (See No. 172, *Somnambulistic Mediums.*)

313. We are fully aware that our severity in respect to interested mediums will arouse against us all those who make money, or may be tempted to make money, by this new trade ; and we shall make bitter enemies of them, as well as of their friends, who will naturally take up their cause ; we console ourselves that the

merchants whom Jesus drove from the temple could
not have regarded him with a favorable eye. We have
also against us those who do not see the thing with
the same gravity; yet we believe we have a right to
our opinion and to express it : we force no one to
adopt it. If an immense majority agree with us, it is,
apparently, because they find it just ; for we see not,
indeed, how it can be proved that there are not more
good chances for frauds and abuses in speculation than
in disinterestedness. As to ourselves, if our writings
have tended to cast discredit on interested mediumship in France and in other countries, we believe it
will not be one of the least services they will have rendered to *serious* Spiritism.

Spirit Frauds.

314. Those who do not admit the reality of the
physical manifestations generally attribute the effects
produced to fraud. They base their opinion on the
fact that skillful jugglers do things that appear like
prodigies when we do not know their secrets ; whence
they conclude that mediums are only another kind of
sharpers. We have already refuted this argument, or,
rather, this opinion, principally in our articles on Mr.
Home, and in the Nos. of the *Review* of January and
February, 1858 ; we shall, therefore, say but a few
words before speaking of a more serious thing.

It is, besides, a consideration that will not escape
any one who reflects a little. There are, no doubt,
marvelously skil.ful prestidigitators, but they are rare.
If all mediums practice juggling, it must be conceded
that the art has made unheard-of progress in a short
time, and become suddenly very common ; as it is

found innate with persons who scarcely suspect it: even with children.

Even as there are quacks who sell drugs in public places, so there are mediums who, without going to public places, betray confidence: must it follow that all doctors are quacks, and that the medical corps is, for that reason, unworthy of consideration? Because there are persons who sell adulterations for wine, does it follow that all wine merchants are adulterators of wine, and that there is none pure? Everything is abused, even the most respectable things, and it may be said that fraud also has its genius. But fraud always has a motive, some material interest: where there is nothing to gain, there is no interest in deceiving. So we say, apropos to mercenary mediums, that the best of all guarantees is absolute disinterestedness.

315. Of all the spirit phenomena, those which most lend themselves to fraud are physical phenomena, from motives it is useful to take into consideration. First, because, addressing themselves more to the eyes than to the intelligence, they are those that jugglery can most easily imitate. Secondly, that, awaking curiosity more than the others, they are more suited to attract the crowd, and are, consequently, more productive. In this double point of view, charlatans have every interest in simulating them: the spectators, mostly strangers to the science, seek them usually more as an amusement than as a serious instruction; and every one knows that what amuses pays better than what instructs. But set that aside, there is another motive not less decided. If juggling can imitate material effects, for which only address is needed, we have not, as yet, known it to possess the gift of improvisation, which requires a degree of intelligence not very com-

mon, neither the gift of producing those beautiful and sublime dictations, often so apropos, which the spirits give in their communications. This recalls to us the following fact:—

A literary man, quite well known, came, one day, to see us, and told us that he was a very good *intuitive* writing medium, and that he would put himself at the disposal of the Spirit Society. As we were accustomed to admit into the society only mediums whose faculties were known to us, we requested him to come and give proofs in a special reunion. He came; several experienced mediums gave dissertations and answers of remarkable precision on questions proposed and subjects unknown to them. When this gentleman's turn came, he wrote some insignificant words, said he was indisposed that day, and since then we have never seen him: he doubtless found that the *rôle* of medium for intelligent effects was more difficult to play than he had supposed.

316. In everything, those most easily deceived are those not of the trade; it is the same with Spiritism; those who know nothing of it are most easily deceived by appearances; while a previous attentive study initiates them, not only into the cause of the phenomena, but into the normal conditions under which they can be produced, and furnishes them also with the means of detecting fraud, should it exist.

317. Deceiving mediums are stigmatized as they deserve in the following letter in the *Review* of August, 1861:—

"PARIS, July 21, 1861.

"SIR: One may disagree on certain points, and agree on others. I have just read, page 213 of the last number of your journal, reflections on frauds in spiritualist (or spiritist) experiments, to which I am happy to give my entire assent. There all differences in matters of theory or doctrine disappear as by enchantment.

"I am not, perhaps, as severe as you in regard to mediums who, in a worthy and suitable way, accept a remuneration as indemnity for the time they devote to experiments often long and fatiguing; but I am quite as much so—and one cannot be too much—in regard to those who, in such cases, supply, on occasion, by trickery and fraud, the absence or insufficiency of the results promised and expected. (See No. 311.)

"To mingle the false with the true, when phenomena obtained through the intervention of spirits is in question, is wholly infamous, and there must be an utter obliteration of all moral sense with the medium who can do so without scruple. As you have so well observed, *it is casting discredit upon the cause in the minds of the undecided, to find it mixed with fraud.* I would add that it is compromising in the most deplorable manner the honorable men who give to mediums the disinterested support of their knowledge and their light, who are guarantees of their sincerity, and in one way their patrons; it is committing a veritable crime against them.

"Every medium convicted of fraudulent maneuvers, taken, to use a common expression, with his hand in the bag, deserves to be ostracized by all spiritualists and spiritists, for whom it should be a rigorous duty to unmask them, and send them adrift.

"If you choose, sir, to insert these few lines in your Journal, they are at your service.

"I am, &c.,

"MATTHEW ———."

318. All spirit phenomena are not equally easy to imitate, and there are those that evidently defy all the skill of practiced jugglers; such are, especially, the movements of objects without contact, the suspension of heavy bodies in space, blows struck on different sides, apparitions, &c., without employing helpers and companions; therefore, we say, what should be done in such cases is, to observe attentively the circumstances, and particularly take into account the character and position of the persons, the motive, and the interest they may have in deceiving; that is the best of all censorship, for these are the circumstances that destroy all cause for suspicion. We think, then, on principle, it is necessary to beware of any one whatever who makes of these phenomena a spectacle, or an object of curiosity or amusement, and who pretends to produce them at will or at a given place, as we have already explained. We cannot too often repeat that the occult intelligences, who manifest themselves to us, have their susceptibilities, and will prove to us that they have their free will, and are not subjected to our caprices. (No. 38.)

It will suffice to mention some subterfuges employed, or that it is possible to employ, in certain cases, to warn sincere observers against fraud. As to persons who persist in judging without studying, it would be labor lost to seek to convince them.

319. One of the most ordinary phenomena is that of raps in the very substance of the wood, with or without movement of the table or other object used; this effect is one of the easiest to imitate, either by contact of the feet, or by calling out little crackings in the furniture; but there is a special little stratagem that may be exposed. It suffices to rest the two hands

flat on the table, near enough for the thumb nails to rest strongly against each other; then, by a muscular movement entirely imperceptible, they are rubbed together, which gives a little dry sound, very much like that of interior typtology. This noise resounds in the wood, and produces a complete illusion. Nothing more easy than to make as many raps heard as are asked, a drum beating, &c., to answer to certain questions by yes or no, by numbers, or even by indicating letters of the alphabet.

Once warned, the means of detecting this fraud are very simple. It is not possible if the hands are separated, and if you are sure no other contact produces the noise. The true raps, however, have this characteristic, that they change place and tone at will, which could not be if they were due to the cause we have mentioned, or any similar, if they go from the table to a piece of furniture no one is touching, on the walls, on the ceiling, &c., if they answer impromptu questions. (See No. 41.)

320. Direct writing is still easier to imitate; without speaking of well-known chemical agents for making writing appear in a given time on a blank piece of paper, which may be exposed by the most ordinary precautions, it might happen that, by skillful trickery, one piece of paper could be substituted for another. It might be that he who might wish to deceive would have the art of distracting the attention while writing a few words. We have been told that writing has been produced with a small crumb of lead hidden under the nail.

321. The phenomenon of materialization is not less accessible to jugglery, and a person can easily be the dupe of a skillful sharper without having recourse to a

professional. In the special article we have published above (No. 96), the spirits have themselves told the exceptional conditions under which they can be produced ; whence it may be concluded that the *easy* and *optional* obtaining of them must be held more or less suspicious. Direct writing is under the same head.

322. In the chapter on *Special Mediums*, we gave from the spirits the common medianimic aptitudes, and those that are rare. Mediums who pretend to have these last too easily are to be suspected, as also those who are ambitious of a multiplicity of faculties — a pretension rarely justified.

323. Intelligent manifestations are, according to the circumstances, those which offer the strongest guarantee ; and yet they are not proof against imitation, at least the ordinary and trivial communications.

It is supposed there is more security with mechanical mediums, not only for independence of ideas, but also against fraud ; for this reason many persons prefer material intermediaries. Well, it is an error. Fraud is everywhere, and we know that, with skill, even a writing basket or planchette can be directed at will. The sentiments expressed will relieve all doubts whether they come from a mechanical, intuitive, auditive, speaking, or seeing medium. There are communications so far above the ideas, the knowledge, and even the intellectual strength of the medium, that we should strangely deceive ourselves in giving him the honor of their authorship. We see, in charlatanism, an extraordinary skill and fertile resources, but we have yet to find it capable of giving knowledge to the ignorant, or mind to him who lacks it.

To recapitulate : we repeat, the best guarantee is in

the known morality of the mediums, and in the absence of all material interested motives or self-love which might stimulate in him the exercise of the medianimic faculties he may possess ; for these same causes may lead him to simulate those he has not.

CHAPTER **XXIX.**

REUNIONS AND SPIRITIST SOCIETIES.

Of Reunions in General. — Of Societies Proper. — Subjects of Study. — Rivalry between Societies.

Of Reunions in General.

324. GREAT advantages may be derived from spiritist reunions, through reciprocal interchange of thought, questions and remarks that each one may make, and from which all may profit ; but in order to draw from them all desirable fruit, they require special conditions, which we will examine, for it is wrong to liken them to ordinary societies. Reunions being collective wholes, consequently the preceding instructions naturally concern them ; they should take the same precautions and guard against the same dangers as individuals : therefore we have placed this chapter last.

Spiritist reunions have very different characters, according to the end therein proposed, and their quality must, for the same cause, also differ. According to their nature, they may be *frivolous, experimental*, or *instructive.*

325. *Frivolous reunions* are composed of persons who see only the jesting side of the manifestations, who are amused with the humor of the trifling spirits, who are very fond of these assemblies, where they have full liberty to say what they please, and are not considered at fault. In these reunions nonsense of

434

all kinds is asked; here is where they expect fortune-telling of the spirits, where they put their perspicacity to the proof to guess ages, what they have in their pockets, to detect little secrets, and a hundred other things of like importance.

These reunions are of little consequence; but as the trifling spirits are often very intelligent, and are usually in an easy and jovial mood, they often produce in them very curious things, from which an observer may draw profit; he who has seen only that, and should judge the world of spirits from that sample, would have as false an idea of it as one who should judge the whole society of a great city by the inhabitants of a certain part of it. Simple good sense tells us that elevated spirits cannot enter such reunions, where the spectators are no more serious than the actors. If persons desire to engage in futile things, they must frankly call trifling spirits, as they would call jesters, to amuse a society; but there would be profanation in inviting thither venerated names, — to mingle the sacred with the profane.

326. *Experimental* reunions have more especially for their object the production of physical manifestations. For many persons this is a more amusing than instructive spectacle; skeptics come from them more astonished than convinced, when they have seen nothing else, and their whole thoughts are turned toward seeking out frauds, for, not understanding any of it, they willingly suspect subterfuges. It is otherwise with those who have studied; they already understand the possibility, and positive facts afterward achieve or finish their conviction; if there should be fraud, they would be safe to discover it.

Yet there is a use in these experiments that no one

should despise, for they were the means of discovering
the laws that rule in the invisible world ; and for many
they are certainly a powerful means of conviction ; but
we maintain that they alone could no more initiate the
science of Spiritism, than an ingenious piece of mechanism could make us understand mechanics, were we
unacquainted with its laws ; if they were always conducted with method and prudence, better results would
be obtained.   We shall return to this subject.

327. *Instructive reunions* have quite another character, and as these are where true instruction can be
received, we shall insist strongly on the conditions
they ought to fill.

The first of all is, to be serious in the full acceptation of the word. We should remember that the
spirits addressed are of a very special nature ; that the
sublime cannot be allied to the trivial, nor the good to
the bad ; if we desire to obtain good things, we must
address good spirits ; but to ask of good spirits is not
sufficient ; express conditions are necessary, to be in
propitious conditions, so that they may *want* to come ;
but superior spirits will no more come into the assemblies of trifling and superficial persons than they would
have come there during their lives.

A society is truly serious only on condition of being
engaged in useful things, to the exclusion of all others ;
if it aspire to obtain extraordinary things, for curiosity
or pastime, the spirits who produce them will come,
but the others will withdraw. In a word, whatever
may be the character of a reunion, it will always find
spirits ready to second its tendencies. A serious reunion turns aside from its end, if it leaves instruction
for amusement. Physical manifestations, as we have
said, have their use ; let those who wish to see them

go to experimental reunions: let those who desire to understand go to reunions for study; thus both will be able to complete their spirit teachings, as, in the study of medicine, some take the course, others clinics.

328. Spirit instruction comprises not only the moral teachings given by the spirits, but, still more, the study of facts; here belong the theory of all the phenomena, the inquiry into causes, and consequently, the verification of what is possible and what is not; in a word, the observation of all that can advance science. But it would be a mistake to suppose that the facts are limited to the extraordinary phenomena; that those which strike the senses most forcibly are alone worthy of attention; at every step in the intelligent communications, which men united for study must not neglect, are met these facts, impossible to enumerate, springing from a host of unforeseen circumstances; though less salient, they are none the less of the highest interest for the observer, who finds therein either the confirmation of a known principle, or the revelation of a new one, which brings him still further into the mysteries of the invisible world: there also is philosophy.

329. Reunions for study are especially useful for mediums, for intelligent manifestations, particularly for those who desire to perfect themselves, and who do not go to them with a foolish presumption of infallibility. One of the greatest dangers of mediumship is, we have said, obsession and fascination; they can thoroughly delude the medium as to the merit of what he obtains, and it may well be understood that the deceiving spirits have full scope when their interpreter is blinded; for this reason, they remove their medium from all criticism: if necessary, they produce in him an aversion even to being enlightened; by means of

isolation and fascination, they can make him accept anything they choose.

We cannot too often repeat it, here is not only the stumbling-block, but the danger; yes, we say it, a real danger. The only means of escaping it is the censorship of disinterested and kind-hearted persons, who, judging the communications with coolness and impartiality, may open his eyes, and make him see what he cannot see of himself. Every medium who fears this judgment is already on the road to obsession; he who believes the light is made only for him, is completely under the yoke; if he takes remarks in ill part, repulses, is irritated by them, there can be no doubt of the bad nature of the spirit who assists him. We have said, a medium may lack the knowledge necessary to understand errors; he may be deluded by big words and pretentious language, be led astray by sophisms, and that in all sincerity; therefore, in default of his own light, he should modestly have recourse to that of others, according to these two adages, that four eyes see better than two, and that no one is a good judge for his own cause. In this point of view, reunions are of very great utility for a medium, if he is sufficiently sensible to listen to advice; because he may find in them persons more clairvoyant than himself, who can seize the most delicate shades by which a spirit may betray his inferiority.

Every medium who sincerely desires not to be the plaything of a lie, should try to be developed in serious reunions, and bring there what he obtains in private; accept with gratitude — solicit even — critical examination of the communications he receives; if he is the dupe of deceiving spirits, it is the surest means of getting rid of them, and of proving to them that they cannot delude him. It is so much the worse for a medium who is irritated by criticism, as his self-love is not at all engaged, since what he says is not his own, and he is no more responsible for it than if he should read the verses of a bad poet.

We have insisted on this point, because, a stumbling-block for mediums, it is also one for reunions, to which it is of great importance not lightly to confide in all the interpreters of the spirits. The assistance of any obsessed or fascinated medium would be more injurious than useful; it should not be accepted. We think we have so fully entered into their development, that it will be impossible to mistake the characteristics of obsession, if the medium cannot recognize it himself; one of the most salient points is the supposition that he alone of all the world is right. Obsessed mediums, who will not be convinced, are like those sick persons who are deluded as to the state of their health, and are lost for want of submitting to salutary regimen.

330. A serious reunion should propose to itself, especially, to drive away lying spirits; it would be an error to suppose its aim and the quality of its mediums a safeguard from them; nothing will save it unless it be itself in favorable conditions.

In order perfectly to comprehend what happens under these circumstances, we beg the reader to turn to what has been said, No. 331, on the *Influence of the Surroundings*. Each individual is surrounded by a certain number of invisible acolytes, who are identified with his character, his tastes, and his inclinations: thus, each person who enters a reunion brings with him spirits who are in sympathy with him. According to their number and nature, these acolytes may exercise a good or bad influence on the assembly, and on its communications. A perfect reunion would be that in which all the members, animated by an equal love of good, would bring with them only good spirits ; in default of this perfection, the better would be where the good would preponderate over the evil. This is too logical to need that we should insist upon it.

331. A reunion is a collective being, whose qualities and properties are the result of those of its members, and form, as it were, a bundle, and this bundle will have as much more force as it may be more homogeneous. If our readers have thoroughly understood what has been said (No. 282, Question 5) on the manner in which spirits are warned of our call, they easily comprehend the power of the association of thought in the assistants. If the spirit is, in some sort, struck by the thought as we are by the voice, twenty persons, being united in the same intention, will necessarily have more force than one alone ; but that all these things may tend toward the same end, they must vibrate in unison ; let them be commingled, as it were, in a one, which cannot be done without concentration of thought.

Then, again, the spirit, entering a completely sympathetic circle, is more at his ease ; finding there only friends, he comes more willingly, and is more disposed to answer. Any person who has attentively watched intelligent spirit manifestations, must have become convinced of this truth.

If the thoughts are divergent, the result will be a clashing of ideas disagreeable for the spirit and injurious to the manifestations. It is the same with a man addressing an assembly ; if he feel all the thoughts to be sympathetic and kindly to him, the impression he receives will react on his own ideas, and give them more fervor; the unanimity of the assembly exercises on him a kind of magnetic action, which doubles his means, while indifference or hostility troubles or paralyzes him; so actors are inspired by plaudits; and spirits, being much more impressionable than human beings, are very much more sensitive to the influence of the surroundings.

Every spiritist reunion should tend as much as possible to homogeneity; of course it is understood that we speak of those that would achieve serious and truly useful results; if they desire simply to receive communications, without caring for the quality of those who give them, it is evident that all these precautions are not necessary; but then they should not complain of the quality of the product.

332. Concentration and communion of thought being the essential conditions of every serious reunion, it can be seen that too many assistants must be one of the causes most directly adverse to homogeneity. There is, certainly, no absolute limit to this number; and a hundred persons, sufficiently collected and attentive, will be better than ten inattentive and noisy; but it is also evident that the greater the number the more difficult to comply with the conditions. It is, besides, a fact proved by experience, that the small private circles are always more favorable for beautiful communications, for reasons already mentioned.

333. There is still another not less necessary point: the regularity of the reunions. In all there are always spirits that may be called *habitués:* we do not mean those spirits that may be found everywhere, and mingling themselves in everything; but those who are either spirit protectors, or those who are most often

interrogated. It must not be supposed that these spirits have naught else to do but to listen to us; they have their occupations, and may, besides, be in conditions unfavorable for invocation. When the reunions take place on fixed days and hours, they manage accordingly, and are rarely absent. There are some who are extreme in punctuality; they take offense at a quarter of an hour's delay, and if they themselves set the time of beginning, it is in vain to call them even a few minutes sooner. Let us add that, as well as the spirits prefer regularity, those who are truly superior are not tenacious on this point. The exaction of a rigorous punctuality is a sign of inferiority, like everything puerile. Beyond the devoted hours, they can come, and do come, even willingly, if the end is useful; but nothing is more injurious to good communications than to call them at random, when the fancy takes us, and especially without a serious motive; as they are not bound to submit to our caprices, they might very well not trouble themselves; then others are sure to take their places.

Of Societies Proper.

334. All that we have said of reunions in general applies to regularly-constituted societies, which, besides, have to contend with some special difficulties, which are born of the very tie that unites the members.

Advice on their organization having been asked of us several times, we will here recapitulate it in a few words.

Spiritism, but lately born, is still too diversely appreciated, too little understood in its essence, by a great number of believers, to afford a powerful bond between the members of what may be called an association.

This bond may exist between those who perceive its moral end, understand it, and *apply it to themselves*. Between those who see only facts more or less curious, there can be no serious bond ; putting facts above principles, a simple divergence in the manner of viewing them may be a cause of division. It is not the same with the first mentioned, for there cannot be two ways of looking at moral questions : also, it must be remarked, that wherever they meet a reciprocal confidence attracts them to each other ; the mutual benevolence that reigns among them banishes the uneasiness and constraint born of sensitiveness, of the pride that is offended at the least contradiction, of the egotism that takes everything to itself. A society where such sentiments reign supreme, where all are united for the purpose of being instructed by the teachings of the spirits, and not in the hope of seeing things more or less interesting, or to make one's own opinion prevail, — such a society, we say, would not only contain the elements of life, but would be indissoluble. Again, the difficulty of bringing together numerous homogeneous elements for this purpose, moves us to say that, in the interest of study, and for the good of the thing even, spirit reunions should be multiplied in small groups, rather than in large agglomerations. These groups, corresponding, visiting, transmitting their observations, may now form the nucleus of the great spiritist family, that will, some day, bring together all opinions, and unite all men in one sentiment of fraternity, sealed by Christian charity.

335. We have seen the importance of uniformity of sentiment for obtaining good results ; the greater the number, the more difficult, necessarily, will it be to obtain this uniformity. In small committees they

know each other better, and are more sure of the elements introduced ; silence and concentration are more
easy, and all are like one family.　Large assemblies
exclude intimacy by the variety of the elements of
which they are composed ; they require special loca-
tions, pecuniary resources, and an administrative machinery useless in small groups : diversity of character,
of ideas, of opinions, is better displayed, and offers to
the meddling spirits greater facility for sowing discord.
The more numerous, the more difficult to satisfy every
one ; each one wants the work directed according to
his liking, that the society should prefer those subjects
most interesting to him : some think that their mem-
bership gives them the right to have everything their
own way ; thence disagreements, a sensation of uneasiness, which, sooner or later, leads to disunion, then
dissolution — the fate of all societies, whatever their
object.　Small committees are not subject to the same
fluctuations ; the fall of a large society would be an
apparent check to the cause of Spiritism, and its enemies would not fail to take advantage of it ; the dissolution of a small group would pass unnoticed ; and
then, if one is dispersed, twenty more would be formed
beside it : also, twenty groups, of from fifteen to twenty, will obtain more and do more for propagation than
an assembly of three or four hundred persons.

It will, doubtless, be said that the members of a
society who would act in such a manner would not be
real spiritists, since the first duty the doctrine imposes
is charity and benevolence.　That is perfectly true ;
those who do this are spiritists in name rather than in
fact ; they do not assuredly belong to the third category
(see No. 28) ; but who can say they are not in some sense
spiritists ?　This consideration is not without gravity.

336. Let us not forget that Spiritism has enemies interested in opposing it, and who view its success with anger : the most dangerous are not those who attack it openly, but those who act in the dark — those who caress with one hand and mangle with the other. These malevolent beings creep in wherever they hope to do harm ; as they know that union is strength, they endeavor to destroy by throwing in brands of discord. Who, then, can say that those who, in reunions, sow trouble and dissension, are not agents of those who are interested in disorder ? Certainly they are neither true nor good spiritists ; they can never do good, but they can do much harm. It may easily be seen that they have infinitely greater facilities to insinuate themselves into large reunions than into small committees, where all know each other ; under cover of their secret plots, they sow doubt, distrust, and disaffection ; under an appearance of hypocritical interest, they criticise everything, form conventicles and coteries, which soon break up the harmony of the whole : this is what they desire. To appeal to sentiments of charity and fraternity with such persons is like talking to persons willfully deaf, for their aim is precisely to destroy those sentiments, the greatest obstacles to their plots. This state of things, grievous in all societies, is still more so in those of spiritists, because, if they do not lead to a rupture, they cause a preoccupation incompatible with concentration and attention.

337. It may be said, if the reunion is on the wrong road, have not discreet and well-intentioned men the right of criticism ? and should they let the evil go on saying nothing, by their silence approving ? Without doubt it is their right ; more, it is a duty ; but if their intention be really good, they will offer their advice in

a seemly and kindly manner, openly, and not in secret; if it is not followed, they withdraw; for one cannot imagine a well-intentioned person remaining in a society where things are done that do not suit him.

It may, then, be established as a principle, that whoever, in a spiritist reunion, causes disorder or disunion, openly or secretly, by any means whatever, is either a designing agent, or, at least, a very bad spiritist, of whom they cannot too soon rid themselves; but the obligations that bind the members are often obstacles to this; and for this reason it is best to avoid all indissoluble engagements: good men are always sufficiently bound, bad men always too much so.

338. Besides men notoriously malevolent who intrude into reunions, there are those who, by their character, bring trouble with them wherever they are; so that we cannot be too circumspect with regard to the new elements introduced. The most troublesome, in such cases, are not those ignorant of the matter, nor even those who do not believe; conviction is acquired only by experience, and there are persons who sincerely desire to be enlightened. Those of whom it is necessary to beware are systematists, skeptics who doubt everything, even the evidence; the vain, who think they alone have the true light, wish to impose their opinion on every one, and look with disdain on all who do not think like themselves. Do not allow yourselves to be deceived by their pretended desire for enlightenment; more than one would be sorry to be forced to acknowledge himself deceived; beware, especially, of those insipid talkers, who always want the last word, and of those who are only pleased when contradicting; both waste the time for others, while

not profiting by it themselves : spirits do not like useless words.

339. In view of the necessity of avoiding every cause of trouble and distraction, a spiritist society about to organize should turn its attention especially to measures that will deprive the fomentors of discord of the means of doing injury, and give the greatest facility for their removal ; small reunions need only a very simple disciplinary rule for the order of the *séances ;* regularly constituted societies require a more complete organization : the best will be where the wheels are the least complicated.

340. Small and large societies, and all reunions, whatever be their importance, have to contend with another danger. The fomentors of discord are not only within them, they are in the invisible world as well. As there are spirit protectors for societies, cities, and nations, so bad spirits attach themselves to groups as to individuals ; they first attack the weakest, the most accessible, of whom they endeavor to make instruments, and gradually try to circumvent the masses ; for their wicked joy increases according to the number they can subjugate. So, whenever one person of a group has fallen into a snare, say at once, an enemy is in the camp, — a wolf in the sheepfold, — and we must be on our guard, for it is most probable he will multiply his attempts ; if he is not discouraged by an energetic resistance, the obsession then becomes like a contagious disease, which is manifested among the mediums by perturbation of mediumship, and among others by hostility of sentiment, perversion of the moral sense, and a breaking up of the harmony. As the most powerful antidote to this poison is charity, it is charity they will seek to stifle. No waiting until the

evil has become incurable in order to bring a remedy
for it, no waiting even for the symptoms, but by every
means endeavor to prevent it ; for this there are two
efficacious means, that may be well employed : prayer
from the heart, and the attentive study of the least
signs that reveal the presence of deceiving spirits ; the
first attracts good spirits who zealously assist those
who second them by confidence in God ; the other
proves to the bad ones that they have to do with
persons clear-sighted and sensible enough not to allow
themselves to be deceived. If one of the members
yields to the influence of the obsession, every effort,
from the first symptoms, should tend to open his eyes,
lest the evil should increase, then to convince him that
he is deceived, and lead him to desire to second those
who wish to help him.

341. The influence of the surroundings is the consequence of the nature of spirits, and of their mode of
action on living beings ; of this influence each can, for
himself, deduce the conditions most favorable for a
society that aspires to conciliate the sympathy of
good spirits, and to obtain only good communications.
These conditions are entirely in the moral characters
of the assistants ; they may be recapitulated as to the
following points : —

Perfect community of views and sentiments.

Reciprocal kind feeling among all the members.

Abnegation of every sentiment adverse to true Christian charity.

Sole desire for instruction, and to advance through
the teachings of good spirits, and to profit by their
advice. Whoever is convinced that the superior spirits
manifest themselves with the view of making us progress, and not for our pleasure, will understand why

they should withdraw from those who are limited to admiration of their style, without extracting the fruit of their teachings, and who prize the *séances* only for the greater or less interest they offer to their own individual tastes.

Exclusion of everything that, in communications asked of the spirits, has only curiosity for its end.

Concentration and respectful silence during the interviews with the spirits.

Associations of all the assistants by thought, in the appeal made to the spirits invoked.

Concurrence of the mediums in the assembly, with abnegation of every sentiment of pride, self-love, and supremacy, in the one desire to be useful.

Are these conditions so difficult to fulfill that it cannot be done? We think not; on the contrary, we hope that truly serious reunions, as there are many already in different localities, will be multiplied, and we do not hesitate to say that it is to them that Spiritism will owe its most powerful propagation; in bringing unto it honest and conscientious men, they will silence criticism; and the purer their intentions, the more respected they will be, even by their adversaries; *when ridicule attacks the good, it no longer amuses, it becomes despicable.* Among reunions of this kind a true bond of sympathy, a mutual solidarity, will be established by the force of events, and will contribute to the general progress.

342. It would be an error to think that this fraternal concert is unnecessary in reunions for physical manifestations more especially, and that they exclude all serious thought; if they do not require so rigorous conditions, it is not with impunity that they are undertaken with levity, and a person would be deceived

should he suppose that the concurrence of the assistants is absolutely null ; we have the proof of this in the fact that often manifestations of this kind, even called out by powerful mediums, can produce nothing in some places.   There is some reason for it, and it can only be in the divergency or hostility of sentiment which paralyzes the efforts of the spirits.

Physical manifestations, as we have said, are of great utility ; they open a vast field to the observer, for it is an entire order of unusual phenomena unfolded to his view, whose consequences are incalculable.   Thus, an assembly may be occupied with very serious views, but may not attain its end, whether of study or means of conviction, if it is not placed in favorable conditions : the first of all is, not faith in the assistants, but their desire to be enlightened, without subterfuge, or determination to reject the evidence ; the second is the restriction of their number, to avoid the bringing together of heterogeneous elements.   If physical manifestations are, in general, produced by the less advanced spirits, they have none the less a providential end, and good spirits always favor them when they can have a useful result.

Subject for Study.

343. When a person has invoked his relations and friends, some celebrated personages, to compare their opinions as spirits with those they had during their lives, he is often embarrassed to sustain a conversation without falling into trivialities.   Many persons think that the Book on Spirits has exhausted the series o questions on morals and philosophy : this is an error ; for this reason it may be useful to indicate the source whence almost illimitable subjects for study may be drawn.

344. If the invocation of illustrious men, of superior spirits, is eminently useful for the instruction they give us, that of ordinary spirits is not less so, though they may be incapable of solving questions of high bearing : by their inferiority they depict themselves, and the smaller the distance that separates us, the greater relation we find to our own situation, without reckoning that they often give us characteristic traits of the highest interest, as we have explained above, No. 281, in speaking of the utility of special invocations. Here is an inexhaustible mine of observations, taking only those whose lives present some peculiarity in regard to their kind of death, age, good or bad qualities, their happy or unhappy position in the world, their habits, mental state, &c.

With elevated spirits, the range of study is enlarged ; besides the psychological questions, which are limited, there may be proposed to them a great number of moral problems, which extend to infinity on all the positions of life, on the best conduct under certain given circumstances, on our reciprocal duties, &c. The value of the instruction we receive on any subject, moral, historical, philosophical or scientific, depends entirely on the state of the spirit interrogated ; it is for us to judge.

345. In addition to invocations proper, spontaneous dictations offer innumerable subjects of study. They consist in waiting for whatever subject it may please the spirits to treat. Several mediums, in such cases, can work simultaneously. Sometimes an appeal may be made to a designated spirit ; more ordinarily those who choose to come are awaited, and often come in the most unexpected manner. These dictations may give rise to a crowd of questions whose theme is thus

found already prepared. They should be scanned with care, to study all the thoughts they contain, and to judge if they bear the seal of truth. This examination, made with severity, is, as we have said, the best guarantee against the intrusion of deceiving spirits. From this motive, as well as for the instruction of the whole, knowledge of the communications obtained outside of the reunion should be given. There, as may be seen, lies an inexhaustible source of elements, eminently serious and instructive.

346. The occupations of each *séance* may be regulated as follows : —

1. Reading of communications obtained in the last *séance*, correctly drawn up.

2. *Varieties.* — Correspondence. — Reading of communications obtained outside of the *séances*. — Relation of interesting facts of Spiritism.

3. *Works of Study*. — Spontaneous dictations. — Various moral questions and problems proposed to the spirits. — Invocations.

4. *Conference.* — Critical and analytical examination of the various communications. — Discussion on the various points of spirit science.

347. Circles are often stopped in their very birth from want of mediums. Mediums are, assuredly, one of the essential elements of spirit reunions ; but they are not an indispensable element, and one would be wrong in supposing that, lacking them, there is nothing to do. Doubtless those who come together simply for experimentation, can no more do without mediums than musicians in a concert can do without instruments ; but those who have serious study in view have a thousand subjects to occupy them, all as useful and profitable as if they could operate them for them-

selves. Besides, the reunions that have mediums, might be accidentally deprived of them, and it would be a pity should they, for that reason, feel that nothing is left for them but to retire. The spirits themselves may, occasionally, place them in such a condition in order to teach them to do without. We will say, further, that it is necessary, in order to profit by the teachings, to consecrate a certain time to their meditation. Scientific societies have not always instruments of observation at hand, and yet they are never at a loss for subjects of discussion ; in the absence of poets and orators, literary societies read and comment on ancient and modern authors ; religious societies meditate on the Scriptures ; spiritist societies should do the same, and they would draw great profit for their advancement by establishing conferences in which they may read and comment upon all that may relate to Spiritism, either for or against. From this discussion, where each could bring the tribute of his reflections, might spring rays of light that might have passed unperceived in an individual reading ; special works, journals swarming with facts, recitals, events, traits of virtue or vice, raising grave moral problems which Spiritism alone can solve — a proof that it is suited to every branch of social order.

We would warrant that a spiritist society that would organize its work in this way, procuring the necessary materials, would scarcely find time to give to the direct communications of spirits ; for this reason, we call the attention to this point of truly serious circles, those who have self-instruction more at heart than pastime. (See No. 207, chapter on the *Formation of Mediums.*)

Rivalry between Societies.

348. Reunions exclusively engaged in intelligent communications, and those devoted to the study of physical manifestations, have each their mission ; neither could have the true feeling of Spiritism if viewing each other with unfavorable eyes, and casting a stone by either would be proof of its being governed by evil influences ; all should agree, though by different ways, in the common end — the research and propagation of truth ; their antagonism, an effect of over-excited pride, by furnishing arms to detractors, could not fail to injure the cause they pretend to defend.

349. These last reflections apply equally to all circles that might differ on small points of doctrine. As we have said in the chapter on *Contradictions*, these divergencies, being mostly only on the accessories, often only on simple words, it would be very trifling to separate for not thinking exactly the same. It would be worse if the different circles in the same city should be jealous of each other. Jealousy between persons who may be prejudicial to each other materially, is easily understood ; but when there is no speculation, jealousy is only a silly rivalry from self-love. As it is certain there is no society that can contain within itself every believer, those who are animated with a true desire to propagate the truth, whose end is solely moral, should be pleased to see reunions multiply ; and if there should be rivalry among them, it should be to see which would do the most good. Those who pretend to have the truth, to the exclusion of the others, should prove it by taking for their device, *Love and Charity ;* for such is the device of every true spiritist. Do they wish to prove the superiority of the spirits

who assist them ? Let them prove it by the superiority of the teachings they receive, and by the application they make of them to themselves : this is an infallible criterion by which to distinguish those who are in the better way.

Certain spirits, more presumptuous than logical, sometimes impose strange and impracticable systems under the venerated names they borrow, Good sense soon disposes of these ; but in the mean time, they may sow doubt and uncertainty among believers, whence arise temporary dissensions. In addition to the means we have given to know them, there is another criterion to measure their value ; it is the number of partisans they recruit. Reason tells us that the system which finds the loudest echo in the masses must be nearer truth than that which is repulsed by the majority ; so, hold for certain that, when spirits forbid discussion on their teachings, it is because they are aware of their weakness.

350. If Spiritism, as has been announced, is to lead to the transformation of humanity, it can be only through the amelioration of the masses, which can only come gradually, and one after another, by the amelioration of individuals. What does it matter to believe in the existence of spirits, if the belief makes us no better, no more benevolent, and no more indulgent to our kind, no more humble, no more patient in adversity ? Of what use is it for the miser to be a spiritist, if he still continues a miser ? for the proud, if he is always full of himself? for the envious, if he is always jealous ? All men may believe in the manifestations, and yet humanity remain stationary ; but these are not the designs of God. All spiritist societies should tend toward the providential end, collecting around them

all who partake of the same sentiments ; then there will be union, sympathy, fraternity, and not a vain and puerile antagonism of self-love, of words rather than things ; then they would be strong and powerful, because they would rest on a firm foundation, good for all ; then they would be respected, and would impose silence on foolish ridicule, because they would speak in the name of evangelical morality, respected by all.

Such is the path into which we are bound to conduct Spiritism. The flag we bear aloft is that of *Christian and humanitary Spiritism*, around which we are happy already to see so many men rally, in all parts of the globe, because they understand that here is the anchor of safety, the safeguard of public order, the signal of a new era for humanity. We call upon all spiritist societies to concur in this grand work ; that from one end of the world to the other, they may stretch out the fraternal hand, and enclose the evil in an inextricable network.

NOTES.

——•◦•——

1. M. Jobert (de Lamballe). To be just, we must say that this discovery is due to M. Schiff: M. Jobert developed its consequences before the Academy of Medicine to give the finishing blow to the spirit-rappers. All the details will be found in the *Revue Spirite* of the month of June, 1859.

2. Communion. The light of the phenomena of the spirit. Talking-tables, somnambules, mediums, miracles, spiritual magnetism; power of the practice of faith. By Emah Tirpsé, a collective soul writing by the aid of a Planchette. Bruxelles, 1858, at Devroye's.

3. This question has been treated in the *Book on Spirits*, (Nos. 128 and following); but we recommend on this subject, as well as on all that touches the question on the religious side, the brochure entitled *Letter of a Catholic on Spiritism*, by Dr. Grand, ex-consul of France (at Ledoyen, price 1 fr.); also one we intend to publish under the title of THE OPPONENTS OF SPIRITISM, *viewed from religion, science, and materialism.*

4. On looking over all we said in the *Book on Spirits* on dreams and the state of the spirit during sleep (Nos. 400 to 418), it may readily be imagined that those dreams which almost every one has expeiienced, in which we seem to be transported through the air as if flying, are nothing but a remembrance of the sensation experienced by the spirit, when, during sleep, it had momentarily quitted the corporeal body, taking with it only its fluid body, that which it retains after death. These dreams may give us some idea of the state of the spirit when it shall be released from the fetters that bind it to earth.

457

5. It may be seen that when it is necessary to express a new idea for which the language lacks the term, the spirits know perfectly well how to create neologisms. These words *électromédiaminique*, *périspritique*, are not ouis. Those who have criticised us as having made the words *spirite*, *spiritisme*, *périsprit*, (literally spirit-covering) which had not their analogies, will be able to do the same to the spirits.

6. See, for further details on the state of the spirit during sleep, the *Book on Spirits*, Chap. *Emancipation of the Soul*, No. 409.

7. *The reality of spirits and of their manifestations*, demonstrated by the phenomenon of direct writing. By Baron de Guldenstubbe, 1 vol. in 8 mo. with fifteen plates and ninety-three *fac-similes*. Price 8 fr. at Franck's, rue Richelieu. Also to be found at Ledoyen's.

8. One of the most extraordinary facts of this nature, for the variety and strangeness of the phenomena, is that which took place in 1852, in the Palatinate (Rhenish Bavaria) at Bergzabern near Wissembourg. It is the more remarkable, that it reunites, and with the same subject, nearly every kind of spontaneous manifestations — racket enough to shake the house, upsetting of furniture, objects thrown to a distance by an invisible hand, visions and apparitions, somnambulism, ecstasy, catalepsy, electrical attraction, aerial cries and sounds, instruments playing without contact, intelligent communications, &c., and, what is not of minor importance, the verification of these facts during nearly three years, by innumerable eye-witnesses, all worthy of belief from their knowledge and social position. The authentic account of it was published in several German papers, and especially in a tract now out of print and very rare. The complete translation of this fact will be found in the *Revue Spirite* of 185 , with the necessary commentaries and explanations. It is the only French publication, to our knowledge. Beyond the great interest attached to these phenomena, they are eminently instructive for the practical study of Spiritism.